TOYOTA
TALENT

TALENT

DEVELOPING YOUR PEOPLE THE TOYOTA WAY

JEFFREY K. LIKER

DAVID P. MEIER

McGraw-Hill

New York Chicago San Francisco Lisbon
London Madrid Mexico City Milan New Delhi
San Juan Seoul Singapore Sydney Toronto

The McGraw-Hill Companies

2 3 4 5 6 7 8 9 0 AGM/AGM 0 9 8

ISBN-13: 978-0-07-147745-1
ISBN-10: 0-07-147745-4

This publication is designed to provide accurate and authoritative information in regard to the subject matter covered. It is sold with the understanding that neither the author nor the publisher is engaged in rendering legal, accounting, futures/securities trading, or other professional service. If legal advice or other expert assistance is required, the services of a competent professional person should be sought.

—From a Declaration of Principles jointly adopted by a Committee of the American Bar Association and a Committee of Publishers

Dedication

To our parents, Jack and Henriette Liker and Louis and Patricia Meier, who set us on a road to developing our true talents.

Contents

Acknowledgments

e both are continually learning and developing new insights into the Toyota Way in many walks of life. So we wrote two sections, one from David and one from Jeff.

Note from Jeff Liker

When David and I completed *The Toyota Way Fieldbook,* I thought we had completed the Toyota series of books. We had the book on the principles and the book on application. What more could there be? But David was not ready to hang up Microsoft Word. He believed there was still a lot to say about the 4Ps. The *Fieldbook* covered a lot of material, and we were only able to skim the surface of some topics compared to the depth of knowledge needed to do justice to each of the 4Ps. David suggested that we needed to provide greater detail on some key subjects. I was a bit skeptical . . . and tired. But I agreed to collaborate again, as long as David took the lead on the content. After all it was David who spent 10 years at the feet of the Toyota masters, absorbing their knowledge like a sponge. He had experienced the level of practice needed to deeply understand the methodologies of the Toyota Production System (TPS).

So here we are again. We have a contract for four more books. You are holding the first. As it turned out we could not even do justice to the People P with just one book. As we delved into Toyota's disciplined process of training and talent development we filled up a book before we could get to other aspects of Toyota's *Human System.* So there will be a book on *Toyota Culture* that covers both the philosophy and important aspects of the people systems. There will be books on *Toyota Process* and on *Problem Solving.*

In this book the division of labor was straightforward. David provided most of the content, and I provided conceptual frameworks, some Toyota examples, and context setting. We agreed to order the authorship alphabetically though by contribution David is the first author. I continue to appreciate David's depth of experience at Toyota and later as a consultant and his "accumulated know-how" of TPS. It is the kind of insight that comes only from repeated experience and intense reflection.

I have been continuing my Toyota studies, visiting operations in Japan, Europe, Indonesia, and the United States. Wherever I go, the dedication to developing people is striking. Miyadera Kazuhiko, executive vice president starting up a Toyota research and development center for Europe, spent hours describing how he had developed his own deep engineering talent and was trying to accelerate the process in Europe. Ed Mantey, vice president of the Toyota Technical Center in Ann Arbor, Michigan, explained the philosophy of training engineers and the relationship to maintaining the "know-how" database. I was privileged to visit Toyota's Global Production Center (GPC) in Japan and satellite facilities in Georgetown, Kentucky. Mike Hoseus arranged a tour of the Georgetown GPC. My thanks to Cliff Jones, manager, who took me through the Georgetown plantwide GPCs and to Caren Caton, assistant general manager, who provided a tour through the North American GPC.

A number of people read versions of the book, painstakingly finding errors or giving feedback on content. Michael Balle read what we had just edited and found a whole new set of errors. My son Jesse Liker is our harshest critic, telling us what statements were "nerdy" or "hypocritical" and generally keeping us honest and helping to refine the prose. Jim Huntzinger has dedicated years to the study of the original Training Within Industry (TWI) program, and he graciously checked what we wrote.

I would like to thank my parents Jack and Henriette Liker who showed me what hard work and commitment can do to develop real talent. I continue to be grateful to my wife Deborah and children Emma and Jesse for keeping me balanced as I continue my quest to study and spread the Toyota Way.

Note from David Meier

In any project of this size, there will always be many people who have in some way played a role, and it is impossible to thank them all personally. There have been hundreds of people along the journey who have influenced my thinking and teaching on the subject of talent development. I want to thank them all.

I owe thanks to Toyota for providing me the opportunity to learn their methods and to develop skills as a teacher. The Toyota philosophy that every leader is first a teacher was a good fit for me because I love to learn and to teach.

I have great appreciation for the original creators of the TWI programs and especially for the Job Instruction (JI) method. Prior to working for Toyota, I had been using similar techniques, and the JI method helped to solidify my thinking and efforts.

In 1987 I had the privilege of working with Isao Kato, who is a Master trainer and Job Instruction expert at Toyota. Mr. Kato has been teaching Job Instruction to Toyota leaders for over three decades and has been personally responsible for the development of thousands of Toyota employees around the world. He has a deep understanding of the material and respect for each of his students. He is a personification of the Job Instruction philosophy.

I truly enjoyed working with Jeff Liker on *The Toyota Way Fieldbook*. So much so that I wanted to do it again! Jeff adds a valuable perspective to the project, and he has the ability to collect my disjointed thoughts into a more unified flow. He is also able to keep up-to-date on the latest happenings at Toyota and to bring the most recent developments to the book.

I owe much thanks to Mark Warren. He is a repository of information on the Training Within Industry program. Mark has extensively researched TWI, and he provided me with the original materials from the 1940s. He has been a great help in reviewing this text.

We were fortunate to have help with the health care examples in the book. We owe thanks to both Dr. Richard F. Kunkle and Mark Graban and his associates for the health care examples they provided and for reading early drafts and providing feedback on the content of the book.

Of course I would like to thank the companies who have allowed me to teach the Job Instruction method and spend time developing talent within their organizations. Thanks especially to my friends at Hoffman, Parker-Hannifin, and MI Windows and Doors.

Other colleagues along the way have provided guidance, ideas, and support. Thanks to Jim White, David James, Bill Costantino, Tim Szymcek, Jodee Bock, Bill Martinson, and Phil Turek for their help.

This project would not be possible without the hard work of the people at McGraw-Hill. Thanks to our editor, Jeanne Glasser, and senior editing supervisor, Maureen Walker, to all of the folks who correct our mistakes, provide ideas and designs for the book cover, and to everyone who handles all of the behind-the-scenes work.

Special thanks goes to my mother, Patricia Meier, who provided valuable help with proofreading and editing. She has a great eye for detail and spotted mistakes that the rest of us missed. This is her special talent.

Finally, I thank my family for allowing me to work on weekends, holidays, and vacations in order to complete this book. To my daughter Jennifer, my twin sons Matthew and Michael, and my wife Kimberly—thank you for your patience, support, and love.

Foreword

It goes almost without saying that our people have always been the most important reason for Toyota's success. From every team member on the shop floor to the most senior executives, Toyota personnel have been carefully selected, trained, and nurtured to be the best in what they do, because it is through their combined skills, motivation, and spirit that outstanding quality and reliability is built into every product we make.

Jeffrey Liker wrote his best-selling book, *The Toyota Way: 14 Management Principles from the World's Greatest Manufacturer,* in 2003, explaining to a wide audience the reasons behind Toyota's management principles and business philosophy.

This year, Liker and coauthor David Meier have published this companion volume. Here you will find significant detail about the methods we use to develop our associates and how they get the comprehensive training needed to meet specific Toyota goals. Since we want to have really good people in the organization, our aim as a company is to give them all the tools they will need to realize their own career potential and job success.

Using Toyota as a model, the arc of the book follows a straightforward approach that any company might want to consider with an eye toward integrating employees into the business of high-quality, lean manufacturing.

Liker and Meier throughout have carefully and admirably detailed our training processes and how we go about doing them. You will learn that our associates develop their skills in an environment of collaboration and teamwork. You will also discover that at Toyota, *how* you achieve the outcome is as important as the outcome itself.

In examining any procedure, for example, we take a disciplined approach to gathering information and finding alternatives, then carefully monitoring and revisiting issues. We call this unique process PDCA, or "plan, do, check, and act."

The culture at Toyota provides our associates not only with rewards, but also opportunities for continued education and career planning. In return, we expect initiative, motivation, and a willingness to assume different roles and responsibilities.

We are serious about fostering an environment in which mutual respect and trust among all employees will lead to individual creativity and teamwork. Our associates know that it's really their company—they are the ones who must stay involved and make important decisions.

As valuable contributors to the company, all Toyota associates strive each day to fully use their capabilities and put forth their best efforts to strengthen and build our business performance around the world. This is the philosophy that we seek to pass on to future generations.

Toyota's commitment to associate education and development has led to the establishment of formal centers of learning at the University of Toyota in California, the Global Production Support Center in Kentucky, the Toyota Institute in Japan, and the Toyota Academy in the United Kingdom.

Developing exceptional people is an old and well-rehearsed story at Toyota. As our company's growth success demonstrates this core value, we think it is one worth repeating that others may benefit.

James E. Press
President
Toyota Motor North America, Inc.

Preface

If only it weren't for the people . . . always getting caught up in the machinery, earth would be an engineer's paradise.

—Engineer Ed Finnerty in *Player Piano,* by Kurt Vonnegut

Unfortunately at times we all feel like Ed Finnerty, the quintessential engineer. Earth would be a great place to live if it weren't for the people. Yet, it is people who make life worth living—and who make the difference between great companies and mediocre ones.

Toyota's phenomenal success is a business story known the world over. How does Toyota continue to be successful through good times and bad? Information on Toyota's production system has been widely available for over 30 years, but no other company has been able to completely duplicate Toyota's results. What is the secret?

The answer is simple: great people, supported by a system that mandates the need for such talent. It is the knowledge and capability of people that distinguishes any company from another. For the most part, organizations have access to the same technology, machinery, raw materials, and even the same pool of potential employees (in any free market economy) as Toyota. The automaker's success lies partially in these areas, but the full benefit is from the people at Toyota who cultivate their success. These individuals work to develop highly dependable suppliers; they strive to create specific technology that will benefit

Toyota; and they collaborate with machinery suppliers to develop equipment that fits the specific needs of their production system—the Toyota Production System (TPS).

If the approach is so simple, why are other companies unsuccessful in copying Toyota's methods? The reason lies mainly in human nature. In, *Building the Bridge as You Walk on It*, Robert Quinn points out that it is not possible to duplicate the success of any other company by merely imitating its techniques. He states, "In discussing techniques, we forget the importance of relationship. Perhaps this is why so many management fads fail. People imitate the technique originated elsewhere but fail to live in the fundamental state of leadership, as did the person who originated the technique. The techniques are valuable, but people cannot learn to make them work if they are not challenged and supported in the process of learning how to make them work."[1] The dilemma, then, is that people merely want to copy the outward appearance of what Toyota is doing, but they do not want to pursue the much harder and time-consuming aspect of changing their own behavior to replicate Toyota's culture and infrastructure.

Ignoring the fact that talent needs to be cultivated and developed is one clear example of copycat mentality. It is much simpler to believe that implementing methods and systems such as 5S standardized work, kanban, and visual factory will yield the same results as Toyota's, rather than pursuing a more challenging path. In *The Toyota Production System: Beyond Large Scale Production*, Taiichi Ohno, the father of the Toyota Production System, indicates an early awareness within Toyota that purely copying an existing method without understanding its importance to, or role in, one's company could be dangerous.[2] He elucidates the fact that it is necessary to consider one's own needs when determining a successful approach. Throughout the book Ohno describes his own personal awareness and devotion to the success of the process even though he doubted his own ability to implement it.[3]

---

[1] Robert Quinn, *Building the Bridge as You Walk on It* (Jossey Bass, 2004), 188–189.

[2] Taiichi Ohno, *Toyota Production System: Beyond Large Scale Production* (Cambridge, Mass.: Productivity Press, 1988), 1.

[3] Ibid, 31 and throughout.

Quinn describes this ability to persist in spite of doubts (which are normal) as a willingness to, "Walk naked into the land of uncertainty."[4] To some extent Ohno had to deal with his own limitations and to face adversity as he moved ahead. He was able to do that because he had a strong personal belief in the need and benefit of the system that was emerging.

The system requires highly capable people to maintain and continuously improve it. Merely installing the methods without the appropriate development of skills and abilities will produce limited benefits, and the primary purpose of the system itself—namely increased performance through the increasing capability of people—will be lost. The concept is simple to understand but very difficult to apply. It requires a dedication to personal change and to the realization that only through facing adversity and hardship will the true benefits be achieved. It is simple, but not easy.

We should point out that while Ohno did not believe in blindly adopting someone else's program, he did borrow voraciously from others. As is discussed further in upcoming chapters, the foundation for Toyota's core approach to training is based on an American creation developed in World War II called Training Within Industry (TWI), and within TWI is a method for training called the Job Instruction training method. This system breaks down a specific job into little pieces; each element of the job is taught in a detailed manner with the teacher demonstrating and the student observing, practicing, and ultimately mastering the element. The little pieces are, in the end, put back together into a whole job. This process takes place on the job, in a collaborative learning environment, and it follows Deming's preaching that we must plan, do, check, and then take further action. Ohno did not blindly adopt the TWI method but took the bulk of it and modified it to fit Toyota's system.

While this book deals with issues related to what has become known as "training and development," it is much more than just a book on training. The term *training* conjures up images of classroom

---

[4] Quinn, *Building the Bridge as You Walk On It*, 9.

study, or of one worker shadowing another as he or she learns the task "on the job." This book is intended to help identify the critical knowledge within the workplace and to provide a means of transferring that knowledge effectively. The acquisition and transfer of knowledge is the only way for people to expand their capabilities and thus improve the performance of the company.

It is essential, however, to place importance on the means rather than the end. If your motivation is simply to do a better job of training because it will reduce problems and help the company, your outcome will not likely match Toyota's. This is what we would call a "results orientation" rather than a "process orientation."[5] Clarify your expectation up front and make sure you have the proper orientation. Do it because you genuinely care about people and are committed to the effort required to help them achieve their greatest potential; in the end, you will get the best results.

In *Toyota Production System: Beyond Large Scale Production*, Ohno summarizes his feelings on training as follows: "In this age, I am painfully aware of the fact that people tend to forget the need for training. Of course, if skills to be learned are not creative or stimulating and if they do not require the best people, training may not seem worthwhile. But let's take a hard look at the world. No goal, regardless of how small, can be achieved without adequate training."[6] Ohno was astutely aware of the relationship between the need for stimulation and challenge in the workplace and the highly capable people needed to meet those challenges. He wanted a better method and realized that he needed better people to support it and that placing more emphasis on people would produce far greater results. He says, "People's desire to achieve the new system intensified beyond description."[7]

In an interview with Art Smalley, Isao Kato, a long-time employee of Toyota and one of the company's initial Master trainers remarked,

---

[5] Thomas Y. Choi and Jeffrey K. Liker, "Bringing Japanese Continuous Improvement Approaches to U.S. Manufacturing: The Roles of Process Orientation and Communications," *Decision Sciences,* 26(5).

[6] Ohno, *Toyota Production System: Beyond Large Scale Production,* 69.

[7] Ibid., 39

"In Toyota we had a saying, '*mono zukuri wa hito zukuri*' which means 'making things is about making people.' If people want to succeed with lean or TPS they have to emphasize people development and making leaders capable of delivering improvements." Additionally, Kato says, "You can not separate people development from production system development if you want to succeed in the long run."[8]

Compare this philosophy to that of other companies, notably General Electric and the "vitality curve" described by Jack Welch in his book *JACK: Straight from the Gut.*[9] Welch suggests that all employees be divided into A, B, and C categories and that within every organization there will always be the "bottom 10 percent" of performers that should be "let go." According to Welch this constant "differentiation" and cutting of the C players will increase the overall performance of the organization. While this argument makes logical sense, it overlooks the responsibility of the company to develop people to their highest potential. This model basically implies, "Either you cut the mustard, or you are out." It does not imply, "We will do our best to help you develop the skills and abilities you need to be successful, but you are responsible to make your best effort." As other organizations attempted to adopt this philosophy, they discovered the shortcomings of this view. The workforce became disengaged and not aligned to the corporate mission making responsiveness to change in the marketplace impossible.[10] To be fair, Welch does explain that the company should first attempt to find a position in which the individual can be successful, but he says nothing about providing people with opportunities to grow in capability.

There is no doubt that within any organization there will be individuals who are unable to perform no matter how much effort is made, but Toyota follows the basic premise of the Job Instruction method, namely, "If the student hasn't learned, the teacher hasn't taught." Every effort must first be made to help all individuals reach a high level of performance. People living in fear of underperformance

---

[8] Interview with Art Smalley, www.artoflean.com, February 2006.

[9] Jack Welch, *Jack: Straight from the Gut* (New York: Warner Books, 2001), 158–162.

[10] B. Morris, *Fortune*, July 24, 2006, 84.

do not spontaneously learn to be top performers. People who are supported and encouraged within a system that requires outstanding performance will respond accordingly. There is little room to hide poor performance within the Toyota Production System. In *Good to Great*, Jim Collins points out that if you "create an environment where hardworking people would thrive and lazy workers would either jump or get thrown right off the bus," the situation will take care of itself.[11] This is precisely how it works at Toyota. The expectations are clear (and high); people are given the necessary tools and support and have a choice to either step onto the bus or to get off. Collins also notes that the companies defined as great[12] "placed greater weight on character attributes (work ethic, dedication to fulfilling commitments, and values) than on specific educational background, practical skills, specialized knowledge, or work experience."[13]

We should note that what we are writing about in this book is based on some of the methods utilized by Toyota, but we do not imply that Toyota uses all these ideas, nor are all ideas utilized consistently throughout all Toyota facilities. In any organization as large as Toyota, it is possible to find pockets of excellence as well as underperformance. We have no doubt that many leaders within Toyota do not completely appreciate the value of developing people and cling to more traditional views. Also many of the ideas and views expressed here were developed by us or were borrowed from our colleagues who areattempting to support other companies. The core method used by Toyota for training team members is the Job Instruction method, and it is taught at Toyota much the same as it was in the 1950s. Additional techniques to enhance the training experience are continually being developed; therefore, this book is not a description of exactly what is happening within Toyota around the world at this given moment.

[11] James C. Collins, *Good to Great* (New York: HarperBusiness, 2001), 51.

[12] Toyota is not on Collins's list of great companies namely because the list is based on long-term stock market performance from 1964 to 1999. Toyota was not publicly traded over that time period and thus does not fit the criteria. We believe Toyota exemplifies the other characteristics exhibited by the great companies profiled.

[13] Collins, *Good to Great*, 51.

We do know that at this moment capable people within Toyota are working hard to identify critical knowledge about the work, are finding more effective ways to transfer that knowledge to each other, and are achieving significant performance levels as a result. Toyota is good, but it is not good enough (nor anywhere near perfect), and it will continuously strive for improvement in all areas including training ability.

Part One

Getting the Organization Ready to Develop Exceptional People

Give me six hours to chop down a tree and I will spend the first four sharpening the axe.

Abraham Lincoln

Chapter 1

What Can We Learn from Toyota about Developing Talent?

If you want one year of prosperity, grow seeds.
If you want ten years of prosperity, grow trees.
If you want one hundred years of prosperity, grow people.

Chinese proverb

The Philosophy of Training and Development within Toyota

A common expression heard around Toyota is, "We do not just build cars; we build people." Every new product development program, every prototype, every quality defect in the factory, and every kaizen activity is an opportunity to develop people. When former Toyota Motor Manufacturing North American president Atushi (Art) Niimi was asked about his greatest challenge when trying to teach the Toyota Way to his American managers, he responded: "They want to be managers, not teachers." He explained that every manager at Toyota must be a teacher. Developing exceptional people is Toyota's number one priority. This has become ingrained throughout the company as a cultural value of the Toyota Way. It is a concept frequently talked about in other companies, but it is one that is rarely practiced.

It is challenging to think of many major corporations aside from Toyota and a select group of Japanese companies that do a great job of developing exceptional people. On the other hand many countries are able to develop world-class athletes and musicians and master chefs and artists and surgeons. There are many professions where top-quality skill is a prerequisite for success. The professional skill is the commodity to be traded in the market, so people make enormous investments in time and energy to develop exceptional talent. For hospitals, having consistently outstanding surgeons can mean the difference between thriving and fighting lengthy legal battles. It seems that it is not so obvious to leaders of most modern corporations that developing exceptional talent is worth the investment. The talented engineer or quality inspector or machine operator or supervisor is not out in front and center for all to see. They are somewhat hidden, and large companies seem to believe it's possible to get by without developing world-class talent.

It is never satisfactory within Toyota to *just get by.* Toyota's many accomplishments and its rise from a small rural-based company to a global powerhouse can be credited to the exceptional talent of its leaders, engineers, team associates, and supplier partners. Toyota's leaders truly believe that the company's only source of competitive differentiation is the exceptional people they develop; that has been their top priority.

Some might debate whether people are born with talent, or whether their talent is developed. Toyota's stance is clear—give us the seeds of talent, and we will plant them, tend the soil, water and nurture the seedlings, and eventually harvest the fruits of our labor. This analogy of planting seeds and growing people is a common one within Toyota, possibly tracing back to the founding of the company in a farming community. Of course the wise farmer selects only the best seeds, but even with careful selection there is no guarantee that the seeds will grow or that the fruits they yield will be sweet. Yet the effort must be made because it provides the best chance of developing a strong crop. Even the best seeds untended will probably not turn out well.

We consider people's native-born gifts to be only about 10 percent of the total talent picture (or less). In other words, natural talent gifts account for only 10 percent of the full capability of an individual.[1] Fully 90 percent or more of what we consider talent in the life of company employees is actually learned through effort and repeated practice. This is the essence of Toyota's success. Begin with a good foundation—a person who has the capacity and desire to learn—and then develop specific talents through repeated effort and practice.

Perhaps the idea that with a basic capability any person can become, if not the greatest, at least great, is not the stuff of legends. It's true that we are all in awe of the greats—Babe Ruth, Michael Jordan, Tiger Woods—the few who are also blessed with pure talent and ability. It's not nearly as exciting to watch the middle-of-the-pack players—the athletes who just work hard and perform well but never have the buzz of greatness. In 2002 to 2005, championship teams like the Detroit Pistons and the New England Patriots were known for having great teams without having the standout stars of their competition.

It is hard to find the ideal people who have exactly the skills that you want. What Toyota has been able to do is gather competent and trainable people from around the world and, with considerable time and effort, develop high levels of talent within the *masses.* It is not a few star performers who make up a strong team. It is a collection of many players with good capability working in unison that makes an exceptional team. Toyota does not hope for the lucky draw of finding the natural talent—it is a rare find. Instead, Toyota leaders work on the known entity—the latent talent in each person who has the desire for personal growth.

In this book we explore the process used by Toyota as the primary tool for teaching and developing this talent. It is not glamorous. It requires dedicated long-term commitment and effort. It will be hard work. It is important to see this process as much more than mere

---

[1] Obviously there are exceptions to this, such as Tiger Woods who was doing miraculous things hitting golf balls when he was barely a toddler. But rarely do jobs in companies require superstar talent like the world's best athletes possess. For the more typical talent pool of individuals working for companies and the typical demands of the jobs, we believe the large majority of talent can be developed.

training. Training for job skills is a starting point, but the development of true talent extends well beyond this level. Understand that the foundational tool used for teaching job skills may also be applied to all other aspects of developing talent. It is the core concept for teaching and learning and thus can be applied to any situation.

In *The Toyota Way Fieldbook*[2] we attempted to demonstrate the consistent applicability of the core concepts and philosophies of the Toyota Production System (building on the 14 guiding principles detailed in *The Toyota Way*[3]) regardless of the workplace in which they are applied. This same idea holds true for the core concepts of teaching and developing people. In *Good to Great*, Jim Collins describes this phenomenon as being similar to the laws of physics relative to scientific application of the physical laws. Collins points out that the general laws haven't really changed much but that our understanding of how they operate and how to apply them has.[4] This is a fundamental element of Toyota's success—don't mess with the basic principle. Rather, deeply understand how to apply the principle in any situation. We do our best to present the core concepts and demonstrate them in some common applications. With some practice you will be able to apply them to any situation that involves teaching and learning.

The philosophy of developing people is so pivotal to Toyota that six of the fourteen principles outlined in *The Toyota Way* are related to it:

> *Principle 1. Base management decisions on a long-term philosophy, even at the expense of short-term financial goals:* Perhaps the most important long-term investment Toyota makes is in its people and the passion to keep team associates employed for their careers reflects that value.

> *Principle 6. Standardized processes are the foundation for continuous improvement:* As we will see, standardized work and job instruction training go hand in hand, and long-term team associates need to learn to see waste and make improvements.

---

[2] J. Liker and D. Meier, *The Toyota Way Fieldbook* (New York: McGraw-Hill, 2005).
[3] J. Liker, *The Toyota Way* (New York: McGraw-Hill, 2004).
[4] J. Collins, *Good to Great* (New York: HarperCollins, 2001).

Principle 9. Grow leaders who thoroughly understand the work and who live the philosophy and teach it to others: Teaching is the most highly valued skill of leaders, and leaders have to deeply understand the work to teach and coach others.

Principle 10. Develop exceptional people and teams who follow your company's philosophy: Teams depend on well-trained people, and part of individual development is learning to work in teams.

Principle 11. Respect your suppliers by challenging them and helping them improve: Suppliers need to have the same talent level as Toyota team associates and are developed in similar ways.

Principle 14. Become a learning organization through relentless reflection and continuous improvement: This was intentionally at the top of the hierarchy of the Toyota Way pyramid because becoming a learning organization is viewed as the highest level of organizational effectiveness.

At Toyota teaching is considered the central part of any manager's job. There is no direct monetary benefit for working to develop people or a formal line on a performance appraisal, but the evidence of this effort is reflected in nearly all aspects of the performance of a manager's group. If the manager does not foster a teaching environment, the group's performance will surely suffer. Toyota has worked to create a culture in which teaching others is highly valued and viewed as the key to long-term success. In fact, as we will see, if people are not adequately developed, the entire system will grind to a screeching halt.

The Unfortunate Reality

For the past few decades it has become a general management trend to talk about the importance of developing people within organizations. "People are our most valuable resource" has become part of the mission statement—a guiding principle for many companies. Human resources management has gained prominence and has become an important entity within most companies (often the vice president of the human resources department is a powerful person in the company). Yet when we visit companies and talk to employees, we find a different reality. We find people who are ill-equipped to perform their jobs, and we can see people struggling to perform even the most basic tasks. We try to work with supervisors to lead lean manufacturing transformations and find that they were promoted because of hard work and company loyalty, but they lack basic skills in the daily management of their work teams. We find managers and leaders who don't have development plans or the ability to create them, let alone have specific methods for developing people. And we are constantly frustrated by companies that see *lean* as a tool kit and do not understand that the main value of lean projects is in developing people who can solve problems and make daily improvements.

If people are truly the most important resource, why has so little been done to improve that asset? Could it be that managers believe they are doing much more than they really are? Or is the statement that "people are our most important resource" intended to be a morale booster to make people feel as though they are a valued part of the company? If it is lip service without action, people in the company soon understand that it is just another attempt by management to get people to feel good about their work and hopefully work harder. "A happy cow gives more milk" is a truism, but in reality there is much more to high performance organizations than gimmicks to boost morale.

Something that is clearly lacking in many companies is an effective method for training people. We work with numerous companies and with people at all levels within these organizations. Every large company has some type of training program in a large variety of areas, from technical to human resources, and many of them have "lean" and "Six Sigma" programs. Often the training is well delivered by competent professionals who have good materials and know what they are doing. Yet, go where the actual work is being done and ask people how they learned their jobs and you get a different picture. People have learned their jobs over time in a relatively unorganized way, and the training courses are interesting but often do not have a direct bearing on the day-to-day job.

One manager explained how he had to "learn the ropes the hard way," and he felt that everyone else should have to do so as well.

Instead of his bad experience becoming a motivation to improve, it became a model for future behavior. Not until he looked at the results of his thinking and behavior—high turnover, mistakes leading to customer complaints, daily firefighting, and a general sense of apathy (indicated by high absenteeism)—did he have an epiphany. By working with all workers as individuals to ensure their success, providing them with the skills needed for the job, and increasing their ability, he found the path to greater success for himself. All great leaders know that they are successful only through the success of those they lead.

Everyone, it seems, understands the need and can see the deficiency, but too few are willing to step up to the situation and do something about it. Why is this? Why is it so easy to recognize the importance of a well-trained workforce, but so difficult to act upon this knowledge? Perhaps there was no effective tool (the Job Instruction method outlined in this book is that tool), or perhaps there are no "trainer types" in the group (unlikely). What is more likely and is highly probable, is that doing a more effective job of training and development is not critical to survival in the short term, and thus it is not emphasized. The current process, as limited and ineffective as it might be, "works." Team members are able to get by. The work happens, jobs get done, and short-term goals are met.

Unfortunately, for most companies, managing their human assets has for years been secondary to the primary interest of the company—manufacturing, health care, banking, construction, or transportation. Certainly people were a necessary part of the company, but in many cases they were viewed as simply a means to achieve an end. Henry Ford is reported to have said: "Why is it that when I want to hire a pair of hands, a brain comes attached to them?" People were necessary for what they could *do*, not for what they could contribute beyond that. Thinking, creating, improving, and developing were activities relegated to the select few with a specific job title—engineer, manager, or vice president in charge of strategic initiatives, for example. Interestingly those engineers and managers were assumed to get most of their knowledge and skills from engineering schools or MBA programs, and rigorous on-the-job training was not much of a focus for them.

The Cycle of Struggle and Firefighting

What we see in most organizations is a struggle of problems, firefighting, some short-lived relief, and on to more problems. It is a vicious cycle—there is never a new outcome. Issues are not resolved; they are simply patched for the moment. As with most cycles, it is difficult to determine where the cycle begins and how to intercede to make a change. We believe that this cycle begins with an ineffective training process, which leads to variable and ineffective results, which is then followed by firefighting (which is totally time-consuming). This leaves little time for effective training. The circle then begins again with an ineffective training process.[5] Figure 1–1 shows this cycle.

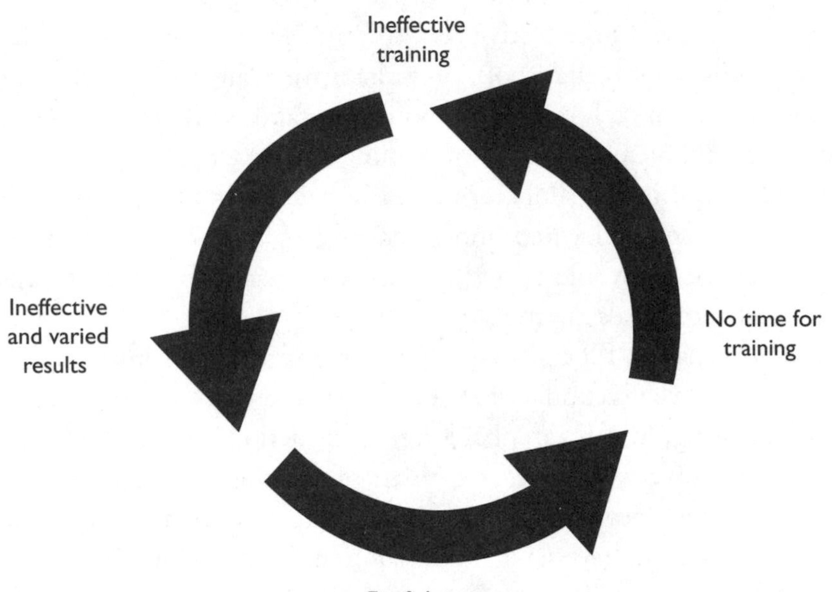

Figure 1–1. The cycle of struggle and firefighting leads to more struggle and firefighting

[5] We believe this to be a bit of an exaggeration. There is time left to do effective training, but firefighting is a convenient excuse to avoid the situation. This may be because people do not know *how* to do a better job with training.

Breaking the Cycle of Defeat to Create a Cycle of Success

Of course, to break this perpetual cycle, it will be necessary to cut in at some point. We believe that lack of time is not the real issue, although it may seem that way to people in the cycle of struggle. The reality is, "You make time for the things you want to do in life."[6] So, if time is lacking, you are simply choosing to do other things, which you are ranking as more important uses of your time. The only way we can see to get off the perpetual wheel is to step off. You must take the time (or find others who can) and invest in your future.

We believe there are three factors that ultimately lead to a deficiency in information sharing and learning, which must be targeted in order to break the cycle.

Defining Critical Knowledge—There is a lack of an effective method for *defining the critical requirements* of a job. It is not clear what is truly important for the successful completion of the work versus what is personal preference, which may vary from person to person. For many years, engineers and other staff members have attempted to identify work requirements and document them, only to discover later that people will perform the actual work differently from what has been prescribed. Knowledge of a particular job is based on "tribal" information, and many workers seem to have their own way of doing the work.

Transferring the Critical Knowledge—Whether the work is well defined or not, the subsequent step of *transferring the critical knowledge* to others is mainly the luck of the draw. If new learners are lucky, they are placed with skilled and competent trainers. This often depends on the particular job opening and availability of preferred trainers. It is often the "best" worker who is relegated to the training responsibility, but very frequently the best worker is not the best trainer and vice versa.

[6] An important lesson from Dr. Donald Hudson, Department of Industrial Technology, Berea College, Berea, KY.

Follow-Up—Perhaps because of the previous two shortcomings, there is generally *limited or no follow up to verify the results of the training effort.* Without well-defined requirements for a job, how would it be possible to determine the effectiveness of the transfer of knowledge? Since there is no systematic and defined method to ensure that the training process is sufficient, the results are unpredictable, inconsistent, and thus cannot be accurately measured.

The cumulative effects of these three factors are similar to a calculation of rolled throughput yield. This is the yield attained from several processes in series when each one produces some quality defects. Suppose that you are 80 percent effective at each element. Multiplying the factor three times (.8 × .8 × .8) would yield an overall effectiveness of the process of only 51 percent! It is imperative that all three elements be perfected in order to support an effective training process. For example, achieving a 96 percent level on the three elements will yield a 90 percent overall result, which will give you great performance.

If People Are the Answer, Selecting Quality People Must Be the Key

In the 1980s when it became clear that Japanese auto companies were producing products superior in quality to those made by American automakers, a common excuse delivered by Ford, GM, and Chrysler was the "superiority" of the Japanese worker. The story line was that the average Japanese worker was somehow more dedicated, more intelligent, and harder working than the average American worker. As with any excuse, there is a fine line between the truth and the "whole truth." This excuse might have been partially true, but the fallacy lay in the avoidance of the whole truth. The Japanese workers did not become more dedicated and hard working by luck, or even by cultural difference. There was a strong concerted effort to develop the Japanese workforce.

Now, 20 years later we often hear a similar excuse with a twist. Now the secret of Toyota's success is attributed to the fact that it hires only the best workers. Because of other extenuating circumstances, Toyota *is* able to pay higher wages and benefits and thus attract and retain exceptional employees. Again, there is an element of truth in this excuse. Toyota does pay good wages, but not the highest in the industry or across the nation.

The problem with these excuses is that they avoid some realities. Toyota has taken one of the worst performing plants in the General Motors system (NUMMI) and turned it into a successful operation. This was done with 80 percent of the original workforce from GM. Toyota has also located manufacturing facilities in Kentucky, Alabama, West Virginia, Indiana, and most recently in Texas. These states rank 35th, 43rd, 34th, 26th, and 24th, respectively, in Morgan Quinto Press's 2005–2006 rankings of the 50 "smartest states."[7] Toyota has taken people from some of the lowest-performing states in the United States and produced incredible results (no offense to any of the states listed). In fact, in Japan, Toyota is mainly located in rural areas of the country where indigent farmers made up the workforce during the early years. Toyota is primarily interested in hiring people with a strong work ethic. It prefers to locate in areas where people are familiar with hard work and have the motivation necessary to learn and perform.

Develop People to Ensure Prosperity

The continuing cycle of firefighting and failing to solve the root cause of the problems must stop. The only way for it to stop is for companies to let go of the excuses and face the reality. In order for change to happen and for that change to lead to the desired result, it is necessary to change our motivation. The development of highly capable people must be a genuine desire. It is not sufficient to state the desire in a vision statement or on a banner over the door. It must be a genuine interest, and the motive cannot be tied directly to an ulterior motive such as short-term financial reward. You must truly have a passion for developing a workforce with the highest skills and know that in doing

[7] Source: www.morganquitno.com

so the financial gain will take care of itself. This is a difficult leap for many executives, and even supervisors, who do not see the performance of their people as being directly linked to their own success. It is much easier to complain about what is lacking and not working rather than to make the investment in change. Change forces us to confront the unknown. It is risky. In many cases past attempts and failures have led us to believe that future attempts will also end with the same result, so we don't try.

There is no doubt that working with people can be extremely challenging and at times frustrating. It may seem that the process of change would be easy if not for the people. The fact is that the process of change would be impossible *without* people. People are harder to deal with than machines or spreadsheets. They have their own opinions and feelings. What allows Toyota to persist in spite of the challenges is the overriding philosophy that only people are able to think, to solve problems, and to improve. People are seen as the key to expanding and strengthening the company. What is needed is a full and unflinching belief that people are the key to success, acting as if that is true, and then developing a system to support people in their efforts. If you say, "People are the most important asset," and then ask, "How many heads can I cut out of the process and send packing for the unemployment line?" you are not practicing what you preach.

The world is becoming hypercompetitive, and managers are struggling to keep up. Companies and smart managers are now realizing that there is an enormous pool of talent waiting to be tapped to aid in the struggle. Some are discovering that without the connection to the talent, it is impossible to survive. As with all things, nothing comes without a price. Companies are finding out about the challenges of "getting people involved." They are discovering that it is difficult to shift their thinking. Furthermore, when people are involved, their feelings, opinions, and perceptions are involved as well. Companies attack this with various human resource programs focused on communication methods and time management methods and ways to improve the work environment, but they miss the core issue: People are not in an environment every day in which they are actively developing skills to be better workers and problem solvers.

Other companies and some managers still harbor the belief that people are interchangeable, need to learn only enough to "get the job done," and are "a cost of doing business." People are not viewed as an asset to grow; they are thought of as a piece of machinery—necessary to perform a function. If only people would behave like machines and not talk back or threaten to strike, things would be easier.

It is in this range of perceptions that we work. On one end are the organizations and individuals who understand the importance of people and want to put into practice new methods, but struggle with changing old ways of thinking and behaving and are not sure exactly what to do to develop true, deep competence in their people. On the other end are the companies and managers who do not even see the need for change. The idea of developing people beyond the base requirement has not entered their minds. A business is a business, and people are a necessary evil to run the business and should be eliminated when possible! This book is intended to provide some guidance for both ends of the range. We can't change your mind or perception, but perhaps we can influence one or the other or both. Our focus is on assisting you to develop your people to be skilled in doing their assigned jobs so they do exceptional work and continually improve their work. In Chapter 4 we will briefly touch on native talent or how to select people who have the natural abilities needed for a particular job. We will not be speaking about the natural inclinations that make people better suited for some jobs compared to others. Certainly we are all different, and some of those differences are hard-wired. Some people will be naturally passionate about going out and meeting people and selling, and others will be passionate about debugging computer programs and working in relative isolation. There are different personal inclinations and personalities and temperaments, and we will not be getting into how to find the best person-job match to maximize the potential of the person. To get the most out of people you must consider the whole person. Our focus is more basic—how can we teach people the core skills needed to do their jobs so they can become comfortable enough with the basics to begin to innovate and grow in their jobs?

It seems as though Toyota is in the news every day, and the news is generally related to some new achievement and the success of the company. It has certainly had some serious stumbles that are given great publicity, but these are minimal in the long term considering Toyota's ability to sustain growth and profitability and recover from stumbles quickly. Few can deny the immense success Toyota has had and appears ready to continue having. It is our intent to explore the connection between Toyota's relentless pursuit of people development and the resulting successes.

Chapter 2

Toyota Works Hard to Develop Exceptional People

People Development Is Critical to Toyota

No one seems to be sure of the exact course of events that led to the development of the Toyota Production System (TPS) as it is today, but we are sure that without highly capable people the current system would quickly disintegrate. We know that in the early development of TPS, its chief architect, Taiichi Ohno, wanted to press forward with some of his ideas and discovered that people were not ready. When he went to work to achieve single-piece flow in a machine shop and he needed multiskilled workers, he encountered resistance and learned that he had to be patient and to think about developing people who would be able to support the methods. He could not simply order people to follow the rules (although he was known as being very forceful when necessary). He needed people with thinking capability because of the challenges presented by the application of his new ideas. In fact, the real purpose of creating flow was to bring problems to the surface, which would force people to think about solving the problems and to help them to develop their abilities.

A select few front-office experts could not possibly deal with all the situations that would surely arise as Ohno pressurized the system, thereby forcing failures. He needed capable *masses*. The development of capable masses requires a clear plan. It requires time and patience.

Above all it takes persistence and the willingness to stick with it and to deal with the individual peculiarities and challenges of each person.

When Taichi Ohno discovered the importance of highly capable people, he sought a method of teaching that would support his needs. He believed he had found such a tool in the *Job Instruction (JI) Method* taught by the American occupation forces after World War II. It has been the primary teaching tool for all of Toyota since the 1950s. Today the capabilities of Toyota employees are a hallmark of the company. We often talk to managers of other companies who view the capability of Toyota employees to be some sort of anomaly or option that is open only to Toyota.

The truth is that Toyota does like to start with good people who possess the *capability* to become exceptional employees. The people whom Toyota selects must have the *capacity* and *desire* to learn. Those are the only absolutes. In fact if one were to look closely at Toyota employees, one would find a broad spectrum of humanity similar to that in any other company—with all the beauty and blemishes found anywhere. Toyota employees bring to bear issues similar to those of other companies, such as attendance problems, resistance to change, lack of motivation, and even reluctance to accept the philosophy of TPS. What allows Toyota to be successful in spite of these challenges is the efforts and interest in drawing out the best of the employee's abilities and initiating possible solutions (rather than a shrug and the "What are you going to do?" attitude we hear from other companies). Perhaps Toyota has recognized the reality of human behavior and limitations, and it has created systems that minimize those limitations or take advantage of human desire.

People are carefully selected to join Toyota based on their potential and a judgment that there is a fit with the job and with Toyota's culture. They must have some general problem-solving capability and be willing to work as part of a team. People develop specific capabilities *after* they are hired at Toyota. It is Toyota's expectation that it will mold the individual to fit the needs of the organization as well as support the interests of the individual. It is this mutuality of purpose that leads to more satisfied employees who are able to perform in exceptional ways. One must not assume that Toyota is completely altruistic in its efforts to develop employees and to provide engaging activities. The objective is to provide benefits for the employees, which in turn also returns benefits to the company.

Toyota often creates situations in which there is an equal balance between reward and punishment in order to encourage the desired behavior. For example, given the critical nature of attendance on the performance of the system, a high emphasis is placed on having great attendance (perfect attendance is preferred). On the reward side, Toyota Motor Manufacturing Kentucky (TMMK) has an annual award ceremony for all employees who achieved perfect attendance in the previous year (over 60 percent in 2005).[1] The award ceremony includes entertainment from some top acts in the country including Jay Leno, Bill Cosby, and Brooks and Dunn. In addition, each person has his or her name placed into a hat, and 14 winners[2] are drawn, each receiving a brand new car (a mix of Camrys and Avalons). To sweeten the pot, each team member with consecutive years of perfect attendance will have his or her name added to the hat an additional time for each year of consecutive perfect attendance. In 2006 there were more than 400 employees who had achieved 15 consecutive years of perfect attendance (the length of the program)!

On the punishment side, repeated unexcused absences are one of the easiest ways to lose a job at TMMK. The policy is fairly strict and is weighted heavily on attendance history and also the circumstances. Consideration is given for good reasons, but repeated absences for poor reasons are sure to lead to discipline. A flat tire is not considered a "good" reason, for example, but the effort a team member makes to reduce the time loss is in his or her favor. If a team member has a flat tire and misses the entire day, it is not viewed favorably. And apart from the fear of being fired, sitting home while all your team associates are at the big bash hoping to win a car is its own punishment.

---

[1] Perfect attendance includes tardies and absences, but the policy allows team members to use "emergency vacation" for certain occasions to cover tardies and absences and maintain "perfect" attendance.

[2] This number has varied over the years as the number of team members has grown.

The Toyota Production System Demands High Capability

Toyota continuously works to improve training methods. Consider the implications of training at Toyota, and it is easy to understand why. The interconnected nature of all processes within the plant makes it necessary to train people without ever slowing the line (doing so would also slow several thousand other people within the plant and ultimately the suppliers). Imagine a new hire working furiously on the line, struggling and not meeting the line speed (known as *takt rate*). The line would be repeatedly stopped. Also imagine that there is no response to the line stoppages, and everyone is watching and waiting as the new hire struggles. When asked about the situation, the group leader shrugs and replies, "He'll get it before long. It usually takes a few weeks before they get the hang of it." Do you think this response would be sufficient within a company like Toyota? Of course not! Unfortunately this scenario is all too common in many other companies.

In reality most auto companies have moving assembly lines and will quickly realize they cannot afford to have incapable individuals who are shutting down the entire line. Some minimum level of competence to at least work within the cycle time is necessary. But Toyota goes beyond this. First, it has stretched the "just in time" philosophy beyond the assembly line by connecting all processes (minimizing inventory between processes) so that if one breaks, the next process in line will quickly be affected. Second, Toyota has built into the tasks quality checks and cross-training that require more than minimum levels of competence. This means that every person must be trained at a high level to work precisely, or the entire operation crumbles like a house of cards. Moreover, training must be accomplished while maintaining the production line pace.

How can so many companies get away with minimal training? The answer is that the "disconnected" nature of processes (separated by inventory buffers) allows varying levels of capability within the system. New hires or trainees do not need to be assimilated carefully, because there are only limited repercussions—if they cannot perform at the required pace, the next operation keeps working using the inventory buffer. This is simply not possible within the Toyota system. The new hire at Toyota must also be developed while maintaining the highest level of quality and safety. If a trainee were to attempt to paint a car body, for example, and she applied the paint thinly, the ensuing defect would not only be difficult to repair, but it might also affect the *heijunka* (leveling) of the production and could possibly result in an empty slot on the production line. This is really the key point of TPS—the system *forces* everyone to be in top form in all aspects, including training. The nature of TPS requires highly capable and competent people—thus the importance of the development of people (and the prominence as one of the four Ps highlighted in *The Toyota Way*). Of course all of the Ps are interrelated. The *P*hilosophy leads to the long-term thinking needed to make investments in the right interconnected *P*rocess so that *P*eople will solve the *P*roblems that surface.

The cyclical nature of the system leads to long-term strengthening as a result of the development of people who are more capable of managing the problems (see Figure 2–1). Simply stated—it is not possible to operate a lean system without highly capable people, and without a lean system it is not mandatory to develop highly capable people who can continuously improve the system.

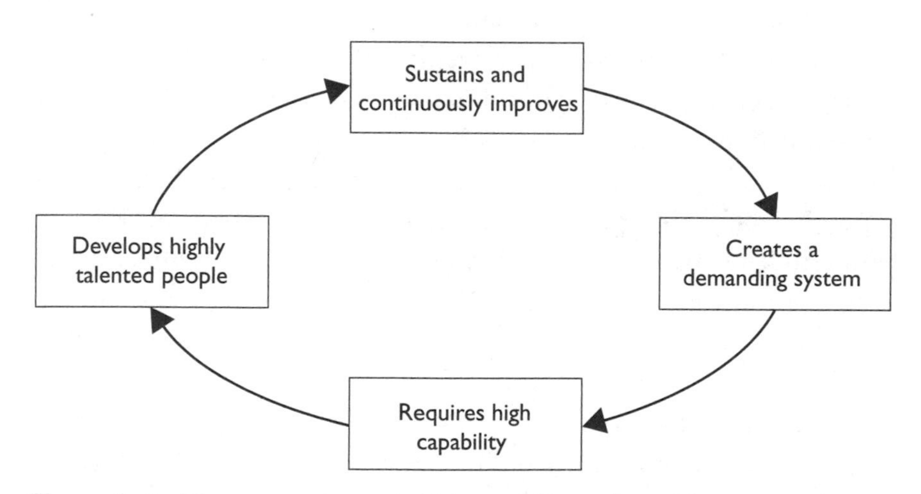

Figure 2–1. The system demands high capability and provides a cycle of continuous improvement

Standardizing Training to Meet Global Needs

Because of the central nature of people to its delicately balanced system, Toyota makes exceptional efforts to train and develop people for success. Toyota is increasing the emphasis on training by opening three regional training centers called Global Production Centers—one in Thailand to support the Far East, one in England for Europe, and the third in Kentucky for all North American plants. Satellite centers are being developed globally at every plant.

The underlying problem facing Toyota as they expand their operations around the world is that of addressing the lack of sufficiently skilled trainers to teach the throngs of new people being hired and assimilated. So it has developed a new system of training (based on the same Job Instruction principles described in this book). Toyota discovered in the process of developing formal training programs, it eliminated a lot of the variation in training methods among individual trainers. Computers are an important part of the training, including interactive learning systems with videotapes of the right and wrong ways to do steps of the jobs. But computers do not drive the training; there are also experienced trainers on site in each center. There is a formal certification process to become a trainer that includes being certified in the individual tasks taught to students.

The Georgetown, Kentucky facility is responsible for teaching trainees from the United States, Canada, and Mexico. At the center, live simulations are used to teach basic skills, such as practicing the installation of screws and tightening bolts on special boards and finally putting the skills together on actual vehicles. Feedback is provided to the students on how they performed each task. For example, in the paint center they practice spray-painting water on a two-way mirror with a video camera behind it. They can then view the patterns of their spraying and modify their technique.

At another station the water the students spray is captured in bottles at the bottom of a wall, and they can see the height of the captured water at various points along the wall to determine if the correct quantity of "paint" is being applied consistently along the surface. The goal is to evenly spray back and forth across the wall, and there are specific acceptable tolerances for deviations from perfect evenness. After practicing, they pull a cord that lights an *andon* to call the trainer over to test them. (The andon is used in the Toyota Production System as a signal that the team associate needs help. It is used in the training to get trainees acclimated to the andon concept.) They must perform each task within the specified tolerances and time allowances before getting certified on that task and going on to the next task. Typically they fail on the first try, get feedback from the trainer, and go back to practicing.

Toyota has already documented reductions in training time as a result of this rigorous and standardized training process. This training is based on the basic Job Instruction method that is outlined later in the book. At the core the Job Instruction method is about teaching the critical aspects of the work and helping the student to develop high capability. In the painting example above, the key points of the task are the thickness of paint applied and the evenness of the application. The method used to develop the proper technique is unique. Toyota devised a way to measure the amount of water sprayed to represent the correct method. Of course this is just introductory practice. The final proof comes when a real vehicle is painted, but this practice to develop "fundamental skills" will greatly shorten the actual learning period.

Skill development occurs with practice, and these standardized fundamentals taught in the production center are used to supplement the Job Instruction method and are being developed to help new hires acquire the necessary skills more quickly. At Georgetown, team leaders and group leaders also were asked to go through the production center training. Experienced team members can go through it at their option. Interestingly, the experienced leaders and members who went through it almost always found it very enlightening. Sometime in the past they learned a way that worked, but it was not always the best way. It is sort of like an experienced golfer getting a lesson from a professional golfer. The experienced golfer over time modifies her swing in response to problems she encounters (e.g., a slice), but often those personal adaptations are a compromise when compared to a better form.

The professional instructor looks at her swing and notices fundamental problems that if corrected can significantly improve the swing and ultimately her scores.

Toyota's Human System Model

Training and development of team members (all employees) at Toyota is part of the broader "Human System." At the core of Toyota's Human System is the development of people, including the ability to attract capable people, engage them, and enroll them as full-fledged members of the Toyota culture. Ultimately, people continually improve the processes for which they were originally trained. There are many supporting organizational and leadership processes to ensure capable and committed team associates at all levels. A version of Toyota's Human System model is shown in Figure 2–2.[3]

As with other aspects of the Toyota Way, no individual component is very complicated. Yet when we consider all the components together as a complete system the integration is very complex and very challenging, even for Toyota. The Toyota Way organizational culture is an extended topic in its own right.[4] Here we use it to put the topic of developing talent in a broader context.

The Human System model reminds us that lean is more than a technical system of efficiently making products. In lean production we evaluate the product *value stream* to identify and eliminate waste. By value stream we mean a series of steps in the process that each add value for the customer. Waste does not add value, but adds cost. But who eliminates waste? There is a companion value stream that produces people who are the creative thinkers and who continually improve the product value stream. Think about the process of how you develop your people, and ask yourself how often steps are taken to make your people better. The components of the human value stream

---

[3] Source: Mike Hoseus, Center for Quality People and Organizations.

[4] The broader human-cultural system of Toyota is explored more fully in a separate book (*Toyota Culture*) by Jeffrey Liker and the Center for Quality People and Organizations. It is scheduled to be released in Fall 2007.

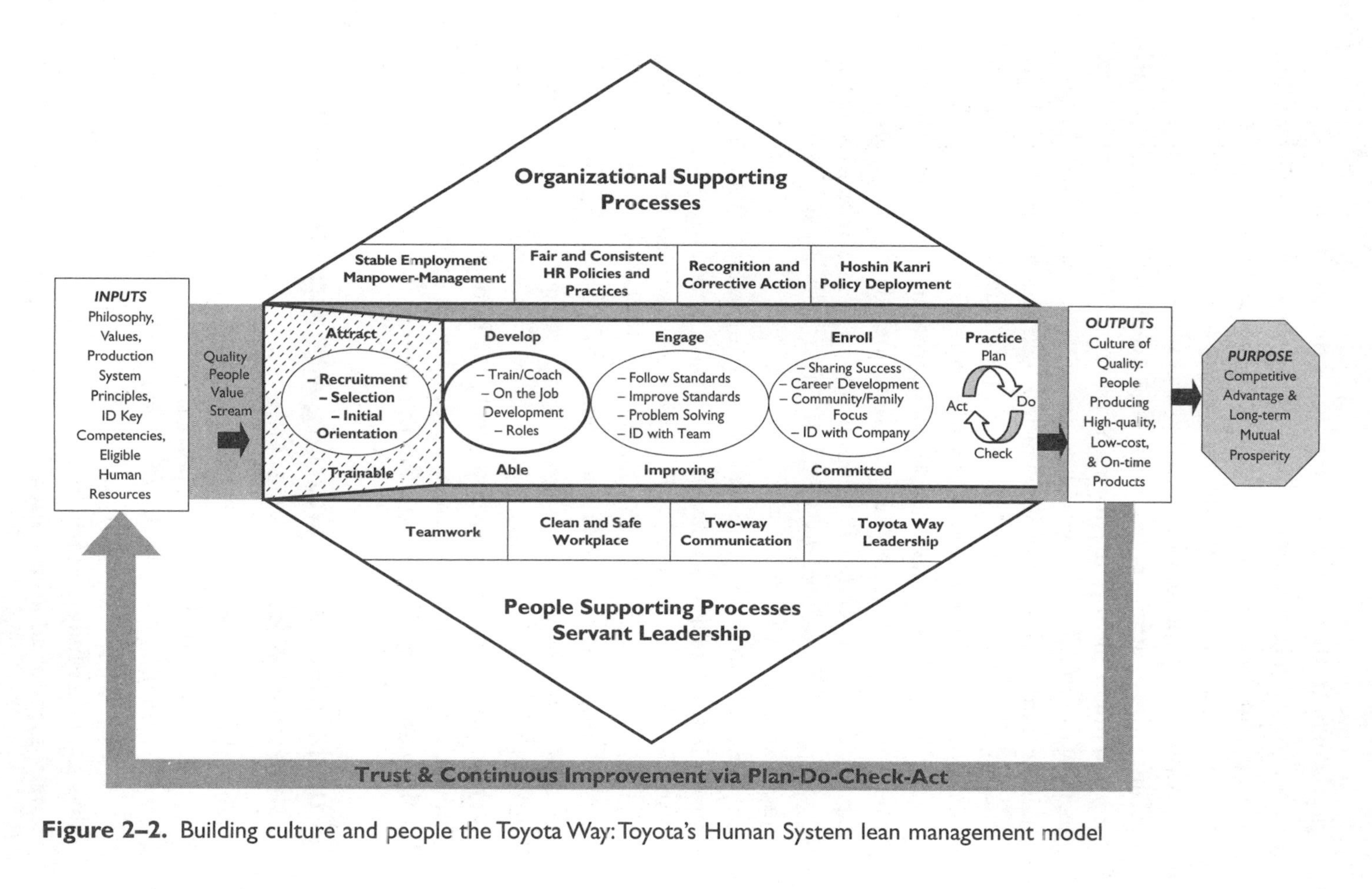

Figure 2–2. Building culture and people the Toyota Way: Toyota's Human System lean management model

clearly reflect the Toyota values of continuous improvement and respect for people who are at the center of the organizational culture. The human value stream is designed to produce employees who are committed to full involvement and participation.

Considering the flow depicted by the human value stream, the initial intent is to attract potential employees, select the most appropriate, and orient them to the Toyota Way. The next step is to familiarize them with job roles and provide them with on-the-job development training and coaching (this is when Job Instruction comes in). As job mastery grows, the task is to encourage individual and team initiative, seek work simplification, and ensure a caring supervisor. The fourth step is to focus on career development, sharing career success with family, and expanding the perspective to include the community. All aspects of this concerted development process are reinforced by an organization that seeks to maintain trust and pursue continuous improvement.

Clearly, from the point of view of the Human System model Toyota moves beyond skill attainment and pursues active *engagement* of the employee. The Toyota Production System is designed to identify and highlight problems, while the Human System model is designed to engage people who are able and willing to solve them. And, as the model's supporting processes suggest, the encouragement of that engagement is extensive. This book is more narrowly focused than the entire Human System model. We will concentrate on those aspects of the core human value stream that center on developing exceptional skills and making associates "able" to perform their jobs.

Fundamentals of Training Are Applicable to Developing Employee Talent

While the core content of this book concentrates on the development of specific job skills, it is important to understand the difference between training for job skills and for the development of a well-rounded employee. Job skills are of course necessary for people to be able to successfully perform their work. This is a basis for further development of additional capabilities. In addition to basic job skills,

Toyota employees are expected to participate in additional activities, such as improving communication skills and leadership abilities, planning, developing new methods or procedures, designing new products, or correcting problems in the work area.

A book by Mike Morrison, Dean of the University of Toyota (part of Toyota Motor Sales) uses a metaphor, which is reflected in the title *The Other Side of the Card,* to remind us we are unique individuals who are more than our official job titles on the front of the business card. In this business novel people take time to realize who they really are and their unique capabilities to contribute to the organization. Examples of "other side of the card" titles include "The Vision-ator," "Captain Courageous," "A Devil for Details," "The Project Meister," and "Cruise Director." These titles represent the unique talents and gifts of each person that often get missed in the routine of daily work. When we think of "talent" we often think about these unique gifts that define who we are as individuals. Nonetheless the core job must get done, and there is significant talent that can be developed to perform the job exceptionally well.

Fundamentally, development is about learning and then teaching others, which is also the basis for learning job skills. The concepts for job training reviewed in this book can be used to teach virtually any subject, including those considered to be related to development. We often hear that it is not possible to teach some aspects of work, especially those related to "creative" endeavors, or those where an individual "style" is necessary. It is our belief that even the creative design and development responsibilities can be taught using a similar method.

Let's consider a very creative endeavor—oil painting. Many of us assume that painting requires artistic talent that is beyond our personal capability (we are not artists). In fact, if we were to sit beside a painter as she created her masterpieces and stopped her now and then to inquire, "What are you doing?" and "What is important about how you are doing it?" we would see that there are in fact identifiable and consistent principles at the core.

For example, if the painter desires to depict "depth" (there is no real depth in a two-dimensional painting, only the perception of depth) between an object and the background, the outside perimeter of the object is highlighted with a darker line and perhaps some shading around the object in the background area. Painters have of course practiced these tricks of the trade for centuries. There are other defined "rules" (in any creative endeavor it is dangerous to define rules because part of the objective of creativity is to create something new, which often defies the rules) such as the placement of complementary and opposing colors to create a certain effect. If we look more closely within any creative endeavor, it is possible to find certain aspects that are easily identifiable and thus teachable.

Those who dream of artistic endeavors can be heartened by the fact that even the artwork of Vincent van Gogh in his mid-twenties was amateurish. He studied principles of color and proportion and worked with other painters to gain an understanding of the key principles. Of course he went on to fame (only after his death) by breaking *some* of the traditional rules of aesthetics, but not the core principles.

One problem is that most people tend to look at any situation and first consider the unique or creative aspects rather than the common and teachable aspects. It is true the exceptional artist, athlete, and designer bring a unique talent that is difficult to emulate, but the reality is that the pure talent may comprise only 10 percent of the total. For example, M. C. Escher created very innovative and different drawings, but as a starting point said he needed to master basic principles of graphic arts. He attended the Haarlem School for Architecture and Decorative Arts, briefly studying architecture to learn rigorous approaches to drawing and design. He then made a switch to decorative arts and learned a different form of drawing as well as wood cutting. He needed to learn the fundamentals of depicting 3-D perspective in two dimensions before he could identify the quirks of perspective to make his unique "impossible structures." He also said: "I believe that producing pictures, as I do, is almost solely a question of wanting so very much to do it well." With the possibility of duplicating 90 percent of any process, it is possible to achieve very good results.

Do not make the mistake of assuming that the techniques outlined in this book are too simplistic, or that your tasks are too complex or require specific talents, and therefore these methods will not work for you. The true sign of mastery of any subject matter lies in the ability to apply the principles in many unique situations. We are confident that if you take the time to analyze your processes, you will find the core issues and will find that there are consistent and teachable key points within all tasks. Identify them and learn how to communicate them effectively to others, and you will be able to develop exceptional talent in your people.

Teaching Fundamental Skills in a Standardized Way at Toyota

In the past, Toyota depended heavily on Japanese trainers to go all over the world and teach the right ways to do the jobs. This worked, but there were a finite number of Japanese trainers, and they varied in the ways they taught. As discussed earlier in the chapter, Toyota's Global Production Center was set up to address the challenging task of developing useful generic training for all of Toyota worldwide. One possibility for such generic training is to teach at the general level, perhaps in the classroom, and to cover some of the basics, allowing the specifics to be taught on the job. But this would violate Toyota's basic principle of teaching: People learn by doing. How do you teach specifics when each shop in Toyota—body shop, stamping, painting, assembly, plastics, and so on, has so many different variations of specific tasks? First, you need a separate training program for each shop. Second, you need a concept Toyota calls "fundamental skills." Toyota analyzed what employees do in each shop and found that there is a surprisingly small set of fundamental skills that account for the large majority of activities in the shop.

Let's take as an example the final assembly process. If you walk Toyota's assembly line, at first it is overwhelming to see the large variety of jobs people do. Even within a work cycle of 1 minute there are many individual elements for each job that require some different activity. But when all of the job tasks were analyzed by Toyota, eight fundamental skills were identified that are the true core content of what goes on in assembly. These skills are:

1. Tightening bolts or nuts on in-line surfaces (fastening plates and surface tightening).
2. Tightening bolts or nuts on any of six angled surfaces.
3. Tightening self-tapping screws.
4. Coupling connectors (e.g., connect wire harness).
5. Inserting hole plugs (includes inserting wire harness through holes).
6. Mistake-proofing (e.g., torque wrenches that only tighten to specifications).
7. Tightening mating fasteners (e.g., tighten flare nuts on ABS).
8. Memorizing manifest (the build specification sheet).

For each of these tasks there is a table set up with a computer monitor on the table and some sort of simulated version of the task. Students review the "video manual," which provides descriptions of the task and key points and illustrates the right and wrong ways to do the task. Students then try the task on the simulated table version with the trainer observing and giving tips. When the students are ready, they pull the andon for the trainer to come and test them. They must complete the task, doing it in the proper way, and in the allotted amount of time.

Even seemingly simple tasks like seating a screw grommet into a hole have been broken down into elemental steps. The first exercise is simply to pick up four or five grommets in each hand and then position them between the forefinger and thumb, ready for insertion. The second exercise is then to actually insert the grommet. This seems like a trivial task, but doing it with both hands without interruption means coordinating picking up grommets, orienting them, and inserting them while picking up grommets in the other hand and keeping both hands moving. It is not as easy as it looks, but with some practice this becomes a very smooth rhythmic process. A metronome is at the workstation to illustrate the rhythm. Safety is emphasized at each station. For example, on the grommet job the student is instructed to rotate wrists as a warm up. Eventually the student will work up to inserting these grommets as part of a complete job on a moving car or cart.

In this process we find one of the fundamental principles of the Job Instruction method—to break the job elements down into small portions so that they can be easily learned. One mistake commonly made by workers who are assigned the training responsibility is to assume that because something is easy for them, it should also be easy for the student. Everything is easy *after* you learn how to do it! Carefully observe jobs in any workplace done by an experienced person, and you see a smoothly executed choreography of fluid motions that look simple. Toyota focuses great attention on identifying these crucial movements and then creates a way to relentlessly practice them until they are mastered. Picking up grommets seems simple enough, but the mastery of that task, fluently moving grommet after grommet from the palm to the finger tips, never missing a beat (and all the while simultaneously moving along the moving assembly line), never dropping a grommet, and never missing an insertion, is the difference between just doing a task, and the level of skill needed to work the line at Toyota. It creates the distinction between good and great.

Pay Now or Pay Later

Obviously there is still a great deal to learn after mastering fundamental skills in the Global Production Center and that is the purpose of Job Instruction training by the team leader—to master a specific job with specific standard work. After the trainees learn the fundamental skills, the trainer can focus on the details of that specific job and not have to spend time teaching the fundamental skills each time the team associate learns another job. The associate will learn the new job more effectively—performing the fundamental skills in the proper way.

We often hear from managers and leaders that they don't have time to go to this extreme when training employees. The truth is that this extensive effort by Toyota shortens the total training cycle and produces much lower total system losses than the method of allowing employees to learn skills while performing the work at their own unscheduled pace. The idea of an initial investment of time in employee development follows the theme of an old commercial for a transmission company. Remember the transmission repair person stating: "You can pay me now, or you can pay me later"? The implication was that if the early preventive maintenance was not performed, the resulting damage to the transmission would incur a greater cost. Unfortunately many people make this mistake when it comes to employee development. They assume that if an employee is in a job position and at least performing at some level, they are getting more initial value, whereas the employee who is still off-line practicing skills is not contributing any value. In the long-run the losses will be greater if employees are not given sufficient training.

Figure 2–3 demonstrates a hypothetical progression curve for the employee who is learning on the job (trial by fire) and the person who is learning basic skills off-line before stepping into a regular position. We can see that off-line trainees are not actually producing anything during the initial learning phase (they are off-line practicing), but that when they do learn the job skills, they quickly achieve full productivity. People learning on the job contribute some productivity during the initial phase, but take much longer to reach full capability, and they may never reach that level because they have not mastered some fundamentals. In addition to productivity losses, there is also increased risk of quality problems and injury with the trial-by-fire method.

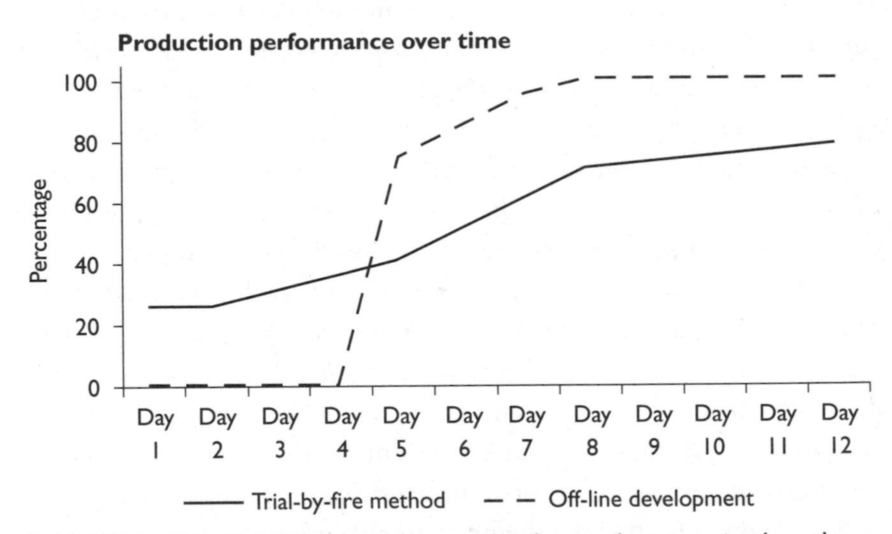

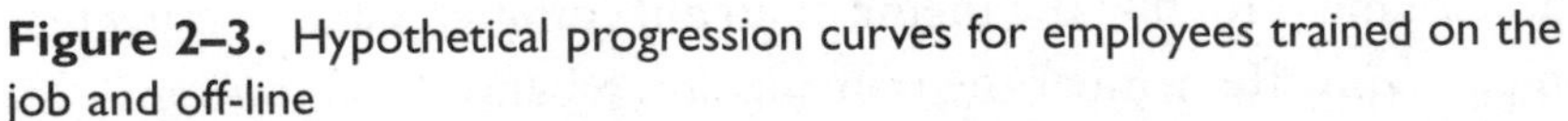

Figure 2–3. Hypothetical progression curves for employees trained on the job and off-line

Of course there are exceptions to this curve; some students will learn quickly on the job, and some will take longer than others with the off-line fundamentals, but generally this is how the performance curve would appear. Also we are representing days in this case, but some more difficult operations may have a longer learning curve for both scenarios. There is no question that the diligent effort put forth by Toyota pays off in the long run.

Can You Achieve Results Similar to Those of Toyota?

We have not had any way of measuring the capability of people selected to be Toyota employees versus those who enter other companies. However, we do not believe that there is anything particularly remarkable about the people selected by Toyota from a traditional academic point of view. Toyota does do an excellent job of selecting capable people with a good work ethic that seem moldable into the Toyota Way of doing things. Several managers who left other automakers like Ford or GM and went to work for Toyota have remarked that, if anything, their previous employers had even higher standards for hiring people in conventional terms such as academic credentials than does Toyota. The secret to Toyota's success is getting extraordinary results from ordinary people.

Of course, even Toyota as an organization does not do a perfect job of training or developing people. It is difficult to be successful in all areas when it is necessary to train thousands of workers, hundreds of line trainers, and dozens of classroom trainers. In this situation there will be natural differences in ability and dedication to the process. Not every leader will place the same importance or effort on the development process, nor will they have the same skill level.

The opening of regional training centers, however, indicates a desire by Toyota to continue improving the training effort. Atsushi Niimi, as senior managing director of training and development, attributes the Global Production Centers to Toyota's desire to "not only get bigger," but also, "We want to get better at the same time." Niimi was the president of Toyota North America and then returned to Japan as managing director, meaning he is one of the small inner circle of leaders who govern the company. The fact that he was assigned to lead training and development is remarkable. In most companies a group vice president would laugh at the thought of leading something as mundane as training and development. At Toyota, it is considered the life blood of the company, and its greatest challenge is to maintain high levels of development as Toyota rapidly expands and globalizes.

Can other companies do this? We believe the answer is *yes.* In part it is as simple as making it a priority. The technology for developing people is not new or remarkable. The commitment to doing it—every day, consistently, at a high level—is unfortunately very rare and remarkable. There are many organizations throughout the world that have to commit to developing exceptional talent; we have mentioned a few such as sports teams and great restaurants. You can do it too if your company is truly dedicated to excellence. In this book we give you some of the hows and whys, but it is up to you to make developing people the highest priority in your company or in your area of responsibility.

Chapter 3

Toyota and the Training Within Industry Program

Training Within Industry

Much of Toyota's way of thinking about training and developing people came from a U.S. program called *Training Within Industry* (TWI). Toyota has modified the material slightly, but for the most part it is used within Toyota today in much the same way as it was taught to Toyota in the 1950s. Because it is so foundational, we dedicate a good deal of this book to the methods first introduced by TWI and as they have been adapted by Toyota. We have added aspects from our own learning through the years, so what you find here will not necessarily be a replica of the TWI program or exactly what Toyota is doing today. The TWI framework also provides a philosophical framework for training in nonrepetitive jobs even when the methods cannot be standardized in detail.

The conquest of France by Germany in the spring of 1940 was a great concern to the U.S. government and greatly accelerated production of war munitions in the United States. One major problem was that many of the skilled workers had enlisted in the military, leaving inexperienced workers to fill the jobs. The need for skilled, experienced workers was identified by the War Manpower Commission, and it moved to establish the Training Within Industry (TWI) program in

August of 1940 in an effort to support U.S. war contractors and other organizations concerned with production of goods for the war effort (World War II).

The objective of the TWI program was to increase production capability so that the war could be shortened and the total cost of production could be reduced. According to *The Training Within Industry Report*, which summarized the entire program, the effort was primarily focused on "immediately increasing production for defense, then for war."[1] At the same time there was recognition of the importance of the methods beyond the war effort. The report went on to say, "No long range objective was set, but there are many implications for the development of the individual and for the improvement of the country's educational system."[2] Dr. Charles Mann, who had served as chairman of the War Department's Committee on Education and Special Training during World War I wrote the following:

> *We all want to meet the demands of war—maximum production through best use of our facilities and talents. But we can also build for the future in meeting the present challenge. The training we give the worker to do a good job for now for war production can be more than an expedient means of getting the job done. It can be suitable to the individual and in line with the native talent and aspiration. Then it becomes education because the worker placed in the line of work he desires, and trained in accordance with his talent and aspiration, is a growing individual—mentally, morally, and spiritually, as well as technically.*[3]

It would appear that Toyota took the goals of TWI to heart, because it has incorporated the concepts of the importance of people and their development into every aspect of their production system and throughout the company, including staff functions.

---

[1] War Manpower Commission, Bureau of Training, Training Within Industry Service, *The Training Within Industry Report: 1940–1945* (Washington, DC: U.S. Government Printing Office, September 1945), preface.

[2] Ibid.

[3] Ibid.

It is said that "there is no new thing under the sun,"[4] and that would appear to be true regarding ideas on effective training techniques. As far back as the early 1900s challenges and issues (such as resistance to change, lack of skills, and lack of motivation) existed that continue to plague businesses today. Aristotle recognized the challenges of education saying, "The roots of education are bitter, but the fruit is sweet."

It also appears that ideas and methodologies proceed in a cyclical manner. A good idea comes along, gains a certain amount of acceptance, and then fades into obscurity, only to be resurrected later. What we call "lean manufacturing" today first started to become popular in Western companies in the 1970s as "just in time," and has been dubbed "kaizen" or even "quality circles" at various times.

This seems to be the pattern with the Job Instruction method. Shortly after the war, the TWI methods fell from use as many of the temporary workers were replaced by returning soldiers who were more experienced. As part of the occupation and rebuilding of Japan, the TWI material was aggressively disseminated in Japan. Manufacturing experts, including some members of the TWI group, were sent over from the United States to teach the Japanese about modern manufacturing. And with the success of Toyota, TWI methods are finally becoming interesting again to American manufacturers.

In fact the concepts underlying TWI go back much further than World War II. In a direct sense they were built on the ideas of Charles Allen who had developed an approach to vocational training in the shipbuilding industry during World War I. Allen had an educational and philosophy background but was very rooted in practice. The vocational training methodology he developed was based on a four-step process: preparation, presentation, application, and testing. We see similarities to the Shewhart cycle (taught by Shewhart to Deming, who then taught it in Japan) of plan, do, check, and act (PDCA) as well as the roots of the Job Instruction training method we describe in this book. One can easily see how this approach fit the philosophy of Toyota's leaders who believed in hands-on learning and the scientific method.

[4] From the Bible, Ecclesiastes 1:9

Today, Toyota continues to use the methods first introduced in the United States in the 1940s with only slight modifications. What appears to be the key for success is not the ability to develop a *new* idea, but rather the ability to continue to *use* and *refine* good ideas. This is perhaps a fundamental key for Toyota, as many would argue that the primary concepts of the Toyota Production System (TPS) were gathered and combined from other sources (Ford, Deming, TWI, etc.). Toyota has been successful at *continuing* to use and build upon good ideas and concepts. Now it appears that the ideas and methods from TWI have come full circle. Based on the success of Toyota, other companies are beginning to adopt the methods of TWI again.

The TWI program contained four primary modules: Job Instruction, Job Methods, Job Relations (and Union Job Relations for unionized facilities), and Program Development. The programs were geared toward the development of internal trainers and supervisors who could multiply their own efforts by each training others. If each person who was certified to deliver the training (lead trainer) trained numerous supervisors (trainers), and each supervisor in turn trained 10 or more associates the success of the program would multiply. A brief synopsis of each training program follows:

- *Job Instruction:* This TWI course was designed to help supervisors "break in" new or unskilled employees and is based on decades of practical experience. Although the material was revised slightly as time went on, the basic premise remained the same—break down a job into its elements, identify the important points, and present the operation until success is achieved. The Job Instruction program introduced a method to Toyota to break down and analyze jobs and to teach them using a four-step method. This technique became a critical factor in Toyota's ability to develop people. Job Instruction training is done on the job by someone capable of doing the job according to the standard as well as with the capability and training to teach others. The intent was to raise productivity by shortening the "break in" period and to improve safety and quality through better worker understanding of critical elements of the work.

- *Job Methods:* This part of TWI provided techniques intended to help supervisors and employees methodically analyze all aspects of a job and to question every detail to determine necessity, sequence, and responsibility for each task. This questioning and evaluation would lead to increased productivity by eliminating "unnecessary" steps and activities, or "waste." This training advocated seeking the ideas of the people closest to the process—the workers—and provided some guidance on an age-old problem—overcoming resistance to change (we often think that resistance to change is a modern challenge).
- *Job Relations (Union Job Relations):* This course was aimed at providing supervisors with methods for handling issues and for improving working relations. Many of the supervisors during the war were inexperienced and had no knowledge of how to effectively handle employee issues and concerns. Topics included providing feedback to employees on performance, handling employee concerns, giving credit for good ideas or performance, communicating events and changes, and utilizing the abilities of each person. For this course there were two different programs depending on whether the facility was unionized or not.
- *Program Development:* It was well understood within TWI that the responsibility for success of the three "J" programs was with the individual plants. Program Development was specifically intended for the person or persons within each plant who would identify specific training needs, develop a plan, get the support of management, implement the plan, train supervisors, and verify the effectiveness of the program. Because of the limited nature of this responsibility (one or two people per facility), this training program was delivered to fewer individuals than the others (but this role will be a key one in your organization as you roll out the Job Instruction method).

Toyota does not teach the Program Development course to all leaders, but the ideas seem to be incorporated into the Toyota Way. The format closely follows Deming's PDCA cycle. The first step is to evaluate and analyze the details to determine the needs. Then develop and implement a plan. Finally, follow up and verify the results and repeat the cycle as necessary. We discuss the development of an overall organizational development plan in Chapter 4, as well as the individual employee development plan established by the supervisor and the employee.

Toyota definitely adopted the three J programs and continues to use them today. Toyota has utilized the Job Instruction and Job Relations materials in nearly their original form (with certain elements modified to "modernize" for current issues). The Job Methods material, based on traditional industrial engineering, mentions "eliminating unnecessary parts of the job" (waste), and refers to "making better use of manpower, machines, and materials."[5] Along with the method itself, these become the four Ms, which are often discussed by Toyota (man, machine, methods, and materials).

Isao Kato, a Master trainer at Toyota and work associate of Taichi Ohno, related that Mr. Ohno felt that the Job Methods material was too narrowly focused and did not include any connection to the idea of takt time, flow, and pull-style production, which Mr. Ohno had been experimenting with. Ohno ordered the discontinuation of the Job Methods training in its original form, and it was replaced by material developed by Mr. Kato and the Toyota training department. This later evolved into a TPS reference manual and specific training for standardized work and kaizen.[6]

We should note that Toyota would never recommend TWI as a stand-alone program. It is deeply integrated into the overall Toyota Production System. We have seen a number of traditionally managed companies adopt only Job Instruction training mainly to accelerate the learning process of new hires, and they are far from adopting lean manufacturing as a system. Taking a traditional mass production environment and dropping in TWI will predictably have limited effectiveness because there will be no clear takt time and no standard work-in-process inventory. In addition there would be incentives for

---

[5] Training Within Industry Service, Bureau of Training, War Manpower Commission, *Job Methods,* 1943, p. 12.

[6] Isao Kato in an interview with Art Smalley, www.artoflean.com, February 2006.

skipping the correct work methods in order to work faster and produce more since work is not synchronized and each operation is encouraged to produce as much as possible and as fast as possible.

Job Instruction Is the Foundation for Developing Talent

The Job Instruction method can be used to teach anyone any task—cooking, surgery, tying shoes, assembly, welding, or hitting a baseball (in fact the idea of having a recipe for cooking arose from the lack of standardization and the need to achieve consistency in the finished product). First, identify in the job to be taught what to do step by step, and then identify what is important about how to perform the steps. If these two elements are achieved successfully, the results of training will surely improve. Any task that is performed can be methodically broken down into these elements, and the information can be conveyed. There are other techniques used to aid in the training effort, but the identification of work elements and key points are at the heart of the method.

All work can be divided into two categories—the physical task that is completed and the related knowledge of the work. Product inspection is a good example of this. The physical task is the inspection process itself. It includes specific motions related to where and how to inspect—a specific visual path for the eyes and/or the hands to follow. What to look for—the defects or specific criteria—is part of the related job knowledge. It includes developing the ability to distinguish variation in the product, to determine acceptable and unacceptable levels, and perhaps to determine the corrective action required.

The Job Instruction method in its pure form is better-suited for teaching the task element of the work, but the principles can also be applied to the development of job knowledge. Don't make the mistake of assuming that the method is suitable only for repetitive tasks. If we were teaching the judgment portion of an inspection task, we would use key points to clarify *how* we make the judgment. There are visual or sensory indicators to distinguish the physical limits of acceptable quality.

We will demonstrate the effectiveness of the primary concepts in many unusual training situations, such as professional jobs, and will concentrate on the use of the Job Instruction fundamentals to teach skills throughout your workplace and company. The method will be demonstrated on simpler, repetitive tasks first because it is easier to understand. If the fundamental ideas are understood, they can be applied to any situation. These concepts will also be applied to non-repetitive jobs, such as tending to complex automated equipment and even engineering (although portions of each are repetitive).

We will branch out to other fields and see how the basic concepts can be applied in the health-care field and other service industries. In every case we will return to the central theme—identify the work elements that define *what* is done, and then identify the critical aspects of *how* the work elements are done. This is the foundation for all teaching and learning. It is a detailed understanding of the fundamental skills needed to do the work that is the foundation of Toyota Talent.

Toyota and the Job Instruction Method

The Job Instruction training introduced three key techniques to Toyota. First, the *job breakdown* provides a method of analyzing the work to determine what is important and how certain aspects of the job should be performed. It provides the basis for Toyota's propensity to study the work very carefully and thoroughly. Breaking down jobs is also an integral part of the standardized work process and is explored in detail in Chapters 5 to 7. The job must be broken down into manageable training pieces so that critical information can be effectively transferred.

Second, the Job Instruction training method is also known as the *four-step method*. The four steps are prepare the student, present the operation, try out performance, and follow up. This is the heart of the process for transferring knowledge effectively.

Finally, the TWI material introduced the idea of developing a *training plan*, which Toyota expanded to include the concept of the "*multifunction worker*." Toyota uses this tool to assess deficiencies in worker capability and to develop a timeline for improving employee talent.

There is little doubt that Toyota has used the original TWI material for training JI trainers very successfully. It is our opinion however, that the material in its original state is too simplistic for today's workplace. Toyota uses the Job Instruction course as a starting point, but over the years Toyota leaders have developed a deep capability to apply the techniques in the workplace. It is our experience that when students complete the 10-hour Job Instruction course originally used by TWI, they will have a limited ability to apply what they have learned. They will need mentoring from an experienced coach.

The limitations of the course include the fact that each student gets to practice the Job Instruction technique one time, and in a "classroom" situation—they teach only a small portion of a job in a classroom setting. This process does not provide enough real practice in the workplace. Don't make the mistake of developing a Job Instruction course, sending people to it, and then expecting them to be "trainers." In the Job Instruction method the follow-up phase of the training is crucial to the overall success. It is necessary to continue working with the student until you know they know how to do the task.

We would also like to point out that Toyota has only made minor modifications to the original content of the training. This does strike us as odd given Toyota's tendency for continuous improvement. The original delivery was very scripted, leaving no room for deviation from the program. While this might add an element of standardization (which we know is important), we find the delivery to be too much like a speaker reciting directly from a PowerPoint presentation.

Like any of the TPS tools, the actual application of the Job Instruction method is adaptable to your situation. We advise maintaining the core method, but certain aspects of the training may be modified to better suit your needs. For example, it is more realistic to practice the demonstrations in the workplace using examples from actual jobs. This is possible when the training session is conducted near the work area. Also the number of students per class session and the total time allotted may be tailored to your particular needs.

The Job Instruction Course

Because the original TWI material is readily available, it is not our intent here to completely outline the Job Instruction course.[7] We will outline some of the more important points (key points).

The original TWI Job Instruction program for training the trainers included a 10-hour classroom session consisting of five 2-hour classes with 10 trainees in each session. A brief summary of the content for each day is shown in Figure 3–1. The course is structured to follow the four-step method of Job Instruction outlined in Figure 3–2. For example, the first session begins by putting the students at ease and follows with discussion aimed at getting them interested in learning about training and the development of people.

During the first class the trainer spends a good portion of the time discussing the importance of effective training and the role of leaders. The Job Instruction method is demonstrated with a simple work example (following the principle of not presenting more than the student can master at one time), and then during subsequent classes the method is repeated by the other students while the trainer provides additional coaching.

Each subsequent session is designed to build on the previous session, and the students are given additional material in small portions.

Each day selected students are asked to prepare a training demonstration for the following day. On the second day the first students to demonstrate their training are at a disadvantage because they have only seen the method demonstrated one time by the instructor. They also have not been taught how to do a job breakdown, and thus their demonstration is generally not very good. It seems that this is an intentional effort to prove to the trainers-to-be what happens when students are not fully trained or prepared and have seen a job performed only one time. (This is what often happens in the workplace. Someone is "shown" the job one time and expected to be able to perform well.)

[7] The original material can be easily obtained from any major university or local library or through interlibrary exchange. For information, contact Mark Warren at www.tesla2.com.

Job Instruction Course Content

Day 1:

- Introductions (put students at ease).
- Get students interested in learning.
- Help students to see the need for effective training.
- Review five requirements of leaders.
- Demonstrate ineffective training techniques.
- Demonstrate correct instruction technique (Job Instruction).
- Review the four-step method.

Day 2:

- Brief review of day 1.
- Training demonstrations from students (2).
- Instruction on breaking down the job (Job Breakdown).
- Review preparation necessary for training.
- Summary.

Day 3:

- Brief review of day 2.
- Review four-step method (recite pocket card).
- Review job breakdown sheets.
- Develop a multifunction worker training plan.
- Training demonstrations from students (3).
- Summary.

Day 4:

- Brief review of day 3.
- Review four-step method (recite pocket card).
- Review multifunction worker training plans.
- Training demonstrations from students (3).
- Handling difficult teaching situations.
- Summary.

Day 5:

- Brief review of day 4.
- Review four-step method (recite pocket card).
- Training demonstrations from students (3).
- Summary and final encouragement.

Figure 3–1. Job Instruction course content

Job Instruction Four-Step Method

Step 1: Prepare the student

- Put the student at ease.
- Tell them the job name.
- Find out what they already know about the job.
- Get the student interested in learning the job.
- Place the student in the correct position to learn.

Step 2: Present the operation

- Tell, show, and demonstrate each major step, one at a time.
- Tell, show, and demonstrate each major step with key points.
- Tell, show, and demonstrate each major step with key points and reasons for each key point.
- Instruct clearly, completely, and patiently.
- Do not give the student more than he can master at one time.

Step 3: Try out performance

- Have the student try the job while correcting errors.
- Have the student do the job again while explaining the major steps.
- Have the student do the job again while explaining the key points.
- Have the student do the job again while explaining the reasons for key points.
- Repeat until you know the student understands.

Step 4: Follow-up

- Assign the student a task.
- Tell them who to ask for help.
- Check their progress frequently.
- Encourage questions.
- Gradually reduce the coaching follow-up.

Figure 3–2. Job Instruction four-step method

A major portion of the class time is spent with students practicing a training demonstration. Each student is expected to demonstrate his or her understanding of the Job Instruction method using a fellow student as a trainee. With 10 students per class and each training demonstration lasting between 20 and 30 minutes, nearly one-half the class time is consumed with demonstrations. Individual experience is considered best, but the intention is that each student would also learn from the other demonstrations. In reality, practicing a new method only one time is not really sufficient to master the skill. In addition, the demonstrations in the classroom are brief relative to actual jobs and include only a small segment of the real job. This does not provide the trainers with first-hand experience with teaching longer and more complex jobs.

The newly minted trainers are to return to the workplace to teach their fellow employees. But with only a brief introduction to the Job Instruction method, the trainers have minimal practical experience in the new skill. At Toyota each new trainer returns to the work area and is mentored by other skilled trainers and the group leader who has also been trained in the Job Instruction method. Each of these leaders has many years of first-hand experience and is highly skilled in the process. Of course Toyota did not always have this deep capability. It started the process at ground zero, just like you will, and had to learn how to deepen its skills as it went along. The key is to begin development with the leaders so that a solid foundation is available to mentor new initiates.

In our experience it is possible to modify the length of the course to accommodate a few more students (or few less) according to your needs. Be careful that the class size does not get too large (over 15 students) because the additional presentations tend to be too repetitious for most students (just watching, but not doing). If the class is smaller, it may be possible to allow each student to practice two times in the classroom. The best situation is to get the students into the hands of experienced leaders who will be able to coach them one-on-one in the actual work area. Toyota has maintained the original format of the 10-hour TWI class, although the class might be shorter if fewer than 10 students are present.

To aid trainers, the basic outline of the Job Instruction method is condensed to fit on a small card that will fit in a shirt pocket (known as a *pocket card*). The front of the pocket card details specific items to do and pay attention to before, during, and after the training activity (see Figure 3–3). The back of the card contains information on the

Considerations for Job Instruction Training

Prior to training activity

- Develop a multifunction worker training plan.
- Determine training needs and develop a schedule.
- Ensure trainer's time availability.
- Make sure the work area is clean and orderly (just as you would expect it to be maintained).
- Have all tools and equipment ready.
- Complete the Job Breakdown Sheet.
- Make sure that your job is covered so that you will not be interrupted.

During the training activity

- Ensure the student's safety.
- Never assume that they know something.
- Evaluate the trainee's learning, and repeat the process until you are satisfied they can do the job.
- Pay close attention to what the trainee is doing.

After the training activity

- Be specific in the job assignment (how much, when).
- Evaluate their work after completion.
- Evaluate for continued good safety habits.
- Check their knowledge by asking questions.
- Provide additional training as needed.

Job Instruction Trainer's Motto

"If the student hasn't learned, the instructor hasn't taught."

Figure 3–3. Considerations before, during, and after the training activity

four-step method (as shown in Figure 3–2). We have expanded some of the text for clarity. In order to fit on a pocket-sized card, the content of the text needs to be abbreviated.

The training process is divided into three stages—before the training session, during the training delivery, and after the training is completed. Both the classroom training and the actual job task training follow the same progression. Prior to launching a training initiative in the company or prior to having a class for trainers, it is necessary to assess the company needs and develop a plan. It is necessary to ensure readiness and to make sure all the bases are covered. The same rule holds true for the trainer who will teach a job task in the work area. The trainer must have a plan, and he or she must make sure that everything is ready.

During any training session the trainer must always assess the current situation and make necessary adjustments. The trainer must never assume that learning has occurred. Learning is always confirmed by observing the student until the trainer is absolutely sure. During the train-the-trainer session, the Master trainer must confirm the capability of each student. The Master trainer may provide additional guidance during the class, and he or she should also review the situation with the student's workplace mentor for additional follow-up. The workplace mentor is someone already experienced and skilled in Job Instruction training who is assigned an area of the plant to coach the new trainer on an ongoing basis. At Toyota this would most often be the group leader, but it may also be a skilled team leader.

The follow-up stage of the process is crucial. After the trainers have successfully completed the course, they will return to the workplace and will require additional guidance. Toyota has been using the Job Instruction method for decades, and it has a strong base of capable mentors for new initiates. A company that is just beginning to use this method may require several years to develop strong mentors. Without available mentors the training would be similar to the "I showed you how, now go do it" training style. It is highly unlikely that students will be capable of effective training after a single 10-hour class.

Toyota has created a structure with "Master" trainers who are responsible for training the Job Instruction classroom trainers (the trainers who will teach the training classes to line trainers). There may be only one or two Master trainers at each facility. The Master trainer must attend a "train-the-trainer" session, which is 40 hours in length (and is required for all employees who will teach the Job Instruction course to trainers). He or she would then learn to teach the train-the-trainer session and be subjected to rigorous scrutiny from another

Master trainer. This is similar in nature to the master and apprentice structure.

The Master trainer is also expected to assess the needs of the organization and to provide training and support to other trainers as needed. Local management and supervision must be skilled in the Job Instruction method and are expected to provide necessary coaching and follow-up to the trainers within their area.

TWI Is a Great Launching Point

We have gone into some detail about TWI and the programs Toyota has created. So how does this help you in your quest to learn from Toyota about how to develop your people to be truly exceptional? TWI was a great launching point for Toyota, and Toyota's approach and thinking can be a great launching point for you.

TWI fits within the way of thinking of Toyota leaders. It is interesting that TWI was a program that filled a specific need during World War II—to quickly get replacement workers up to speed to keep America's factories going—yet it was actually much more. TWI was built on the philosophies of Charles Allen and his team and then was broadened to a system of management in the workplace, which has implications beyond the factory floor. There were a lot of key assumptions about the right way to teach and manage, including:

1. People learn gradually over time, in small chunks, by doing and being coached and learning small pieces of the process step by step.
2. Putting the pieces together into a whole takes additional time beyond learning the pieces and requires ongoing coaching as the work is being done.
3. The pieces need to be defined and put together into some form of a standardized process in order to be effectively taught to the student.
4. Training and development are ongoing processes in the workplace and create a harmonious relationship between the supervisor (coach) and the worker.

5. The key role of the supervisor is to be a teacher and coach and to develop the people doing the work.
6. Ultimately quality and productivity are the result of this long-term development process.

These were not necessarily explicitly stated as assumptions of TWI, but they were at least implicit and fit the Toyota Way as it was evolving. They fit the sensibilities of the leaders who were building on what the Toyota family founders had started. Toyota, after all, evolved from a farming family in a farming community. They were practical, hands-on people. For centuries parents taught their children the craft of farming. They knew how to teach, and TWI provided a foundation to continue the teaching methods that had worked for centuries.

With this foundation we are suggesting that many different types of companies with many different types of jobs have a lot to learn. If we start with the basic philosophy of TWI and consider how people learn and the value of developing people, we can significantly increase the performance of any organization. The rest of the book shows you how to do this.

Chapter 4

Prepare the Organization

Start at the Beginning[1]

We know you are anxious to begin the journey of developing exceptional people and to dive right into figuring out a training plan. But you are not quite ready. You need a broader plan to prepare your organization. Before you begin any journey, it is helpful to understand both where you currently are and where you intend to go. We begin with a process that is essentially the same as that used for problem solving. The first step of the problem-solving process is to define the current situation and to explore the background information. There are important questions to explore, and then you must develop an understanding of what the journey's end will look like. If you don't do these things, how will you know if you are on the correct path?

Two things that Toyota is famous for are meticulous planning and preparation. We strongly suggest that you emulate Toyota in this regard. It is much easier to spend a little extra time in planning and preparation in order to avoid the hardship of correcting mistakes later. We know this may not be the "fun stuff" and that there is a strong bias

[1] March Hare, *Alice in Wonderland.*

for "getting going," but it is crucial that you properly set your sights and understand the requirements ahead. You must consider many questions, such as, "How long will it take to reach the desired level?" "What resources will be necessary to reach the objective?" and "How will the resources get training?"

In this chapter we begin to cover in detail the Toyota Talent Development Process. The overall process is summarized in Figure 4–1. In this chapter we discuss the organizational preparation required before you can get started on the actual Job Instruction (JI) process. You must understand the organization's needs, develop an organization structure for training, develop plans for who will be trained and developed, and select and develop the trainers themselves. In Part 2 of the book we look at the process of identifying critical knowledge, which includes breaking down the job into manageable pieces that can be absorbed by the trainee. Once you have the job broken down and you know what you are going to teach, you can begin the training, which has four steps that are described in Part 3—prepare the student, present the operation, try out the performance, and follow up until the

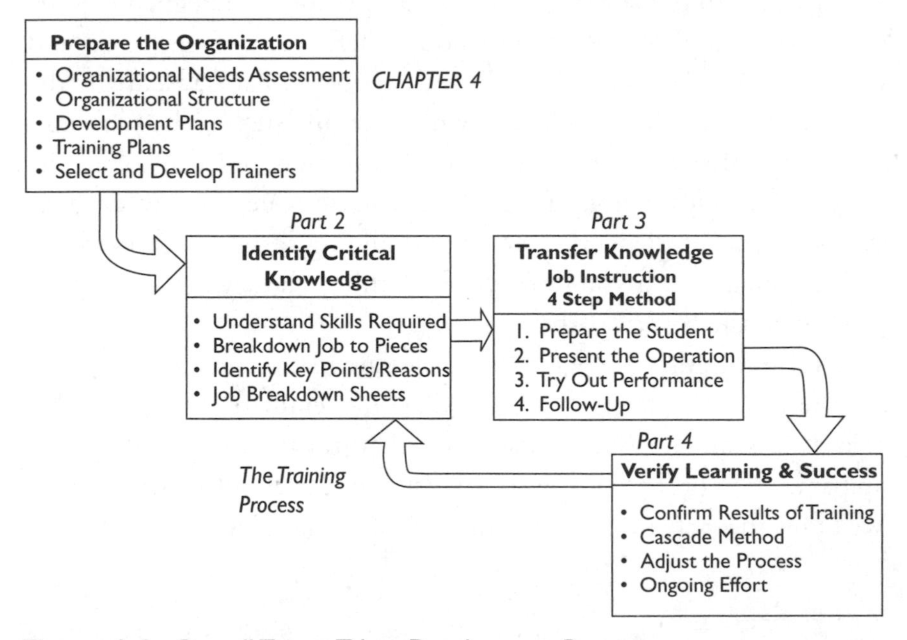

Figure 4–1. Overall Toyota Talent Development Process

student is capable of working alone. Finally you must verify learning and success and continuously improve the process as discussed in Part 4. Each of these steps has its own challenges and must be learned over time.

If it is not already painfully obvious, we remind you once more of the effort required to complete this task and to make sure you are prepared. Perhaps you have seen a movie where the young, ambitious upstart begs the experienced master to teach him to achieve success (think *The Karate Kid* with Pat Morita). The student starts with great enthusiasm until he discovers the amount of work required (in the case of *The Karate Kid,* it was the routine and mundane activity of waxing the car over and over).

In Hollywood the upstart always discovers the secret wisdom of the activity (the reward) just before he gives up in frustration. We don't want to dissuade you, but there may not be the quick and dramatic gratification we see in a Hollywood ending. You will work exceptionally hard and will need to be patient before expecting to see the reward. But we can assure you that, if you practice these methods diligently, the reward will be there and will probably surpass your expectations.

Define the Organizational Needs and Objectives

The first question in the Toyota Talent Development Process is, "Why do you want to develop the talents of your employees?" To answer this question, we suggest you consider the current market conditions of your business. Talented employees will surely improve your business results, but it is better to more specifically define the scope of your need before beginning. We don't want to go about randomly getting talented. We want the talent to support the needs of our business. Remember that the training process is part of an overall comprehensive course of action—implementing your version of the Toyota Way.

Consider what you want and what the needs of your business are. Is the market expanding? Is the company struggling to meet the customers demand? If so, the talent development process can be structured to emphasize the improvement of productivity (e.g., specific key points to improve efficiency and job analysis for the elimination of waste) or support additional staffing for expansion. Your people can focus on developing skills to quickly and effectively train new or existing employees. It is important to state the immediate need when you establish your process. You state, "We need to use this process to improve our productivity," or "We need to use the process to more quickly and effectively introduce new people to our operation and teach them the necessary skills."

Do you have a need to bring products to the market more quickly? Do you want to use the process specifically to accelerate your product design process and your ability to get the product to the market sooner? If you are in a service business, it is always your aim to improve the customer experience. Hospitals can concentrate on improving patient care and the patient experience (including the side customer—the family of the patient), cost reduction, and the speed of processing patients through the system.

Have you established an objective to be a market leader in your business? Do you want to achieve the highest levels of customer satisfaction in your industry? You must understand your objectives and then see the connection between them and the development of your people. This is an important step—to understand the needs of your business from an *external* standpoint. That is, to identify what is necessary to be competitive and to grow the business and become a market leader. Of course, over the long-term you are trying to establish a core of talented people who can work on whatever your highest priority objectives are at the time. The next step will be to consider the needs from an *internal* perspective—those things that are necessary to improve conditions within your organization, such as employee retention and satisfaction. Table 4–1 provides a review of some of the common indicators of both internal and external business conditions, and we discuss ways to evaluate your situation.

We can assure you that Toyota faces the same challenges as anyone else in business. Its competitive edge is well-defined systems and highly capable people who know how to run the systems. Toyota has used

Table 4–1. Business performance analysis

Measurement	Negative performance	Flat performance	Improving performance	Comments
Safety incidence rate	X			Higher than industry average
Quality—internal cost			X	
Quality—external customer		X		
Productivity/ efficiency	X			
Profitability		X		
Total cost		X		
Employee involvement				
– Quality circles	X			QC program stopped
– Suggestion program	X			No suggestion program
Unexcused absence rate		X		
Employee turnover	X			Losses within first year
Other				

the Job Instruction method as a means to achieve success. It has learned how to adapt the tools on a case-by-case basis to achieve specific results. This means that the process can be tailored specifically for particular situations. Of course it can be used in a general way for overall performance, but it can also be used to highlight specific needs. Many people view standardization as being inflexible, but in reality it is quite the opposite. As with a mechanic, a standard set of tools can accomplish a multitude of tasks—all depending on the need at the time.

Assess the Current Situation

You must completely understand the current situation of your business, both internally and externally. There are a variety of ways to do this and multiple indicators in any organization. We suggest a review of business performance metrics, interviews with management and employees, first-hand observation and interaction, and other sources of information, such as customer feedback or employee opinion surveys.

Table 4–1 provides an example of a business performance metric analysis. The idea is to look at the trends over the past few years. Essentially, if the organization is not trending upward this indicates stagnation in the growth of employee capability and talent.

We suggest that you begin by analyzing past and present business performance, such as profit growth, productivity gains, quality levels, and safety. If the performance indicators do not show continuously improving results, it is an indication that people are not developing. It is also important to understand whether the condition is getting worse or staying the same. If results are declining, the urgency to address the situation becomes greater.

Notice that Table 4–1 is a very simple summary rather than detailed charts and graphs (which should be looked at to get to this simple summary). These indicators will assist you in establishing both the need for improvement and specific areas to target during the training. For example, if the quality indicators are showing a negative trend, the root cause may be that quality-related key points are not being effectively identified and communicated during the training process or that people do not understand what is important for ensuring quality. This assumption can be confirmed during employee interviews (explained in the next section of this chapter) and also by having employees demonstrate how to perform their jobs. If this is an area of weakness, it can be specifically targeted in the implementation plan and during the training process.

Other factors, such as turnover and absenteeism, are also indicators of overall satisfaction. Note that Table 4–1 shows a comment regarding the turnover of employees with less than one year of service. This is an indication of potential problem areas regarding assimilating new hires effectively. If people are dissatisfied with the work, they will recognize it early and may cut their losses quickly. This is an especially troubling indicator because all investment made in the individuals' development is lost. Turnover of long-time employees may suggest other factors, such as pay rates at competing companies, and may not indicate overall dissatisfaction with work conditions.

Any negative shift in the absentee rate may indicate a more pressing problem. People need challenge and stimulation. If they are not adequately challenged and stimulated by having learning opportunities, they become bored and will begin to avoid the issue—they will avoid work. Absenteeism is often a precursor to turnover and should be viewed as a serious warning of future problems. You should use this process as a means to actively engage people in challenging and stimulating activities (and developing deep understanding of the work content and teaching others is certainly challenging!).

Actual data may not be available for all indicators in your organization, and it may be necessary to use subjective information in those cases. The collective opinion of several people may be an accurate indicator and can be used. It is not necessary in this case to have precise indicators, but rather it is important to understand the general performance and the need for improvement.

Go to the Source for Information

Next we suggest that you interview employees. If you have a small organization, it may be possible to talk with each employee directly. In larger organizations it may be necessary to interview a representative sample. This is preferable to an anonymous written survey because you can clarify any comments. An example of possible questions to ask is shown in Figure 4–2.

Ask employees about their experience when they started with the company or more recently if they have transferred to a new area. The purpose is not to identify specific names of people who are not doing a good job of development, but rather to understand the overall situation and shortcomings of the current system (ultimately everyone bears responsibility for shortcomings unless they are specific to one area).

You may notice that some employees shrug off the fact that they weren't given adequate training to perform their job. They may be the type of people who are tenacious and will find a way to succeed in spite of having little information. Note that these are the type of people who are likely to work through the challenges and may not jump ship, but

Needs Assessment Employee Interview

- What is your current job?
- How long have you been in your current job?
- What was your previous job?
- How long were you in that job?

Employees with less than one year on the job—ask the following questions:

- How was your first day on the job?
- Were you welcomed and shown important things such as emergency exits, break areas, restrooms, smoking areas, etc.?
- Did your supervisor spend time reviewing expectations and work requirements?
- Were you assigned to a trainer who was responsible for your learning?

All employees:

- When was the last time you learned a new job?
- What was the training like? (Was adequate time, attention, detail, etc. shown by the trainer?)
- Do you feel that the person who trained you knew the job well enough?
- Do you feel as though you know the job well enough to perform it and meet expectation?
- Do you know what the requirements for safety are? (explain)
- Do you know what the requirements for quality are? (explain)
- Does the supervisor know and understand the requirements for your job?
- What suggestions do you have for improving the training process?

Figure 4–2. Sample questions for needs assessment employee interview

there will be many others who will not be willing to stick with the job if there is little training and support.

Ask employees questions related to how much time was spent on introducing them to the work area before they began work. Were the policies and procedures explained carefully? Did the supervisor review safety procedures and emergency evacuation procedures? In many cases we find supervisors who appear so eager to begin getting value from employees that they overlook the need to "get acquainted" and to make employees feel welcome.

Another way to find out the current situation is to ask various employees to teach you how to do their jobs. This can be a very enlightening activity. Pay particular attention to their explanation of critical safety and quality points. Often we hear employees training others and stating, "I have my own particular way of doing this, and others have a different way." This is an indication of inconsistencies in both the method of training and in the content of the work itself. This will be one of the items that you will target—to achieve greater clarity and consistency of the critical elements of the work. Evaluate the depth of detail and understanding of the work as it is explained. You may want to develop a better understanding of standardized work and job breakdowns, which are explained in Chapters 7 to 10 before doing this step. Then you will have a better understanding of whether people know the different elements of the task and the degrees of importance of certain aspects of each element.

Establish the Organization Structure

After you have assessed the situation, you must determine the resources necessary to accomplish your objective. The resource requirement is mostly dependent on the number of employees in your company or facility. We recommend a minimum of one person qualified in Job Instruction for every 10 employees. The people responsible for Job Instruction would not be full-time trainers who belong to a training department. They would instead be people from within the work group who have been certified through the Job Instruction class to train others. We refer to them as "workplace trainers." Within Toyota each team leader and group leader is a qualified workplace trainer, so the ratio of qualified trainers to team members is approximately one person skilled in Job Instruction for every four to six employees on average.

If your company has more than 300 employees, you may consider a structure like the one shown in Figure 4–3. There should be a high-level manager who acts as the champion or sponsor of the program. This individual should attend the Job Instruction training, but he or she does not need to be deeply qualified (although it won't hurt). With

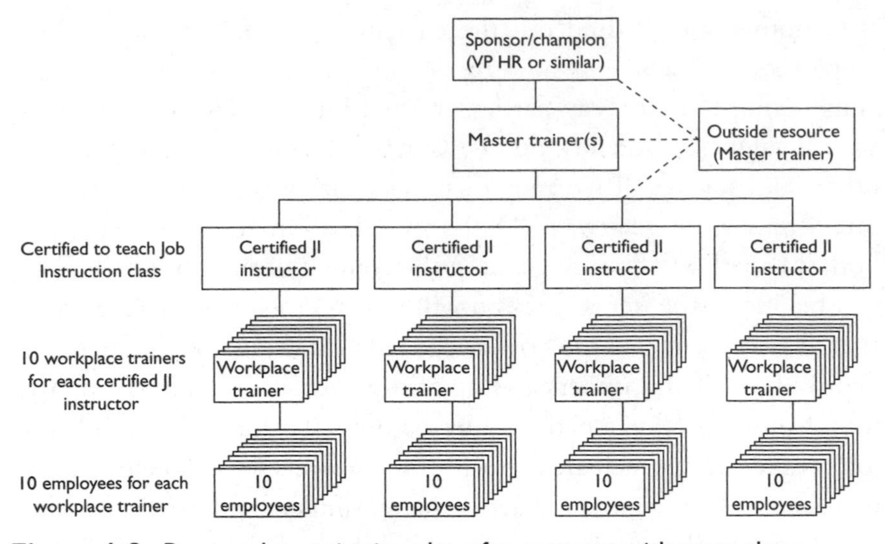

Figure 4–3. Proposed organization chart for company with more than 300 employees

over 300 employees, it is helpful to have a Master trainer who will oversee the entire process and ensure the consistency of the effort. The Master trainer must receive training to become certified as a trainer of other trainers; this person must also have organizational skills to be able to plan and outline a process for achieving the desired result. Below the Master trainer are additional people who are work-certified trainers. Depending on the size of the organization, the Master trainers will be responsible for certifying and supporting "certified JI instructors." The certified JI instructors can also train workplace trainers and would generally be from the supervisory ranks. Overall, the more people you have who are deeply qualified the better; however, there is a trade-off with time and cost to develop this structure. It is also a challenge to achieve depth of capability across a wider group.

Smaller companies will not need the same amount of training resources, but the ratio between employees and trainers should remain about 10 to 1 as shown in Figure 4–4. In this case a Master trainer to oversee the process may not be necessary. One of the certified JI instructors should act as a coordinator of the process. He or she will be responsible for planning and overseeing of the process, including

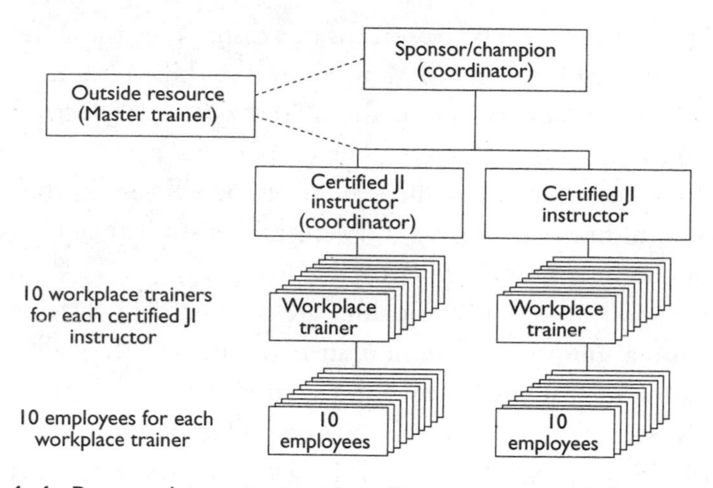

Figure 4–4. Proposed organization chart for companies with fewer than 300 employees

verification of results. Since there are fewer trainers in this case, the responsibility for some activities must be assumed by the certified JI instructors and process champion of the company. For example the process champion must assume some responsibilities for the development of the process that would otherwise be done by a Master trainer in a larger organization.

You will most likely find that some people in your organization have a strong interest in teaching and developing others. This should be your starting point for developing a structure that fits your organization. It is our belief that every supervisor should be required to attend a Job Instruction training class and that the supervisors should be responsible for supporting the trainers within their work areas. For promoting the process and assisting with the development of other trainers, we recommend using employees who volunteer to participate rather than requiring that people participate as a part of the job function.

Selecting Trainers

Many people make the incorrect assumption that the most skilled person on a job will be the best person to train others. Unfortunately, this is not always the case. The reason for this disparity is the difference in skill sets required for each task. For example, a skilled trainer does not have to be the fastest person at the task in order to effectively teach others to be fast and competent. The trainer only needs to know how to teach the techniques that allow people to be efficient in their movements. With time and practice the well-trained student can master the skills and become proficient.

We should note that companies are organized in different ways. Toyota has a unique organization structure on the shop floor and a similar structure for engineering and support groups. There is a group leader (salaried in manufacturing) who has team leaders (hourly in manufacturing) as direct reports. The group leader is responsible for developing the training plan, and the team leaders (with an average of about five to six team associates in their team) assist in training. The team leaders know all the jobs in their area so they are able to train for all jobs. In this way the people in each area who know the work are training others to do the work. Selecting team leaders and group leaders includes looking for the characteristics that make a strong trainer. We want to reiterate that the trainers are not in a full-time training position. The responsibility for employee development is part of their overall responsibility. We do not advise the use of full-time trainers to teach the team members job tasks. The trainers should be active members of the work group.

Since on-the-job training is a distributed responsibility within each department, you will not have the luxury of developing a small training center with a few hand-selected teachers. Not every department is going to have people who will make the ideal trainer, but you should plan for who will do the training, seeking or developing as many of the desirable characteristics as possible. Some of the characteristics you are looking for can be developed, and others are largely a part of a person's personality and, as such, are not necessarily learned or easily changed. You will need to do your best with what you can get. But, by analyzing strengths and weaknesses and selecting and developing trainers who are the best possible, you will have a huge multiplier effect on your success rate.

Natural Talents Necessary to Be an Effective Trainer

The model presented in Chapter 5 (Figure 5–2) proposes that all jobs are made up of fundamental skills, core job-specific knowledge, and accumulated know-how. In addition, there are personal traits each person has that also help in the performance of any task. These traits are hard to quantify. Sometimes they are referred to as "natural talent," or we may refer to them as "intuitive ability."

When selecting trainers, we must consider the skills required for the job. Fundamental skills are teachable and can be developed with repeated practice. Because they can be learned, we don't need to find people who already possess these abilities. It is possible to develop them. Almost anyone can learn the fundamentals of training. Intuitive skills, however, tend to be inherent in the personal makeup of the individual. It is possible to bring out latent abilities in individuals, but it is easier if the basic raw material is present to begin with.

In the case of a trainer, we may think of these intuitive abilities as character traits or personality characteristics. Longitudinal studies have shown that some basic characteristics of individuals are stable over time. It is not that people cannot change certain tendencies but that they are hard to change and unlikely to change. Introversion-extroversion is one such personality dimension. Some people are energized by being the center of attention (extroverts), while others find this draining and prefer to focus inward (introverts). This personality tendency does not generally change a lot over time. Interestingly, one might assume that a good trainer should be an extrovert, but that is not our experience. Extroverts may be better at holding attention in large lecture situations, but introverts can be excellent trainers, particularly in one-on-one mentoring. So this particular tendency should not have much impact on someone's ability to do Job Instruction training.

In our experience there are some intuitive abilities worth considering when we select trainers. We are not claiming that these are the results of psychological research, and we believe that some of these are more easily learned than others. We should also note that lack of any single trait is not a showstopper. Finding the complete package in any one individual is challenging.

Willing and Able to Learn

Teaching others is as much about learning as it is about teaching. Albert Einstein once said that the definition of insanity is, "Doing the same thing over and over again and expecting different results." Reversing the logic a bit would suggest that it would be insane as a teacher to expect different results without ever adapting to varying situations. The true master trainer is also a master student. A trainer must have the *desire* and *ability* to continually learn and grow and to reinvest his or her own learning into the teaching. This trait is generally observed in people who make efforts on their own to learn and accept new challenges.

Adaptable and Flexible

Every training circumstance will be different. For example, there will be differences in the material covered, the ability of the student, the current conditions in the workplace, and the amount of time that will be set aside for the training. Skilled trainers must have core competency in the training method, but they must also be adaptable to the moment. People who are rigid in their method and approach will surely be faced with Einstein's version of insanity. It is not possible to approach the varying conditions in the workplace with the same teaching style and method every time and expect a successful outcome.

Genuine Caring and Concern for Others

Trainers must care about the student. They must genuinely want the student to become successful in the task, and as a person overall. This desire includes respecting others and the ability to be empathetic to each person's situation as a student. People can easily sense when a trainer is genuinely interested in them. If trainers do not have genuine caring and concern, their attitudes and behavior will negatively influence the student, which can have long-lasting consequences. It is relatively easy to spot this characteristic in people. They are the employees who naturally make efforts to help others learn—without being asked to do so.

Patience

Training requires a great deal of patience. Conditions for the ideal training situation rarely occur, and challenges are plentiful. Each student will have different abilities, and some will need lots of practice to master the job. If the trainer is easily frustrated or is not able to stick with the process until the student is successful, the student may sense frustration from the trainer and may not be able to relax and concentrate on the task. A successful trainer must be able to put trainees at ease prior to beginning the training session.

Persistence

A trainer must stick with the learning process until the desired outcome is achieved. Skilled trainers understand that each student has different needs and abilities, and they must be willing to persist in the face of numerous obstacles. A trainer who is easily defeated or who believes that showing someone the job a few times should be enough would struggle in many training situations. One mistake that skilled and capable individuals often make is assuming that everyone will have the same ability that they have. If the student does not "get it" quickly, some trainers assume that the student is incapable of learning. This is an erroneous assumption and causes endless grief for the trainer and the trainee. Persistence should not be confused with belligerence or doggedness. Relentlessly pestering the student will lead to resentment. *Persistence* is the ability to stay with the process (while modifying the approach) until the desired outcome is achieved.

Taking Responsibility

The responsibility for a successful outcome rests with the trainer. There are many adults who try to do a good job, but not all are willing to take responsibility, particularly for an outcome they believe is not in their control. In the case of training, if the student fails, the trainer has failed. The trainer must make numerous decisions throughout the training process. If the decisions lead to undesirable outcomes the trainer must take responsibility for the decisions and develop a new plan in order to obtain a better result.

Confidence and Leadership

Trainers should be confident and self-assured. Students view trainers as the subject-matter experts. Trainers should have confidence when challenged in terms of their capability, questioned regarding rationale, and be seen as an authority but not necessarily as an autocrat. Trainers must lead by example in that they should demonstrate proficiency in the subject they are training. Nothing is more frustrating to a student than a teacher who does not know the material. Trainers need to provide some guidance without being too overbearing or too lax.

Questioning Nature

The final characteristic that trainers should have is a questioning attitude. Trainers must question why there was a particular outcome of the training and what must be changed, if a different outcome is desired. They must question the content of the job and fully understand why each step is important and what happens if each step is not completed correctly. They are not satisfied with, "I think this is correct." They must know for sure. Students are full of questions, and great trainers have already asked the questions and pursued the answer on their own and are willing to share what they have learned with others.

Fundamental Skills and Abilities That Are Learnable

The following are fundamental skills and abilities that can be mastered by anyone with the desire to do so. Some people possess greater natural abilities in these areas, but with continued practice and guidance from an experienced mentor, nearly everyone can become proficient.

Observation and Job Analysis Ability

The ability to carefully observe and analyze any situation is also tied to the need for adaptability. If trainers are unable to pick up subtle signs from the student regarding how well the training is going, they will be unable to make necessary adjustments. All trainers must have the ability to observe and analyze the training during three distinct phases. Trainers must have:

1. *The ability to observe the current work method and to identify the specific portions that are critical to the success of that work (known as* key points*).* This ability may require observing others, and it may be self-reflection as the trainer performs the task on his own. Or it may be a combination of observing others and self-reflection. These observations are then transferred onto a job breakdown sheet in preparation for the actual training.
2. *The ability to observe the student during the training session and to detect problems.* Perhaps the training is progressing too slowly, and the trainer needs to pick up the pace. Perhaps the student is not grasping the concept, and the trainer needs to break the content into smaller pieces. Or perhaps the student is struggling with a particular step, and the trainer must adapt and concentrate on that single step.
3. *The ability to analyze the final result and determine the effectiveness of the method and to incorporate this learning into subsequent training sessions.* Trainers must continue to observe the student until they are 100 percent certain that the training is complete and has been effective.

Effective Communication Skills

Communication skills go well beyond the ability to speak clearly. In fact in some training situations speaking is not possible (such as in a hazardous environment where the trainer and student must wear protective clothing that prevents them from speaking or when there is a language barrier). Communication is also about body language. Does the trainer present a relaxed yet confident air? Does he or she show interest by watching closely and providing positive confirmation when the steps are completed properly? Communication via gestures is a key component of successful training. A trainer must demonstrate correct posture and positioning by pointing, posing, and emphasizing certain work movements.

Of course trainers must have the ability to speak clearly and concisely. Some people can talk freely—at times too freely as they struggle to stay on task while rambling on about unrelated subjects. This overloads the student who is trying to focus on the important task at hand.

The ability to listen effectively and to interpret questions accurately is the other side of the communication equation. This is often called *active* listening—the ability to go beyond taking in the words, to actively interpreting what is being seen and heard.

Attention to Detail

Attention to detail is related to keen observation ability; however, attention to detail is also about being thorough and complete. It means making sure that preparation of the work site is thorough and complete prior to training, and it means that the trainer has made arrangements to conduct the training without interruption. The trainer must confirm that the critical details of the work are performed precisely as specified. Although attention to detail may reflect a personality characteristic, it can be taught sufficiently for people to make it a part of how they function.

Knowledge of the Job

A trainer must have a solid knowledge of the job. This may seem obvious, but we need to clarify the meaning of "knowledge." We are not referring to a cursory understanding of how to do the job—that is fairly easy to attain. We are referring to an understanding that is deeper and is developed over time—with experience. Knowledge of past quality issues, for example, helps the trainer to identify the correct key points that are necessary to prevent defects. Trainers should also have an understanding of the knacks that are used to perform the work efficiently. They are able to draw from a variety of knacks that are used by others to complete the task successfully—again demonstrating adaptability in the immediate training situation.

Respect of Fellow Employees

Let's face it. People are more likely to listen to and accept feedback from someone they respect than from someone they don't respect. Respect is earned and given if a person possesses the traits and abilities listed here as well as by demonstrating respect for others. If trainers are not seen as hard-working, knowledgeable, and caring, they are not likely to earn respect and will not have credibility with others. This is not really a fundamental skill, but certainly with effort a person can work to gain the respect of fellow employees.

Selection Process

We have summarized these selection characteristics in Table 4–2 which can be used as an evaluation tool. We show some hypothetical individuals being considered for a training role. We have separate averages for personal characteristics and teachable skills as well as an overall average. Note that while some individuals may have a higher score than others, we should also consider the difference between the averages for personal tendencies and teachable skills separately. For example, Emma's overall average is below Jesse's, but she is slightly stronger in personal tendencies. Emma's weaker areas are in those skills that can be taught, such as attention to detail. All these individuals could become effective trainers, even Matthew whose average is slightly above 2 or "meets expectation."

The selection criteria and scores for each characteristic should be used as a guide and not a definitive decision maker. A candidate who initially has lower skills and abilities may make a better trainer in the long-term, but they will need more development before they become proficient trainers. We advise taking the long-term perspective and working to develop all interested candidates. It never hurts to have more skilled people on the team!

Of course there may be other factors to consider as well. We believe that one of the most critical factors is a strong desire to be a trainer. If people have a strong desire to achieve an objective, they will

Table 4–2. Example of trainer capability evaluation sheet

Trainer Capability Evaluation Sheet					
		Name			
		Emma	Jesse	Matthew	Michael
Intuitive ability/personal characteristics	Willingness to learn	4	3	3	2
	Adaptability and flexibility	3	3	2	3
	Caring and concern for others	4	2	3	3
	Patience	3	2	2	3
	Persistence	3	3	2	4
	Taking responsibility	3	2	3	3
	Confidence	2	3	3	3
	Questioning nature	3	3	2	2
	Average for personal characteristics	3.1	2.6	2.5	2.9
Fundamental/ learnable skills	Observation and analysis ability	2	4	2	3
	Communication skills	3	3	2	3
	Attention to detail	2	4	2	2
	Job knowledge	3	4	2	4
	Respect of fellow employees	3	3	3	3
	Average for fundamental skills	2.6	3.6	2.2	3.0
	Overall average	2.9	3.1	2.4	2.9

Scoring
0–1 = Below expectation
2–3 = Meets expectation
4 = Exceeds expectation

be more likely to succeed. If trainers are selected arbitrarily, they may view it as a burden rather than an opportunity, and that feeling tends to rub off on students. People who are drawn to the opportunity by desire have a much greater chance of success and will exude enthusiasm to the students. This is a much better situation than having a person who does not want to be a trainer who is forced to become one.

Making Development Plans for All Employees

All leaders should devote a major portion of their time to the development of every employee (including themselves). Smart leaders know that people who are learning and growing are happier and more productive. People with more abilities are able to support the leader and the company more effectively. When people are able to utilize their talents, they provide greater benefits to themselves, the company, and to their work team. It is impossible to separate the performance of the individual from the success of the team or company.

A development plan goes beyond only identifying jobs and skills that you want an employee to learn, or improving weak areas in performance. There are three considerations when creating employee development plans. They are:

1. Ensuring that employees learn the necessary job skills to perform their work;
2. Planning for the development of related job skills such as becoming a trainer, learning problem-solving methods, or becoming proficient with specific tools and equipment such as computers or programming machine tools; and
3. Considering the personal growth and development of each employee in areas such as leadership development or pursuing other objectives such as acquiring a degree or pursuing opportunities in another department (for example, a production team member becomes a production planner or acquires a degree in accounting and moves to the accounting department).

Smart leaders will achieve greater success when they pay attention to the development of the complete individual beyond basic job skills. Take the time to understand what team associates want for their future. Sometimes this means that an associate may pursue other opportunities in the company and that you will lose your valuable asset and investment. In the long run you will be doing everyone a greater service by making this sacrifice.

In one situation at the Toyota plant in Georgetown, a production team member indicated that he had aspirations of becoming a skilled trades member (maintenance). The leader saw this as an opportunity to benefit the team in the short term, and the employee and company in the long term. As part of his development plan, the team member was asked to participate in continuous improvement efforts within the team. He could practice and develop his skills by assisting with the construction of various items suggested by the team, such as new workstations or jigs and fixtures. The leader had experience in welding and fabrication and was able to instruct him in these areas. The team benefited because it had one of its own members who could assist with the development of their ideas. The team member benefited because he was more engaged in his work and more satisfied overall. The company benefited because the spirit of continuous improvement was fostered and a skilled team member was being developed (and maintenance people were always in short supply). Of course the leader benefited as well because he had a more productive team member and a more satisfied team. In the end the team member was accepted into the skilled trades apprenticeship program—a long-term sacrifice for the leader, but a benefit for the team member and company.

Development for Personal Achievement

The third type of development relates to specific interests that may or may not be beneficial to the work currently being done. Working on the personal development of individuals may seem like a waste of time to some managers. Why should a manager develop a plan to help someone learn something that ultimately may take him or her away (as in a plan to become an accountant and to transfer out of the area)? Here the prudent manager understands that there is generally a connection (albeit a loose one) between a person's interest for development and the needs of the organization. In his book *The Seven-Day Weekend,* Ricardo Semler shares the wisdom of helping employees of Semco explore their self-interests and what he calls their "reservoir of talent" and, at the same time, fulfill the agenda of the company. He states, "If there's a match or alignment between what we want and what they want, the results will be twofold: While they're busy satisfying themselves, they'll satisfy the company's objectives, too. They succeed, we succeed."[2]

---

[2] R. Semler, *The Seven-Day Weekend* (New York: Penguin Books, 2004), p. 42.

The leader must make a conscious decision to support people and to help them achieve what they desire, knowing that in the long run this decision will make people want to support the leader and the company. People who feel constrained in some way, who are unchallenged, or who are unable to engage in activities that interest them, will not deliver their best work.

Take for example the employee who expressed an interest in entering the skilled trades program (maintenance) discussed above. He had a natural aptitude for this work and had previously learned some skills. At Toyota, having an individual on the team who had an ability to build things is very beneficial when it comes time for implementation. It is always preferable to have a person implement his or her own idea if possible, or to work together with a fellow team member, so having someone in the group who wants to learn these skills is a plus.

It is not necessary for the leader to provide the training. The leader only needs to provide the opportunity for the employee to get the training. The employee must take personal responsibility for development of skills that are not related to the work. This is also a good way to test commitment (it is easy to think that we want something, but an entirely different matter if we actually have to *do* something to get it!) and to have the student assume some responsibility for his or her development. In this area there is no defined time limit for completion. The employee would determine this.

A colleague, Bill Martinson with the Minnesota Manufacturing Extension Partnership, was teaching a course in operations management at the local community college. Christian, a student in the class, expressed an interest in the type of work that Bill was discussing in the classroom and asked if he could accompany Bill when he was working with one of his client companies. As it turned out, we were conducting a class in Job Methods Improvement, another of the Training Within Industry courses, and Bill suggested that Christian attend the session. Christian was accepted by the people from the company and jumped into the process wholeheartedly. He made a great contribution to the company—at no cost to the company—but more importantly he demonstrated willingness to invest his own time to discover whether he was interested in the work. For that effort he was rewarded with a great experience and the opportunity to find out firsthand without risk, whether that type of work was what he really wanted as a career before finding and accepting a job in that field. A valuable lesson indeed!

In *First, Break All the Rules*,[3] Marcus Buckingham and Curt Coffman point out that one mistake many managers make is to focus on developing the weak points of employees rather than working with people to capitalize on their strengths. Rather than sending employees to "sensitivity training" annually because they are "abrasive," look for ways that their positive natural talents and abilities can be applied. Every employee brings with him some personality or character trait that is undesirable. Buckingham and Coffman stress the importance of positioning employees where their natural deficiencies can be minimized while their strengths can be used effectively.

It is fairly easy to assess people's strengths and weaknesses for performing the tasks required at work. What is more difficult is to find natural interest, which often points to unused strengths or talents that, if used, would spark a fresh desire and renewed commitment to the work. One way to find out what interests people is to ask them! Initiate a conversation to find out what their hobbies and interests are. You may already know the hobbies, but in this case you are trying to find out more. You want to know why they like what they do. For example, does their hobby require analytical ability such as solving puzzles? If so, they may naturally be drawn to work tasks that require analysis skills.

During a recent training session on problem solving, the idea occurred to us that some people seem naturally drawn to the problem-solving process, while others are not. Wanting to build on the idea of appealing to people's natural inclinations, we needed to discover who liked this type of activity. We decided that we might get an understanding by asking what types of games people liked to play. For example, did they like puzzles and analytical games, or did they like games

[3] Marcus Buckingham and Curt Coffman, *First, Break All the Rules: What the World's Greatest Managers Do Differently* (New York: Simon & Schuster, 1999).

of strategy or games such as word searches or crossword puzzles? As is usually the case, the answers were fairly surprising. Just when you think that you have someone figured out, asking these types of questions reveals that you may not know as much as you think. Remember the old adage about assuming anything! Some people indicated that they liked chess. Chess is a game that requires several skills—strategy, advance planning, counterstrategy, and organization, to name a few. It is a complex game that moves slowly and methodically. What type of work activities might be of interest to a person who enjoys chess?

In addition to asking what games they liked, we also asked why they liked them to see whether people were consciously connected to what it is that they enjoy about the game, and whether they would be able to connect to similar activities in the workplace. We often find that people are unable to see connections between what they enjoy doing as a hobby and similar activities at work.

A few people simply stated that they do not like games of any kind. This would require further exploration. Perhaps they are "practical" and see games as a waste of time. (Would a practical approach to situations be a possible strength?) The question was intended to get a better understanding of what motivates and interests people in order to connect those interests and motivations to similar situations at work. If you are able to find these connections and help people maximize their exposure to what they truly enjoy, you will be richly rewarded. One beleaguered manager quipped, "If only I could figure out a way to make work more like fishing!" That is one connection we have not been able to make—yet.

The Talent Development Process

This book is divided into four parts that follow the talent development process. This chapter completes the first part—getting the organization ready to develop exceptional people. This critical step establishes a foundation for a successful process, and while some parts of this first step may be repeated or evaluated in the future, it is generally a one-time process. The next three parts outline the actual process that must be followed to develop exceptional people, and these steps will be repeated continually. Things in the work area change constantly, and it is necessary to reevaluate the work methods, share new information, and make modifications to existing work methods.

The next three steps (presented below) will also require a great deal of work, and a lot of time, to truly develop exceptional people. We suggest that you begin gradually and deepen your ability before attempting to conquer the entire process. We suggest that you select a target work area where you can go through each of the three steps completely with your certified trainers and learn how to effectively develop the process before expanding into other areas of your facility. Make sure you do a thorough job in each step before moving to the next step. There is little point in trying to transfer incomplete knowledge of the work and then have to repeat the process later (waste of "correction"). It is typical, though, that once you delve into the process and your ability increases, you will discover even more details. Expect to circle back a time or two initially as you are learning.

1. *Identify critical knowledge:* Identifying critical knowledge is the first thing that must be done after the needs analysis and development plans have been completed and before actual training begins. It is best to have this performed one job at a time by a trainer and workers who are proficient at the job. We recommend selecting an initial trial work area with a few trainers. Then have the trainers and workers dig deep into the work to identify the critical knowledge (the job breakdown). After this is completed and the trainers have developed their ability to process the information, the method can be applied to other work areas. We refer to this as "going deep" before "going wide." Many people make the mistake of attempting to go wide before developing depth of capability. The end result is usually superficial and cannot be sustained. Be sure you develop sufficient depth of capability before attempting to apply the process across the organization.

   Because there is often confusion and disagreement about what is important and how certain aspects of the work are to be performed, this phase will be very time-consuming the first few times. After the initial knowledge is captured, subsequent changes resulting from new learning or process changes will be relatively small.

This is a crucial phase because if the correct information is not identified, it will not matter how effective the training method is. Incorrect information perfectly delivered will not yield the desired results. During this phase there may be significant disparity among the workers regarding the "correct" way to do a job. It is important to effectively identify the approximately 20 percent of the total content that is absolutely crucial to achieving consistent results, followed by the important items that will make up nearly 60 percent of the work content. That means that roughly 20 percent of the entire job may have some degree of variability, but the desired results can still be consistently achieved.

Before we get any disagreement on this, let us clarify. Suppose that the job is the task of stapling a packing carton (a simple example). In this task the important items are related to the correct placement and number of the staples while maintaining the correct hand position outside the hazard zone. In reality, the only absolutes are the quantity of staples and keeping the hands out of the hazard zone. The placement of staples and hand position allow for *some* variation within a range, provided they don't exceed the quality or safety requirements (e.g., it is acceptable to position the hands farther away from the hazard zone, but not into the hazard zone). Because of the importance and challenge of identifying absolutely critical information, we devote a significant portion of Chapter 9 to identifying "key points."

The training process is not initiated as a stand-alone activity. It is closely linked to standardized work and the development of the basic job method. Completion of standardized work prior to beginning training will provide a basis for the work method and will simplify the task of identifying the critical information. Also, standardized work provides a consistent and repeatable process. If the work is random and unstable, how will it be possible to train to achieve consistent results? It is difficult (perhaps impossible) to train someone when randomness is present in the work. This does not mean that the sequence of the work activities are always the same, but *how* the work is done is the same. In Chapter 6 we review in detail the connection between standardized work and Job Instruction.

2. *Transfer knowledge using the Job Instruction method:* Just as poorly identified information transferred perfectly will not produce the desired results, perfect information transferred poorly will also not yield the desired results. Training is more than simply telling someone what to do. There are effective techniques that can be used to accelerate learning and to increase the retention of information. Job Instruction provides a method whereby the trainer will "tell, show, and illustrate" (to explain or make clear) the task. In addition the trainer will learn to use gestures and voice inflection to stress certain elements. In Chapter 12 we review methods used to present the training. Also, Chapter 14 contains information regarding especially challenging training situations and how to handle them.
3. *Verify learning and success:* One important item that is often overlooked or not confirmed is verification that the student has actually learned and is fully capable of performing the job task. Often we find people who are "turned loose" too early, and they struggle to perform. Perhaps this is rooted in the incorrect assumption that, if the trainer showed the student the job, the student actually learned the job. Perhaps managers "trust" the trainer and assume that they will ensure the full ability of the student before the student is released to perform the job.

   Students must never be released to work alone without support from the trainer until they have demonstrated consistent capability to perform the work. This is partially a judgment call, but it should be founded on actual performance measures. For example, the trainer must evaluate the quality performance of the student. The trainee must be capable of performing the task repeatedly without error. For tasks that require "finesse," the time to develop skills will be extended. The trainer is obligated to check and confirm that the work is being completed successfully during this learning period.

It is unacceptable for the performance indicators to show a worsening condition during the training period. It is true that a new student may make more errors than someone with experience, but it is unacceptable for those errors to result in injury or defects passing to the customer. In order to prevent injuries or the customer receiving faulty merchandise, the trainer must pay absolute attention to the trainee during the development period. The trainer must also utilize "off-line" skill development activities (practice the job in a simulated work environment). In this way, a trainee at worst will have a very slight negative impact on the performance results (e.g., increased scrap).

Development Is a Long-Term Commitment

The three steps of the talent development process—determine what is important to teach, teach it, and then verify that learning occurred—will be repeated continually as new work methods are developed or as new processes are introduced. The effort required for "maintenance" of the process will be less than the initial effort because the time-consuming activity is digging into the details of each task and developing a full understanding of them. It is often possible to transfer some of the knowledge from one operation to another similar one. An example is a nurse administering medication through an IV. The medication itself may change, but the basic method will stay the same. The location where the IV is inserted may vary, but the basic working of the IV apparatus will be the same.

By now you should have a good understanding of why you want to pursue the process of developing talent in your employees. You should have evaluated the status of your organization as it is now, established some objectives you want to meet, and finally determined how you will create a structure to support the process.

You can see that the development of talented people is a long-term commitment. This is not a "project" that has a defined completion and afterwards you move to another project. You cannot work at developing people just one time and then abandon future development. This process will require continued sustained effort *forever.* Development has no upper limits. There is no threshold at which point you would say, "Okay. Now people are developed enough. Let's move on." Why would you place such limitations on the greatest potential within your organization? It is a serious commitment.

Part Two

Identify Critical Knowledge

The object of all work is production or accomplishment and to either of these ends there must be forethought, system, planning, intelligence, and honest purpose, as well as perspiration.

Thomas Edison

Chapter 5

Begin at a High Level to Understand the Skill Requirements of the Job

Start with the Broad View

In this section of the book we begin to explore the first phase of the training process—to define the critical requirements of the work. In the next phase we will learn to transfer the knowledge and skills to others. This step is the first hurdle as you begin to develop talent in people. Jobs are complex. They have a great deal of variety. Most jobs are not like the mundane and repetitious factory jobs of yesteryear. How is it possible to capture the wide variety of information and then effectively teach that information to someone?

We begin in this chapter with a way to first classify jobs and work. Any analytical process should begin with a broad understanding and move toward details. If we were to begin at the detailed level, we would see jobs involving a wide variety of activities and no clear patterns of sequence or repetition. We would conclude that it is impossible to define the job because it is never the same. You might have an employee tell you, "You'll never be able to standardize this job because it is always different. I'm never doing the same thing, and I am always running."

In this chapter, we start with the big picture view and organize the elements of the work according to broad categories. After we see that all work is a mix of specific skills, tasks, accumulated knowledge, and the ability to make appropriate decisions based on our knowledge, we can begin to move into details in a logical and organized manner.

In Chapters 6 to 8, we take the total job and begin the process of dissecting the work, looking for similarities and common characteristics that will be grouped together. This is done in two steps. First, we must analyze and break down the work for the purpose of defining the method and standardizing the work. We explore this analysis in Chapters 6 and 7. Second, we organize the work in a manner that is best for transferring the information to others. A defined standard is the foundation for teaching. But to effectively teach, it is necessary to break the work into different pieces to facilitate learning. The two steps have different objectives and thus are approached in different ways. The details of the work must be organized specifically for effective teaching. We detail this step in Chapter 8.

Are Service and Technical Jobs Completely Different from Manufacturing Jobs?

We realize there is more to the world than manufacturing, and, in fact, the service sector has been growing every year. We can talk about work breakdown structures and standardized work and detailed Job Instruction training for repetitive manufacturing jobs, but does this apply to the task content within service jobs? When we think of Toyota, the first image that comes to mind is the assembly line. On the assembly line the worker is doing a repetitive job that has a total cycle of one to two minutes. Toyota breaks the cycle time down into foundational elements that can be dissected and taught in intervals of a few seconds. But those who work in service operations are likely to believe this is irrelevant. They might say, "We are in the service sector, not manufacturing. Our jobs are different."

We don't really need to go outside of manufacturing to hear this same argument. Within the manufacturing sector we hear comparisons between assembly line work and non–assembly line work, between work for customized products versus work for standard products, and between short-cycle repeating work and very long-cycle nonrepeating work. There is a general assumption in the world that it is possible to standardize only work that is predictable and repeatable minute by minute.

There is certainly some truth in the assertion that manufacturing and service jobs are different. But there is also a tendency to generalize too broadly about the differences, be they cultural, structural, or technical. If we ask, "How are the jobs different?" The response may be, "Well, everything is different." If we ask for specific examples of what is different, the reply might be, "We do not have a car moving down an assembly line. We do not have a highly engineered and specific process. We do not have a person standing in one place physically building the same product over and over 400 times per day. We have people in offices doing some work at a desk and moving to a copy machine and going to meetings."

These certainly are differences, but it is easy to forget the fact that Toyota has a lot more going on than workers on an assembly line. There are maintenance workers and material handlers, and truck drivers and people in the kanban room running computers and an office complex of production planners, engineers, logistics people, trainers, and on and on.

So we have established that there are a variety of different types of jobs inside manufacturing. Now let's journey to the amorphous "service sector." We see some people madly dashing from meeting to meeting with no obvious order to their day, and others thinking deep thoughts in front of a computer screen, creating artwork or complex engineering designs. We also see people at McDonald's filling routine orders of standard products. We see people in hospitals doing material handling work making routes to refill stores of tools, equipment, and supplies. We see call centers full of people sitting at desks making phone calls with a standard script repeated every minute.

The point here is simple: Avoid overgeneralization when it comes to differences between industries or sectors. The variation within an industry rivals the variation across industries. In other words, start with a question about the specifics of the work and then look at the reality to get the answer to that question.

The question relevant to this book is, "What are the characteristics of jobs that call for different approaches to developing people?" We are not interested in the manufacturing versus service sector or in the shop floor versus the office. We are interested in the job. If we can isolate the job characteristics that matter, we can then start talking about implications for training and development approaches. Then we can look at any operation, whether it is a service operation or a manufacturing operation, and we can analyze each individual job to determine what its characteristics are and how to go about standardizing what can be standardized, identifying the unique skills that are not so standardized, and developing the talent needed to be exceptional at that job.

When learning any new skill, it is best to begin with fundamentals and move toward mastery of the more complex techniques. We believe if you can understand the basic principles and concepts, you can apply them in any situation. Clearly, repetitive manual work on the shop floor is easier to break down and standardize than most other jobs. But what are the principles we can take away from the training approach that will apply to any job?

We have included some examples from other fields, and we believe that instead of focusing on exact job content, you will see common patterns that apply to any work. Make an effort to focus on the common characteristics of the work rather than on the specific type of work. We begin with a well-established academic framework that can help put this into perspective.

A Framework for Classifying Jobs

If we followed a nurse making rounds in a hospital and observed an engineer sitting in front of a CAD (computer-aided design) terminal and then watched an assembly line worker, we would see many differences in the types of tasks they do. How can we classify these differences? We might notice the nurse moving around a lot more and having direct contact with patients, answering specific questions and doing specific things appropriate for each patient. We could observe the engineer designing a product and making a lot of mouse and keyboard movements at the CAD terminal, but the important activities are happening in his brain and are not visible to the observer. Both are obviously doing tasks that are very different from the repetitive, visible manual work of the assembly line worker.

So how can we classify the differences between the manual shop floor assembler and service or technical jobs? Charles Perrow presented a useful framework in a 1967 academic article.[1] It has become a staple of university textbooks on organizational behavior and design. He identified two factors that can help us classify different jobs—task variety and task analyzability. From the perspective of skill development, we can define these as the number of different types of skills required to do the job (task variety) and whether the job can be broken down into a cookbook-like set of standard steps that can be easily taught (task analyzability). Let's start by defining each concept.

1. *Task variety:* How many different types of tasks does the job require? Do workers spend most of their time doing the same types of tasks, or are they equally likely to move between different types of tasks? Note the issue is not simply having a lot of tasks but having a variety of tasks that require different types of skills. Tightening a bolt and then inserting a spring would be considered similar types of tasks. But entering data into a CAD system to create a drawing and then going to a meeting with marketing to understand the product requirements are very different types of tasks. Even if there are a lot of different skills required but most of them are rarely used, the job might still be low on task variety. Note that jobs with very short cycle times like automotive assembly work are not likely to have a great deal of task variety even though there is a long list of tasks performed by the worker.
2. *Task analyzability:* To what degree can the job be broken down into a set of clearly specifiable tasks that can be easily taught? By this we mean, can we specify what the content of each task is and the sequence of each task in such a way that we can standardize the task? In lean manufacturing terms this is like asking,

[1] Charles Perrow, "A Framework for the Comparative Analysis of Organizations," *American Sociological Review* 32 (1967): 194–208.

"Is it possible to develop standardized work for this set of tasks that make up a job?" The distinction between explicit knowledge and accumulated know-how is another way to think about this. Highly analyzable tasks can be defined in a set of explicit procedures, like a cookbook. Those low in analyzability are "intuitive" based on accumulated know-how and cannot be easily explained. You learn the art of doing the job over time from an experienced mentor like the master chef teaching an apprentice the subtleties of seasoning different dishes by tasting the dish to decide what else should be added.

Based on these two simple variables, Perrow developed a whole theory of organizational design. He put these two factors together in the matrix shown in Figure 5–1 with two levels each—high and low—and, based on the position in the matrix, he predicted the most effective type of organization for different types of jobs. He ended up with four generic types of jobs, each with different training requirements. Let's discuss each of the four types of jobs:

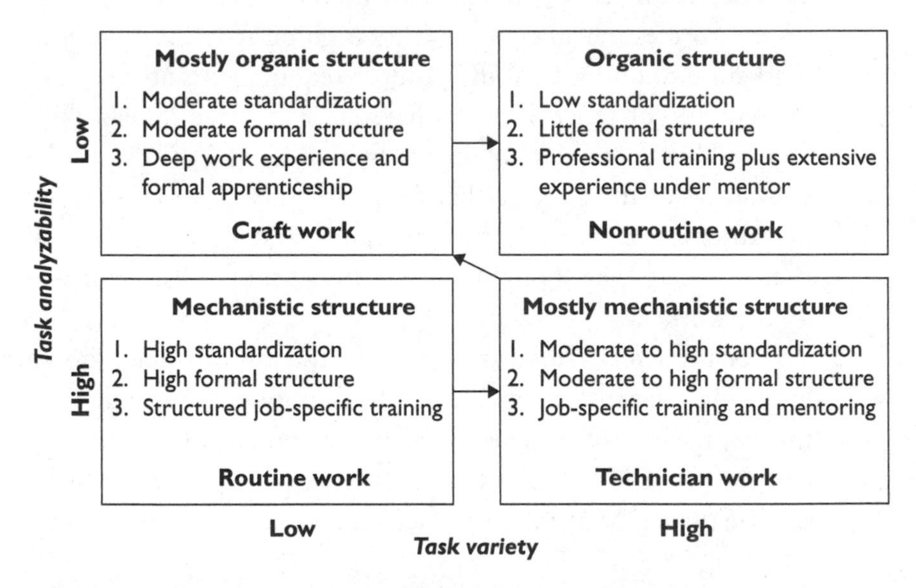

Figure 5–1. Classifying different jobs by the task requirements
Source: Modified from Charles Perrow, "A Framework for the Comparative Analysis of Organizations," *American Sociological Review* 32 (1967): 194–208

1. *Routine work:* When you combine jobs that are high on analyzability with low task variety, you get routine work. The short-cycle assembly job is in this category. The reason we can create a standardized worksheet on a single sheet of paper to represent the job is because it is routine work. This does not mean the skills required are trivial. It takes some native ability and persistence to consistently do the job within takt time, even when the cycle time is 60 seconds. But it can be explicitly taught, and Toyota can even effectively use temporary workers because the work is routine.

   Of course Toyota is not satisfied with the team associate simply using rote memory to perform the job mindlessly over and over. Toyota wants the associate to be critically evaluating what happens each day and developing suggestions for improvement. This problem solving would be classified as accumulated know-how that is not high on "analyzability." The more creative parts of the job are the contributions to the kaizen process, for example, participation in quality circles, the detection of deviations from standards, and solving problems when there is a deviation from standard. Problem solving at Toyota is a more complex skill that cannot be taught in cookbook fashion but must be learned over time through experience and coaching. For the work that is highly routine, Perrow found it can be best managed using a relatively "mechanistic" organizational structure (Figure 5–1). By this he means there is a lot of structure given to the individual by the boss with clearly specified roles, responsibilities, work procedures, and detailed daily time schedules. There are also clear measures of efficiency and effectiveness, which can be closely monitored day by day.
2. *Technician work:* We think of a technician as someone who perhaps does testing in a quality lab. Or, in some highly automated manufacturing plants, "operators" are called technicians because they are monitoring highly sophisticated equipment and are responsible for responding to problems and minor maintenance issues. In a hospital someone who operates the CAT scan machine might be regarded as a technician. The term *technician*

refers to jobs in which there are a variety of tasks, and the sequence can vary depending on the situation, but each individual task can be prespecified with cookbook-like instructions or answers that can be looked up in tables or procedure manuals. In reality "technician work" is more complex than this, and it often takes a great deal of accumulated know-how to solve real technical problems that arise, but a lot of the day-to-day checking and data collection and analysis are routine. Thus much of this work can be broken down into clearly specified tasks and can be taught in a structured way. But this must be supplemented by one-on-one mentoring on the job so the technician learns the know-how parts of the work. Perrow said this type of work could be best managed in a "mostly mechanistic" organization, which is a combination of a structured work environment with a degree of autonomy for the worker (Figure 5–1).

3. *Craft work:* The skilled maintenance crew in a Toyota factory that is trained to repair and rebuild the robots is doing craft work. There are a definable number of different tasks required of these jobs, but every situation the workers face is somewhat different from others. Team associates do routine cleaning and maintenance as part of their daily Total Productive Maintenance. The skilled maintenance team members are problem solvers. They face each situation anew and have to troubleshoot and come up with creative solutions to the problems. Of course over time they see patterns and similar problems and can use similar solutions. They develop "accumulated know-how" that over time they can pass on to an apprentice. There are some basic skills that can be taught in a structured way including standard ways of troubleshooting equipment, but the most critical and challenging parts of the job are learned through deep experience facing multiple situations over years while working up from an apprentice to a master craft worker. Management of the craft worker should be mostly "organic," which suggests a more flexible organization with fewer rules and formal polices that give considerable autonomy to the worker

and also require teamwork and excellent communications to integrate across specialties. Rules and standards are guidelines to be used selectively by the craft worker.

4. *Nonroutine work:* The lean expert you are trying to develop and are teaching TPS methods to is doing nonroutine work. So are managers of departments. The body engineer at Toyota who is responsible for development from concept to launch is doing nonroutine work. The head of a software team developing new user interfaces is doing nonroutine work. These people are often moving from task to task, and each situation is unique thereby calling for spontaneous thinking and reasoning and decision making. They must adapt to the situation while taking in complex data to make complex decisions. They must have a large repertoire of people skills to know what to say, how to say it, and when in each new circumstance to say it. There are some fundamental skills needed for these jobs that can help tremendously, and some of this is taught through formal professional education including technical training or university. But the most critical aspects are what the expert or manager does on the fly in day-to-day interactions, and this can only be learned on the job over time in a career path by those who have "it" and have been selected for promotion to higher levels of responsibility. "It" is a difficult-to-define quality. There are various candidates for promotion, and somehow (hopefully) it seems clear to those above who has "it" and who does not. Management of these people must be more "organic." That is, they need a lot of freedom and flexibility to use the judgment they have honed through years of accumulated experiences.

A Note on Standardization in Mechanistic versus Organic Organizations

We have described routine work as best managed in a mechanistic organization, while highly nonroutine jobs are appropriately managed in organic organizations. When we think of a mechanistic organization, we think of a machine—rigid, fixed, specialized parts. Each part is easily replaced without affecting the functioning of the machine, single purpose, or whatever. We might think of a rigid bureaucracy as being top down with many written rules and procedures. An organic organization is more of a human system—adaptable, flexible, and focused on learning. Substitute one person for another, and the system changes. We think of work in a mechanized setting as boring, mind numbing, and controlling. In an organic organization we have freedom to develop and express ourselves creatively.

We believe people by and large want to have freedom and to express themselves at work, even if they are doing routine work. Most people think of themselves as belonging in an organic organization and having autonomy. If you suggest standardizing their work, a red flag goes up. "How can you make my work routine when it takes so much creativity and is different in every situation?" People tend to think they are unique, that they have a unique way, and that they have a better way. They erroneously believe standardization means they will become like robots.

In *The Toyota Way,* Jeff Liker introduced a different perspective on this issue that was well captured by Paul Adler and his observations of NUMMI—Toyota's joint venture with General Motors in California.[2] He argued that Toyota had developed a different type of bureaucracy. We think of bureaucracy as red tape—inefficient and overly mechanistic. He said that at NUMMI he was observing a highly structured environment that was full of standardization, but with a great deal of individual initiative and creativity. The creativity was channeled to improve the standards.

Toyota views standard work as a tool for continuous improvement. It is a tool for operators to improve their work. Of course when they are performing the job, they are doing routine work in a prescribed way over and over. But they are expected to think about how to improve the job. Creative professionals at Toyota are not immune to

---

[2] Paul S. Adler, "Building Better Bureaucracies," *Academy of Management Executive* 13:4 (November 1999): 36–47.

standardization. Even the product engineer is expected to use a wide variety of standard processes and standard parts and standard rules for good design. But the bumper engineer is improving on the bumper design standards and within the constraints of those standards has a tremendous range of design alternatives. In fact, having some parts of the job specified as routine gives the engineer more opportunity to focus on the creative parts of the design.

Adler refers to the form of bureaucracy he witnessed at Toyota as "enabling bureaucracy" as opposed to the "coercive bureaucracy" he was used to seeing in most companies. In enabling bureaucracies, rules and standard procedures help the organization perform consistently at a high level. Unfortunately, employees who for years have lived in coercive bureaucracies are fearful that any new rules or procedures are going to be like chains preventing them from using their real skills to do high-quality work. And unless the culture of the organization changes, they are probably correct.

Developing Exceptional People in Different Types of Jobs

Obviously different types of jobs require different approaches to how you develop people. Let's consider each of the four general types and the implications for staff development. We have summarized the people development implications in Table 5–1 and in the list below.

1. *Routine work:* Many of the examples in this book focus on training and developing team associates who do routine work. Much of the actual job can be analyzed, broken down, and specified to the second. When a team member masters well-designed standardized work, the job becomes fluid and natural. The team member no longer has to consciously think about each action. Actually most people prefer doing a job in this way as opposed to constant starts and stops and interruptions. When the physical actions are almost unconscious, the person is able to consciously focus on other things. This can be daydreaming, or in the case of Toyota the desire is for the person to focus on two

Table 5-1. People development requirements for different types of jobs

Type of work	Example jobs	What can be standardized?	Accumulated know-how requirements
Routine (low variety, high analyzability)	Assembly line work, fast food server, bank teller, data entry clerk	Work elements, sequence, timing, fundamental skills, product specifications, workplace layout—tools	Recognition of problems, problem response, problem solving
Technician (high variety, high analyzability)	Inspection, material handling, lab data analyst, computer technical support work, equipment maintenance	Generic procedures, core processes, fundamental skills, product specifications, workplace layout—tools	Troubleshooting ability, intuitive problem solving, mental map of problem situations
Craft (low variety, low analyzability)	Group leader, nurse, buyer, some engineering jobs	Generic procedures, fundamental skills, product guidelines, workplace layout—tools	Intuitive problem solving, reading situations
Nonroutine (high variety, low analyzability)	Program manager, R&D scientist, development engineer, surgeon	Generic procedures, fundamental skills, product criteria, workplace layout—tools	Creative-innovative ability, intuitive problem solving, reading situations

Note: There is wide variation in the content of jobs across companies and industries and even within companies. So the same job category, e.g., engineer, will fall into different job type classifications depending on the content of the job.

things. First, Toyota wants the person to notice any deviations from standard and stop the operation by pulling the andon cord. This requires the skill of vigilance—paying intense attention to each part and each task. Second, Toyota wants people to think about ways to improve the job and then later participate in problem-solving activities.

While doing the routine job is highly analyzable and repetitive, detecting deviations and problem solving are "intuitive" skills. It might take a month or two to master an individual routine job, but it may take years to develop strong skills in detecting deviations and then becoming a part of a problem-solving group. We talk about people doing routine work as "team members" because they are in fact working as part of a team. In addition to their role of performing routine manual tasks, they have a number of roles as a team member, including how to work with others to establish rotation schedules, to agree on changes to the standard work, perhaps to help in training others, and to be part of problem-solving activities.

2. *Technician work:* It may be of interest to note that in the academic world when a professor who is expected to be a leader in research is referred to as a "technician," it is considered a criticism. "He is a good technician, but not a good researcher," is a negative comment. The assumption is that technicians mindlessly perform routine tasks. In reality good technicians are creatively applying well-understood tools and principles to solving problems. Perhaps it should be a compliment.

Toyota's training for nonroutine jobs like equipment maintenance is certainly different from training for routine jobs. Yet there are still some fundamental skills that can be defined and taught in a structured manner. We were interested to learn that Toyota's Global Production Center (GPC) has developed fundamental skills training even for skilled trades workers like die makers. These skills have longer cycle times and take longer to learn than do shorter-cycle routine jobs. For example, student die makers have a four-week class in the center just to learn how to do die finishing (a hand operation to smooth out the die and fix minor defects), one of many tasks in die making. The center even teaches basic skills in troubleshooting. For example, it has automated equipment and a computer program that can program faults into the process. To make it realistic, real faults from previous days' operations at the Georgetown plant are programmed into the system. Then students are asked to identify and solve the real problems.

This simulation of real problems with real supervised troubleshooting is the type of training needed to teach intuitive skills. It goes beyond simply lecturing about specific topics.

Responding to these simulated problems only begins the process of learning for actual troubleshooting of equipment. Each situation is unique. On the job the maintenance worker will see many individual situations and begin to develop a mental map of the types of problems that occur and how to respond to them. But the simulated experience begins that process and shortens the learning curve of actual on-the-job training.

Toyota recognizes that performing maintenance on complex equipment requires a great deal of basic classroom knowledge that cannot be taught in the Global Production Center, including basic math skills like geometry and trigonometry and reading blueprints and more. In Kentucky, Toyota contracted these courses out to a local community college and housed them in the Regional Production Center. The company still wants to exercise a good deal of control over the content and quality of the education, but it is leaving the actual teaching to professional educators. Toyota also realizes many of these skills will come from on-the-job apprenticeship training from an experienced maintenance person.

3. *Craft work:* Think about the blacksmith of old. How do you learn to be a blacksmith? For centuries it has been understood that such jobs require complex skills that go beyond simple mechanics. There is an element of art to them, and a skilled master has always done training over a long period of time. The most important training is on the job. Nonetheless we will see there are more opportunities than may be apparent at first glance to standardize certain aspects of the job and to teach in a systematic way. We are pretty certain the master blacksmiths taught certain fundamental procedures in a specific way, as they were taught, and expected these to be repeated as taught. The artistic part of creating and using imagination can really begin only after the student learns the basics.
4. *Nonroutine work:* The challenge of teaching nonroutine work is similar to that for craft work but is amplified still further. By definition there is little about this work that is repetitive, and

variety is what characterizes the job. But we have professional schools that prepare students for these nonroutine professional jobs. Essentially what is being taught is fundamental skills that have been identified over many years. A company like Toyota does not assume that the students entering the workplace have learned the right fundamental skills or that they have learned them the way they are practiced at Toyota. There is rigorous training set up within Toyota to develop these professionals. As we move through the book, we will give examples of how Toyota trains engineers as they move through their careers. There is a well-defined training curriculum for the first year, the next two to five years, and so on as the engineer advances to increasingly higher-level positions that are less and less routine. Of course a large portion of what needs to be learned is taught through very deliberate mentoring on the job. As Toyota has been developing engineering competence in the United States where there is more movement of engineers in and out of companies, Toyota has been working to make more of the unwritten techniques of engineering explicit. It is developing comprehensive "know-how databases" that include key points and the reasons why it is important to follow these key points of engineering.

Move from Broad Classifications to Specific Skill Requirements

We should point out that jobs do not necessarily fit neatly into only one of the categories defined by Perrow. If we look closely, we will likely see that many jobs include a blend of the job classifications. It is not important to find the correct box and label your jobs accordingly. It is only necessary to understand the distinctions between the work categories. These distinctions mainly apply later when we begin to explore the best method to define and teach each type of work.

In Figure 5–2 we created a model that takes the basic job classifications of Perrow and categorizes specific types of tasks and knowledge necessary to perform each type of job. Our intention in the rest of this

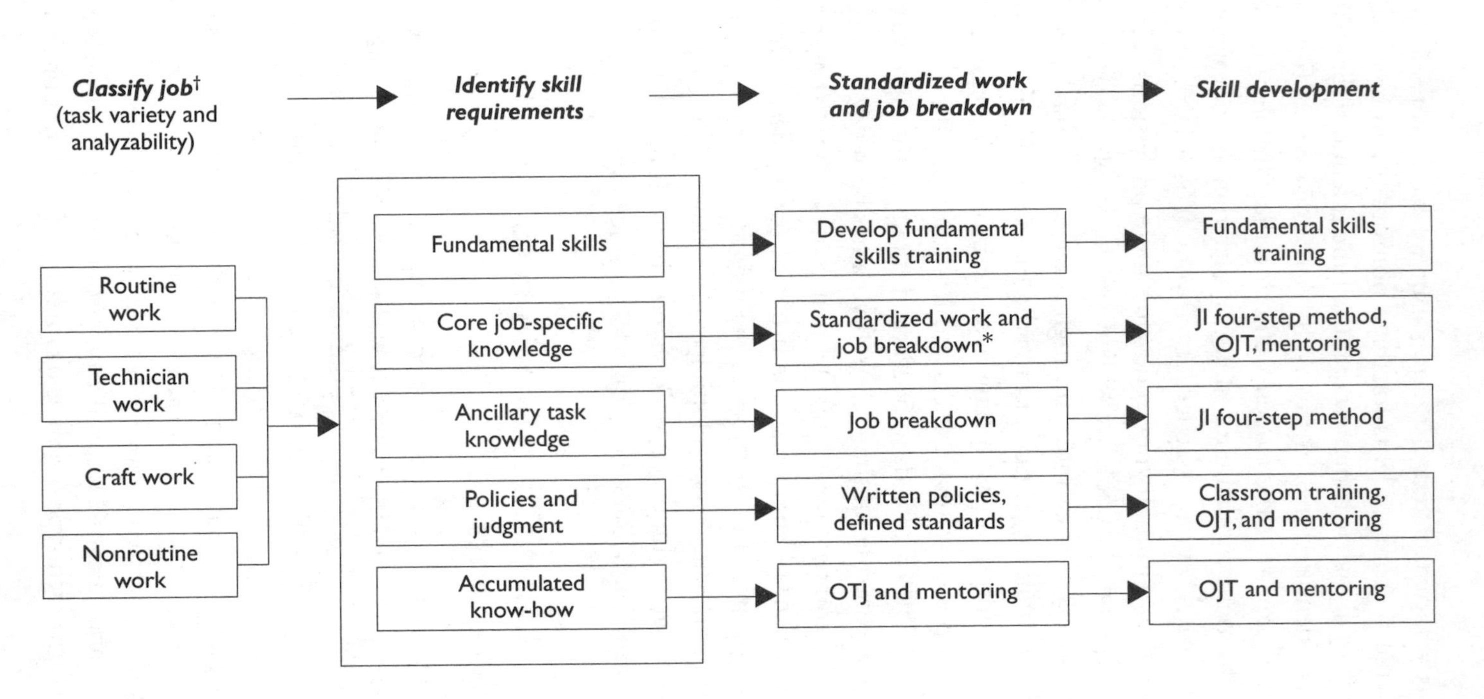

† Some jobs may include a blend of classifications.
* Jobs will vary in the degree to which the work can be standardized.

Figure 5–2. Flow diagram of training for different job types

section is to show how to proceed through the process of defining the elements of the work and to document them appropriately. In the next section of the book, we discuss the method used to transfer the knowledge and develop the skills and knowledge in others. The model in Figure 5–2 is intended to show the broad framework for how we move through these phases.

In this model we start with the broad classification of the job and then look at the skill requirements. Let's apply this model to an example that most readers will be familiar with—driving a car. We would classify driving a car as a "technician job." There are a variety of tasks to learn that require different skills, and most of these skills can be analyzed, broken down, and taught effectively using standard procedures. The correct classification of jobs in a particular category is not critical. It is important to understand how to break each subcategory task into successively smaller pieces until the majority of individual tasks are definable.

We started by asking, "What are the fundamental skills required for driving?" Fundamental skills are those that are applicable to all driving situations. They are equivalent to learning to use common hand tools for assembly operations. The fundamental skills for driving may be learned in a classroom setting, such as a driver's education class or directly with a teacher. In either case they would most likely be learned "off-line" meaning not on the road in an actual driving situation. Fundamental skills are practiced prior to the actual task (like in the Global Production Center at Toyota). The list of fundamental skills (may not be a comprehensive list) follows:

- General maneuvering
- Accelerating
- Steering and handling
- Braking
- Parking (parallel and angle)
- Parking in garage
- Three-point turn
- Putting the car in gear
- Backing up (straight and turning)

Fundamental skills are completed as a part of the primary job, but they must be combined with other skills and accumulated know-how in order to do the complete task. They may be either routine and repetitive or nonroutine and repeated in a random sequence. It is possible to actually do a portion of the driving task without knowing how to do everything necessary to drive on the highway. For example, perhaps the first thing to learn is how to accelerate and drive the car straight for 50 feet and then to stop. This portion of the total task could be repeated over and over in an empty parking lot until some competency is gained. Then another portion of the task, say turning, would be added. Typically the fundamental skills are first learned off-line if possible, and then after basic competency is achieved, they are transferred to the actual workplace. This depends on the importance of the task and the risk associated with working in the actual condition. It is not advisable to have a new student driver practicing in city traffic!

Ancillary tasks are secondary and supportive in nature. At some point it will be necessary to learn to do these tasks, but it is entirely possible to perform the core task without ever doing the ancillary tasks (however, someone will have to do them). It would not make sense to attempt to teach the ancillary tasks in the same session as the core tasks. The trainer should teach each ancillary task separately. These items may be covered in classroom training, but this must generally be supplemented by on-the-job mentoring. Examples of ancillary tasks for driving are as follows:

- Starting the car
- Adjusting mirrors
- Buckling seat belt
- Adjusting lights and controls
- Turning car off
- Filling the gas tank
- Checking oil and tires
- Servicing per manufacturer's recommendation
- Licensing (plates) and insurance

Most jobs today in any field require a certain amount of knowledge of policies and use of judgment—the rules of the road if you will.

In the case of driving, every student will likely study the driver's education handbook. The handbook explains traffic signs and lights, speed limits and laws regarding emergency vehicles, school busses, and driving in a school zone among other things. Students must learn how to interpret traffic signs and symbols. This type of information is generally written and may be studied independently from the actual job task. Examples of policies and judgment for driving include:

- Traffic signs
- Traffic lights
- Speed limits and zones
- Emergency vehicles
- Laws
- Rules of the road (e.g., use of headlights in the rain)
- Rules for right-of-way

After the student driver has mastered the fundamental skills, has sound judgment regarding acceleration and braking, and understands the legal policies of road driving, it is time to put it together on the actual job—driving on the road. This is the core task. The learning process moves from off-line to "online." The student learns to apply the fundamental skills in the context of the actual work and must deal with real-world conditions such as other vehicles on the road, moving through intersections, merging into traffic, and passing other vehicles on the highway.

The student is still under the watchful eye of a trainer and begins to acquire knowledge on the job that will enable them to know instinctively what to do. We call this "accumulated know-how." This is the ability to compile a mass of experience and turn that into correct actions. There is no substitute for experience. The experience may be gained by first studying policy knowledge (the driver's handbook describes these conditions). The skills must be repeated numerous times before the mentor can be assured the student is capable of handling the novel situations he will face on his own.

As the students get more and more practice, they experience many different conditions and accumulate know-how concerning what to do under different conditions. Because this knowledge is acquired over time, in actual practice people mistakenly believe that there is no defined element of the task for training purposes (no step-by-step procedure). The fact is that each of these tasks is by itself definable from the standpoint of identifying specific key points (discussed in Chapter 9) that must be learned for each task. For example, when people are driving at night, there are specific adjustments that must be made. Vehicle speed should be adjusted down to compensate for reduced visibility. The driver learns to judge the position of the vehicle relative to the line on the road. Night driving combined with country driving will change the parameters. There may not be lines on the road, and country roads may be narrow, winding, and perhaps hilly. Visibility is reduced further in these conditions. Specific key points can be identified for each condition, and with experience the driver will learn to apply them instinctively.

Don't make the mistake of assuming that this knowledge will be attained automatically with time (as we have seen with supervisors waiting for employees to figure out the job on their own). Specifics must be taught, and with time they will become automatic. You would never expect a new driver to learn to handle each of these situations without guidance. It would be far too risky. This is how you must view this type of knowledge pertaining to your work. Examples of accumulated know-how include:

- Driving in various conditions
  - Nighttime conditions
  - Winter conditions
  - Driving in the countryside
  - City driving conditions
  - Driving in fog
- Response to near-accident situation
- Two-way traffic
- Divided or limited highway access
- Intersections
- Driving etiquette

Figure 5-3 shows how the various tasks and skills fit together to build complete job skill. Fundamental skills are common skills that

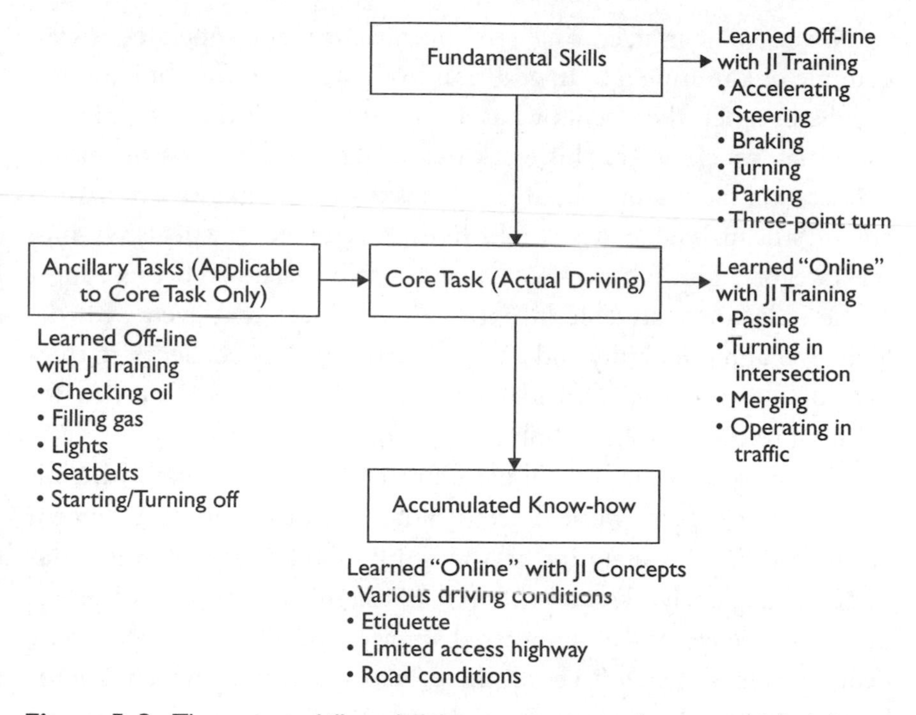

Figure 5–3. The various skills and abilities necessary to become a skilled driver

support the core task, but by themselves they do not provide complete capability to perform the core task. Ancillary tasks support the core task, but it is not necessary to learn them to complete the core task (they can be performed by the trainer). Accumulated know-how is gained from repetitive practice, and the key knowledge can be identified and taught using a modified version of Job Instruction concepts.

Remember this—everything that is done by a human being in this world is potentially learnable by any other human being, special talent aside. You may not be able to shoot or jump like Michael Jordan, but you can learn the fundamentals of the game. You may not develop the techniques of the great masters like Monet and Picasso, but you can learn the essential skills of a painter. Inherent talents play a part in the mastery of any skill, but most people, with effort, effective training, and practice can attain the majority of any skill.

As we go through the rest of the book, we will be using three different jobs to present the fundamentals of effective talent development. These jobs represent some of the more common types of work.

We use a manufacturing job (bumper molding operator) as an example of a routine job. In addition to the routine work of completing the bumper, the operator has a portion of work that fits into the technician category. For this work the operator tends to various needs of operating the machine itself. These tasks are not repetitive in nature, but are still analyzable. Many jobs in the service sector will also fit into this category. This job may be the easiest to break down because most of the tasks are analyzable in nature. We will see that even with the high level of repeatability and analyzability, it is a big challenge to carefully define this work and identify the critical elements needed for teaching routine, repetitive jobs.

For the service job we will use a nurse in a busy hospital, which is more technician type work. There is not a repetitive core task element of the work. The majority of the work is made up of numerous nonrepeating analyzable tasks as well as a significant portion of procedural knowledge and accumulated know-how. There are also more nebulous types of skills (we call these "native abilities") which include bedside manner and an inherent desire to serve others. Because this work is primarily made up of analyzable tasks, the breakdown will be similar to that for the manufacturing job. There is no repetitive core task with this job, but the nonrepeating tasks are analyzed in the same way as repeating ones are. It is not possible to develop a standard sequence for the work, but the work itself is standardized. Procedural knowledge and accumulated know-how may be learned in a classroom setting or with on-the-job mentoring, but we will see that the core concepts of job instruction can still be applied. There are still key points that must be identified and transferred to others.

The work of an entry-level design engineer is a mix of technician work and a dash of craft with a multitude of small nonroutine activities added to the mix. Certainly the job includes some routine work, but the primary work is not routine. We will see how Toyota uses certain tools in an effort to standardize as much of the work as possible (knowledge databases and check sheets) and to communicate key points that are relevant to the task. Still this work is predominately an accumulation of know-how pieced together over many years. There is a logical progression that Toyota has developed, but the cycle extends out over years. In this situation we can see the training cycle is repeated many times over an extended period.

Keep in mind the same basic idea applies to all training. For a short-cycle routine job there may be a few training events within a few days or weeks allowing for practice of newly learned skills in between. For technician-type work there will need to be several training events—one for each of the tasks and for other procedural types of knowledge. This may extend over several months as each of the tasks occurs and repetition of each task is necessary to fully develop the skill. Some of the task repeatability frequency may occur over several months. The engineering training events will be spread out over years. If the engineer learns to design a product for one model car, it would be several years perhaps before he or she had an opportunity to repeat this task. We see, however, the accumulated know-how is at least partially transferable to other design tasks of similar nature.

Begin with Simple Tasks

We demonstrate through the flow of this book an important training concept—begin with simple tasks and advance to the more complex. The easiest tasks to analyze are the repetitive and repeatable tasks, and we focus on them first. Because of the notoriety of Toyota, we need to address the specific issue of standardized work. As we have shown in this chapter, only a portion of any job is analyzable and therefore possible to define in a standardized way. In the next chapter we attempt to clarify the process and tools of standardized work as defined by Toyota, and we also use Toyota's process as a framework for analyzing other jobs.

You may think that because your work is not routine in nature, you should skip Chapter 6. We suggest you read the chapter, and you may find much more of your work is of a routine nature than you imagined. Also the process of standardized work is about much more than just defining work and documenting it on paper. It is as much about the analysis of work for waste, which is present in *all* work, and the ongoing activity of continuously improving work methods to eliminate the waste.

Chapter 6

Standardized Work and the Job Instruction Method

Build a Foundation for Effective Training

You will notice that what we are doing is working down the chain from the highest level—planning the overall training program—to more detailed levels of breaking down jobs and classifying them. We first determine what talents we want our employees to omit be have, and then we establish a method to get them the knowledge and skill they need to develop those talents. We presented a high-level view of classifying jobs and breaking down the work in Chapter 5 (Figure 5–2). In this chapter we continue down the ladder to the much more detailed task level using the process Toyota calls "standardized work." We show that it is necessary to first analyze the work from this perspective even if the work itself does not appear to be analyzable or routine. We distinguish the standardized worksheet from the job breakdown we do for Job Instruction (JI) training, but note each builds on the other. From Toyota's view it is impossible to separate the standardized work process and the development of talent.

All work may not be repeatable and predictable, but all work involves *muda* (waste), and one of the primary purposes of standardized work is to analyze the work for waste and to systematically eliminate it. During the systematic search for waste, the work method is also defined and then serves as a foundation for training. The intent of the two processes is very different, and we need to understand their relationship; we must not confuse the two. We don't use standardized work as a teaching tool. We don't break down jobs for teaching in the same way we do for standardized work. We will see that this is a meticulous procedure, and it takes considerable time and attention. We estimate that Toyota spends five times as much time detailing work methods and developing talent in employees as any other company we have seen.

Standardized Work Is Part of an Overall System

Standardized work is the process used by Toyota to develop work methods. It describes an overall process that is intended to produce specific outcomes related to the work. Every organization strives to generate consistently high results. The key to success is the development of superior talent and the establishment of excellent work methods. Thus standardized work goes hand in hand with Job Instruction training, which is the method used to develop talent.

It is often said that "lean" is a *systems* approach to high performance. Yet we continue to see companies attempting to implement individual pieces of a system in the hope it will get the system benefits. Unfortunately this does not work. Standardized work and training your people to be the best they can be actually go hand in hand. This is part of an overall system. Creating standardized work reduces the variation and chaos in a process and thus yields superior results. If the work method is random, undefined, and undisciplined, how would it be possible to effectively teach it to others so they can perform the work in a reliable way?

Before we start discussing how to train people to perform at a high level, we need to clarify the connection between standard work and Toyota's method for training team associates—Job Instruction training. It might already be clear to many readers that standardized work is the foundation for efficient and effective work methods, but we also see that the ability to study a job from the teaching viewpoint, and to dissect it into critical elements, is a necessary part of defining the standardized work. In this chapter we explore the connection between these two processes, namely how to dissect any job task and break out specific details for the purpose of defining the correct method to perform the work, and for establishing a basis for teaching the important elements of the work to others.

TWI and the Roots of Standardized Work

The introduction of material from Training Within Industry (TWI) discussed in Chapter 3 brought to Toyota two key elements of its production system—a process for analyzing, improving, and defining the work methods and a technique for training workers in the carefully defined methods. But Toyota went beyond TWI in the way it eliminates waste from work methods. Today, Toyota employees utilize a process known as *standardized work* to create well-defined and efficient work methods. Knowledge, talent, and skill are transferred with the basic Job Instruction method developed by TWI in the 1940s. It is difficult to separate these two approaches because the knowledge of good work practices without the ability to transfer this knowledge to others is wasted, and teaching ability without a deep knowledge of the work and the ability to distinguish the critical aspects passes on only minimal or incorrect information.

It is believed that Taichi Ohno (the father of the Toyota Production System) felt the original Job Methods material presented by TWI was too narrowly focused. Ohno and his followers went beyond the TWI ideas to pursue one-piece flow as a primary means to reduce *muda* in the operations. This objective led to the connection with the customer demand rate (*takt*) and line balancing, which are necessary to create smooth flow. Over the years Toyota has refined the Job Methods material and integrated it with other concepts such as kaizen, takt time, line balancing, and visual control to create a standardized work process that better fits its needs. Job Methods provided a starting point, but Toyota has expanded the concepts to establish standardized work in its current manifestation.[1]

Standardized Work Applies in All Companies

Of course other companies have used the basic idea of standardizing procedures with great success. In the book *The Spirit to Serve*, Bill Marriott shares his thoughts about standardizing procedures, which are similar to those of Toyota. He said, "Maybe we *are* a little fanatical about the way things should be done. But for us, the idea of having systems and procedures for everything is very natural and logical: If you want to produce a consistent result, you need to figure out how to do it, write it down, practice it, and keep improving it until there's nothing left to improve. (Of course, we at Marriott believe that there's *always* something to improve.)"[2] Marriott goes on to describe the detail to which some items are taken—for example, the 66-step procedure for cleaning a room in 30 minutes or less. Paying attention to the details where they are most important is what will lead to success in the development of standardized work.

If we were to identify the single greatest difference between Toyota and other organizations (this includes service, health care, and manufacturing organizations), it would be the depth of understanding among Toyota employees regarding their work. It is our perception that most other companies detail the work process to no more than 25 percent of the level achieved by Toyota. It seems to us that at most other companies there is only a superficial understanding of the work, and a great deal of uncertainty exists pertaining to the critical elements of the work. Much is left to individuals to figure out, and people make gallant efforts to produce good results. It has been our experience that in the absence of valid information, people will find some way to get the job done.

---

[1] There is much debate over this issue. Many people view the Job Methods program as the foundation of standardized work in the Toyota Production System. There are clearly similarities, and JM was surely introduced to Toyota, but the current work improvement method used by Toyota is much different from the original JM material.

[2] J. W. Marriott, *The Spirit to Serve* (New York: HarperCollins, 1997), 16.

Unfortunately, if everyone is figuring out something different, the resulting variation will be significant. We have seen instances where equipment setup time variation is as high as 100 percent, and production output varies by as much as 50 percent among full-time operators. This is usually shrugged off by the supervisor and attributed to the normal learning curve. The lack of detailed understanding of the work method leads to confused and frustrated employees (and leaders) who spend vast amounts of time struggling with the resulting problems. As we show later in this chapter, work at Toyota is analyzed at great depth, and the work content is broken down into numerous segments, which leads to deep understanding of the work and to continuous improvement.

There are many situations we see in our daily lives, of companies that have done exceptionally well in the area of standardizing work procedures. Many of the fast-food restaurants, such as McDonald's, Wendy's, and Subway (and others to varying degrees), have implemented procedures to ensure your visit is consistent no matter when or where you visit.

Mindless Conformity or Intentional Mindfulness?

Whenever we mention the use of standardized work, we get some typical responses. "How can we possibly get our people to do the work in exactly the same way?" Also we hear, "People are not robots. If we make them do it the same way as everyone else, they won't be able to use their creativity."

It is easy to understand why people come to these conclusions. The term *standardized* after all means to make the same, and certainly some companies have used standardization as a way to control and stifle employee creativity. It is clearly not the intention of Toyota to develop mindless employees who are no more creative than robots.

Toyota places a very high value on creativity, thinking ability, and problem solving. A common term used around Toyota is *monozukuri*—the art of making things. Within Toyota this is viewed very much as an art, and a very high value is placed on the artisans who build the car using standardized methods. Artisans are continually challenging the current standards and then improving the standardized methods. Teruyuki Minoura, senior managing director of Toyota, began referring to the Toyota Production System—TPS—as the "Thinking Production System." He recounted a story about being asked by Mr. Ohno how he would solve a particular problem, "I don't think he was interested in my answer at all. I think he was just putting me through some kind of training to get me to learn how to think."

This is certainly a challenging issue for most companies. It is true that one purpose of standardized work is to create consistent results and to control undesirable variation. Also, standardized work is meant to evolve and to be continuously improved. How is it possible to allow for creativity and change and at the same time create consistency? In fact we do want to create consistent work where it matters, but we can allow some degree of variation in less critical situations. How does Toyota resolve this conflict? The question perhaps is best answered by clarifying how much of the total operation should be standardized and how strictly the standardization must be followed.

What Toyota leaders do is identify the most critical and commonly repeated aspects of every job, learn how they can be performed flawlessly, document these practices, and then diligently train people to follow the standard procedures (the way it's done at Marriott). There are other portions of most jobs that are less critical, have a broader range of acceptability, or are performed very seldom and thus do not need strict control. By focusing efforts where they yield the greatest benefit and adhering tightly to the most important aspects of the work, Toyota is able to consistently produce great results.

Bill Marriott describes the criticism often placed on Marriott and the misunderstanding others have regarding standardizing procedures. He said, "Mindless conformity and the thoughtful setting of standards should never be confused. In our case, the latter has proved to be one of the main engines of our success."[3] Marriott continues, "Even the most maniacally detailed procedures can't cover every

---

[3] Marriott, *The Spirit to Serve*, 17.

situation, problem, or emergency that might arise.... What solid systems and SOPs [standard operating procedures] do is nip *common* problems in the bud so that staff can focus instead on solving *un*common problems that come their way."[4] So, the key is the thoughtful setting of standards for the most important and common aspects of the work, thereby allowing people to perform the work without having to "figure it out" on their own. Employees then are free to focus their energies on the more intuitive activities such as problem identification and problem solving.

We find some concern among managers and supervisors regarding setting a correct work method and then expecting people to follow it. There is a proper way to do any task—to do it in such a way as to produce the desired results. What is wrong with showing people the correct way to do the work and then expecting them to follow that method? Generally people don't begin a job thinking, "I sure hope that no one shows me how to do this work so that I can struggle with it on my own." But if people are not shown the proper method and they are expected to deliver a result (get the job done), they *will* find a way to get the work done *somehow*. Generally people will get very defensive if they are told later their method is wrong if they were never shown a correct way.

Supervisors often argue this point and proclaim, "I told them the right way, but they didn't listen." Most likely the breakdown in communication occurred because the correct method was not defined to a detailed enough level. Specifics of the job were not communicated, which creates a discrepancy between the two parties—the workers, who think they are doing what they were told based on rather general instructions, and the supervisors, who believe the workers are not listening to them and that their instructions were perfectly clear.

This breakdown of communication is the responsibility of the supervisor. The solution is to analyze the work in detail and establish the critical and important aspects that must be performed exactly as prescribed. To complete the loop, the Job Instruction process requires

[4] Marriott, *The Spirit to Serve*, 25.

follow-up and confirmation that the task was learned and applied correctly. You will find that rather than feeling restricted by this exactness, people will find comfort in knowing the correct thing to do.

We often hear leaders comment, "I can't get them to do the job the correct way." How is it possible that the decision to follow the work methods is optional? It can never be optional to do the work correctly. Determining what is correct, however, entails some discussion and evaluation. Perhaps what the leader is really saying is, "The best method has never been defined, and I don't want to take the time to define it and teach it to people." Closer examination often reveals that the decision to do work in a certain manner is based on some "urban legends," the pesky uncertainties and misinformation that are often spread like a virus. If people are pressed to define what is truly critical in an operation, we will likely hear, "I think this is the correct way," or, "I was told this way." Very few people truly know what would happen if tasks were not performed a specific way or what would happen if the methods were changed. The understanding is on a very general level.

One of the techniques picked up from the Job Methods improvement portion of TWI is to question every detail. "Why is the work done this way?" "What is the purpose?" "How should the work be done?" "Who should do the work?" These are some of the questions Toyota rigorously asks when analyzing work methods. Experimentation is an important part of the discovery process. If the answers to these questions were not known, an experiment would be devised to find the best solutions. It is important to remember, however, the "best" solution is only the best that is known today. It is possible that a more effective method will be found and used later, at which time the standard is changed.

Standardized Work Is a Prerequisite for Training, and Job Instruction Is a Prerequisite for Standardized Work

We have a chicken-or-egg situation. Does standardized work come first, or does Job Instruction come first? Generally speaking, you will want to develop standardized work for a job to eliminate waste before further breaking it down to teachable elements. If you try to teach a task without the foundation of standardized work, what will you end up with? If you teach a nonstandardized task, you will surely end up with nonstandard results. If chaos is the foundation, the teaching effort will be chaotic. In practice the detailed breakdown we do in order for us to teach is one more integral part of the standardized work. We do not get the whole without both parts.

Isao Kato, a former Toyota manager and Master trainer, who, under the direction of Taichi Ohno, developed much of the training material used, believes the Job Instruction method is an integral part of developing standardized work. Kato explains, "I don't think you can do a good job of implementing standardized work or several other elements of TPS without the JI skill set in place. I have observed quite a few companies struggle with implementing standardized work, kaizen, and other items. Often the short-term gains companies obtain fall away over time. One direct reason why is no proper plan was ever put in place to train people to the new method, and the JI technique provides the exact skill set required to do this work. I can't see how standardized work can function without JI in place underneath to support it in the long run. If you do JI properly, you can eliminate so many problems that plague operations. You can stabilize the operation, improve productivity, enhance quality, and establish the fundamental elements of the job on paper for analysis. Then it is a much smaller step to next balance the line to takt time and to add the other elements of standardized work. This was the order at least in Toyota that we taught and had success with."[5]

We often see people struggling to teach tasks that have not been standardized. They are not sure what really matters and what does not, which things are their preference versus those that are truly critical. With this confusion there is nothing to say other than, "This is the way I do it." So people have "their own way," and the results are inconsistency, lack of true understanding, and endless frustration from attempting to get people to "do things correctly."

---

[5] Isao Kato in an interview with Art Smalley, www.artoflean.com, February 2006.

In addition, without an understanding of the Job Instruction method, is it possible to understand *how* to standardize? As we will see, with the Job Instruction method we learn to identify the critical aspects of the work, to ask questions like, "Why is this important?" If we can understand the importance of certain aspects of the work, and those aspects are critical to the success of the work, we standardize them and make them part of "the best way."

In reality it is necessary to learn to use both tools simultaneously. Use the Job Instruction method to identify work elements and key points necessary to successfully complete the task and then incorporate them into the standardized work. Analyze the work for waste, refine the method, determine "the best way we know how—today," and then teach everyone to do it that way—until such time when improvements are made and retraining is necessary. Figure 6–1 shows the relationship between standardized work and Job Instruction.

We can see in this relationship a perpetual loop connecting the defined method of doing the task, the process used to teach people to

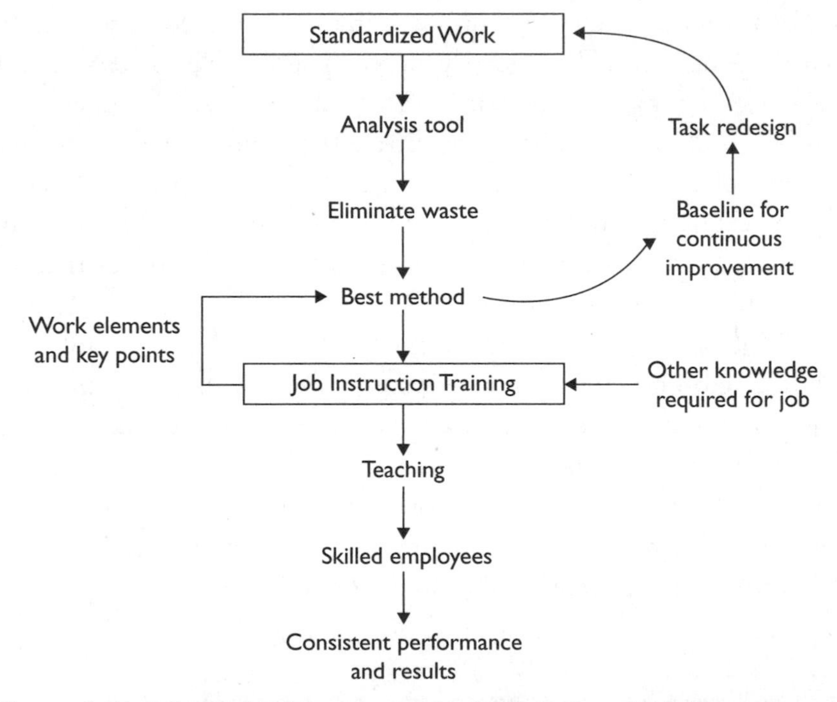

Figure 6–1. Relationship between standardized work and Job Instruction

follow the defined method, and then back to a new definition of the work. Throughout this book we must assume this relationship is understood, but the focus is on the training method rather than the development of the work method. Our objective in this book is to focus on the development of talent, but effective training is not possible without also defining the work method. It is not our intent to delve into standardized work in its entirety. We are looking at the part that is specifically related to the teaching process.

Standardized Work as a Process and a Tool

The standardized work process includes numerous tools and worksheets (Table 6–1), one of which is called a standardized worksheet. This can be confusing, and people mistakenly believe the standardized worksheet *is* the standardized work process. Standardized work is the entire integrated process that includes Job Instruction as a

Table 6–1. Tools and documents comprising the standardized work process

Tool or document	Purpose
Standardized worksheet (standardized work chart)	Primary tool used for the identification of waste in repetitive work tasks. Used to document the basic work flow, capture information to balance operation to takt, and show standard work-in-process quantity.
Work combination sheet (work combination table)	Used to analyze the relationship between an operator and machine to effectively synchronize work and eliminate time the operator is waiting for the machine. Also used for multiple people working on the same item simultaneously.
Process capacity sheet	Used to analyze production capacity of equipment and factors in tool changes, setup time, and other planned losses.
Operator work instruction (work instruction, operator instruction)	Used to detail important cyclical and noncyclical tasks especially those that are performed infrequently. This document is a reference document and is not posted in the work area.
Cycle balance chart (stack chart, Yamazumi chart)	Used to compare cycle times to takt for balancing operations to takt and eliminating uneven work. Often used to identify opportunities to combine work, eliminate muda (waste), and reduce the labor requirement.

means of teaching people to achieve efficient work consistently and flawlessly.

To complicate matters further, there are derivations such as work instruction sheets (also known as *operator instructions*) that are similar to the job breakdown sheet used in Job Instruction. These sheets primarily serve as a reference for certain tasks that may be performed infrequently or for critical or complex tasks. In an effort to streamline the tools, lean implementers often attempt to combine several functions into one form. Unfortunately all top mechanics understand that a multifunction tool may get the job done, but it is not as functional as the specific tool designed for the job.

As you can see, there are several variations of the terms used to describe the tools. Don't worry so much about the specific name of the tool. Rather, understand the intended use of each tool. It is a challenge to decide which tool to use and for what application. For example, if the work process being analyzed is a single operation (no product flow down a line), there is no need to use the cycle balance chart to balance multiple operations with one another (although the single operation will still need to be balanced to takt time).

Also if the work is strictly manual with no automated machine cycle (the machine operates independently from the operator), there is no need to use the work combination sheet. The work combination sheet is used whenever there is a person/machine interface and the machine cycle is independent of the operator. The intent is to ensure that the operator's work is synchronous with the machine so no operator time is wasted waiting for the machine. It is also applicable when there is more than one person simultaneously working on the same product at the same time. Again, the purpose is to synchronize the work steps to avoid any waiting.

The standardized worksheet is used on any job with repeatable steps (it is primarily used to analyze for efficiency of motion). It is not really a detailed account of the specifics of the work; rather, it focuses on movement of the worker (and the concept can be used to study machine movement as well). Depending on the nature of the work, the analysis will be made on larger motions such as walking, or, if the work involves smaller hand motions, the analysis will be done at that level of detail.

There is a difference between what Toyota calls standardized work and having defined and standardized work methods. Toyota attempts to standardize all elements of the work, but generally the routine cyclical value-adding portion of the work is analyzed, documented, and posted in the work area. As we will show, other aspects of the work that are nonrepeating and are performed outside the routine cyclical work are defined and standardized, but they are not documented on the same form. This includes the ancillary tasks related to tending the machine and other policy knowledge such as safety procedures.

There are several reasons for this difference. One is because the out-of-cycle work is usually non-value-adding, and Toyota does not want to standardize waste into the process (this is part of TPS thinking—if you standardize waste, you are essentially accepting it). Of course this is not always true (some out-of-cycle work may be value-adding), but it is the general philosophy. Another reason, which we explore in this chapter, is that attempting to combine routine cyclical work and noncyclical work together in one document is an exercise in futility.

What most people see when they visit a Toyota plant is the final outcome of the process—standardized worksheets posted in the work area. Having documented work methods is just one outcome within the total process and should not be considered the primary end objective. The end objective of the process is actually to create consistent results through the elimination of variation in the processes.

The problem with understanding Toyota's process is the exact method and set of tools vary according to the work situation. To an inexperienced visitor to Toyota, there appears to be a variety of methods, forms, and worksheets used. The various departments within Toyota do not use the sheets in exactly the same way.[6] The process that is supposed to provide standardization and consistency does not appear to be consistent. If we look at the task-specific level, we see

---

[6] One example is the use of standardized work in assembly. The vehicle moves through the work area during the task, and the team member's relative position changes during the job cycle. It is difficult to capture a dynamic work process on a static piece of paper. The objective however, is the same—to study operator motion and the flow of the work to eliminate variation and waste. There is a method called *scrolling* that helps capture this movement of the vehicle on the standard worksheet.

apparent inconsistencies, but if we look at the process level, we can see a consistent process applied to varying situations.

On a visit to a Toyota plant in Indonesia, Dr. Liker noted a laminated standard worksheet in color with digital photos and inquired about it. The plant manager explained that as Toyota has become a global company, there has been a need to become more formalized about the process of standardized work. So there are now global standards being developed for particular common jobs on the assembly line along with key points. These are updated regularly through the Internet. He can take particular work elements and mix and match them as they are rebalanced for different job assignments. He can also modify them, and the work teams have some discretion on changes. He had spent several years in Japan and clearly understood the philosophy of TPS. The plant manager made clear that there was a trade-off between standardization coming from a central office and kaizen at the work site. Kaizen at the work site was always a top priority.

Lean implementers often ask for specifics of how to *do* standardized work, or which software tool to use, when the real question should be, "What are we trying to achieve with the process?" The answer is, "We want to achieve the most efficient work with the least amount of waste, performed consistently and flawlessly by highly skilled people." If you were to ask a Toyota *sensei* the question, "How do I do standardized work?" the answer would be a simple, "It depends," which at first is frustrating because we just want to be given the solution so we can implement it correctly. The problem is there is not "one best way." You must consider the situation before a specific course of action can be determined. It is necessary to understand the various tools and how they may or may not be applied to each unique situation.

This reminds us of the joke about the mechanic who is called in to fix a problem with a machine. After careful observation, the mechanic removes a hammer from his tool bag and lightly taps on the side of the machine. The machine is fixed! The mechanic replaces his hammer and presents the client with a bill for services. The bill is $500, and the client is shocked. He asks the mechanic, "How can this simple service of tapping the machine with a hammer be worth $500?" Unfazed the mechanic says, "You are right; let me adjust my bill." He writes out a new bill itemizing his charges as follows, "Tapping with hammer = $1. Knowing *where* to tap = $499." It is important to develop a deep understanding of how to use the tools of standardized work in a variety of situations. This deep understanding can only come from hands-on experience. No one can give you an easy answer. The type of work being analyzed will dictate the exact tool to use.

Think Like a Rice Farmer

One can easily become preoccupied with the message of this chapter to the point of paralysis. How can we possibly develop our people until we have broken every job down to the tiniest level of detail and have decided exactly how it should be done with clear documentation? It might take years to do that. We visited one "lean model plant" with beautiful standardized worksheets hung at every workstation. Managers there explained they had visited a Toyota plant and were not impressed by their standardized work. So they decided they would outdo Toyota at standardized work. For example, they decided to have photographs of each step of the job on their standardized worksheets, while the Toyota plant used only words. And they wanted all the standardized worksheets to look the same and have the same high quality, including good English. So, how did they get every department to do such a good job? At first they asked the departments to do it, but the results were too inconsistent and it was taking too long. So they hired a high school English teacher who had the summer off, and she completed the standard worksheets. Have they changed since then? Of course not! They are "standardized."

Clearly they missed the entire point of standardized work. They had not outdone Toyota. They had simply misunderstood what they saw on their tour of the Toyota plant. Their standardized work meant having standardized worksheets posted, but when we watched people doing the jobs, their motions were anything but standardized. And the work teams were clearly not using standardized work as a continuous improvement tool. Beautiful-looking standardized worksheets do not guarantee good work methods.

As we go through the rest of the book, please remember to always step back and ask, "What is the purpose?" Most often if you ask someone from Toyota the essence of TPS, he or she will answer, "Common sense." After all it did not start at a university. It started with rice farmers in the Nagoya area of Japan. Think like a rice farmer—an intelligent rice farmer who knows the right tool to use for every situation and knows how to improvise.

Chapter 7

Analyzing Routine Work and Ancillary Tasks

Analyzing Routine Work

If we revisit the model in Figure 5–2, we see the first step is to capture the elements of an entire job and then to group them according to the skill requirements. From here we can see how best to proceed with standardized work and the teaching steps.

Let's start with the easiest to analyze—the routine manufacturing job. In the case of routine work, there is a repeatable, cyclical portion of the work we call the "core" job task. The first step for analyzing routine work is to separate the total job task into individual elements and to separate the consistent "core" from the inconsistent ancillary tasks. Another way to look at this is to separate the total job task into two primary categories—the main part of the job task, in which the value-adding activity is done, and all other work necessary to perform the value-adding task. In a repetitive manual task, the core work will generally be the work performed during each cycle—the in-cycle work. The ancillary tasks will generally be done out of cycle on a periodic basis.

Keep in mind there are exceptions to every situation. Some jobs may be completely in-cycle work, and other jobs may have little if any in-cycle work. Perhaps the work you are analyzing has multiple portions of work that are cyclical but separated by noncyclical tasks. It is important to identify common and repeatable tasks. The objective is to group the items with the highest repeatable frequency and lowest amount of time variation. It is important that you take time to study the work. Observe the similarities or consistent items. On first glance the work may appear to be completely random, but if you look deeper, you will begin to see the tasks that occur consistently. In the beginning, you may need to spend some time standing in the Ohno circle and observing for several hours or maybe even days before the pattern emerges. After you are more experienced, this activity will not take as much time.

For our example of a routine job, we are using the rear bumper-molding operation at Toyota where David Meier was a group leader. Some of the details have been modified for clarity, and some have been omitted for brevity. Our intent is to demonstrate the basic concept. This job is typical of any job that involves an independent machine operation and a production task that is performed by the operator during the machine operation. As we say in Chapter 5, this job is a mix of routine work and technician-like work. It is a bit more complex in nature than a purely routine job because of the nature of plastic molding. It is typical of any job that includes a consistent repeatable core task as well as a variety of tasks that are consistent in their method but vary in the frequency of their performance. Some of the "random" tasks have consistent frequency, others are more inconsistent, and some are "as needed" and completely unpredictable.

When dissecting the job, begin with just the more routine high-level elements that are generally easier to understand than all the details and variants. Always move from simplicity to complexity. One mistake often made is to worry about the details before first understanding the basics. As we will learn, this "routine" manufacturing work is actually fairly complex when we uncover the critical details necessary to complete the work successfully. Table 7–1 shows the first separation of the bumper-molding operator job into the routine and nonroutine core tasks and other ancillary tasks (noncyclical). At this step we have not identified other policy or judgment-related

Table 7–1. Separation of bumper-molding job into task categories

Rear Bumper Molding Operator		
Routine core tasks	**Nonroutine core tasks**	**Ancillary tasks**
De-mold bumper	Spray mold release	Machine start-up
Set bumper in trimming nest	Mold release touch-up spray	Machine cycling
Mold release touch-up spray	Full mold cleaning	Mold change
Trim flash	Partial mold cleaning	Machine shut down
Sand parting lines	Mold preparation after cleaning	Miscellaneous
Inspect	Buffing mold surface	
Load on rack	Quality-related tasks	

tasks or considered accumulated know-how. Remember to start with simplicity and move toward complexity. It is also important to develop value-adding skills first. We define the procedural and judgment knowledge later.

The routine core task is fairly straightforward in terms of identifying specific steps and can easily be put on a standardized worksheet as shown in Figure 7–1. (Note: This job has no standard amount of WIP, and the quality checks and safety items are not shown here). The finished standardized worksheet looks fairly simple overall. Don't be fooled by the apparent simplicity! We will see that the details of *how* to perform these routine tasks are quite involved, and developing exceptional talent requires much greater depth of understanding.

The standardized worksheet is mainly used to analyze the work motion and to define and depict the most efficient movement of the operator as he or she performs the work steps. The standardized worksheet lists the work steps, diagrams the movement, defines the standard work in process amount, and shows each work element time (in seconds) and the takt time for the complete operation.

Note that the descriptions of each step are fairly general and the placement of the work steps on the diagram shows the approximate location of the operator's feet during that step. It is a very superficial representation of the work method. This tool helps us to understand the work pattern and to determine if it is the most efficient movement of the operator, but this is a far cry from detailed instruction on how to

Standardized worksheet Date: 9/1/20___

Plant:	Group: Bumper molding	Part Name: Rear bumper	Prepared By: David Sullivan	Required Qty. per shift: 190
Department: Plastics	Operation: Rear bumper operator	Part #:	Standard WIP None	TAKT Time: 135 sec.

#	Work Elements	Work Time	Walk Time
1	De-mold right side	4	3
2	Push off left side	4	3
3	Set in trimming nest	2	3
4	Spray right core	14	3
5	Spray left core	14	3
6	Retract platen and start cycle	4	2
7	Trim left side flash	13	2
8	Trim gate flash	7	2
9	Trim right side flash	13	0
10	Sand right side parting line	14	3
11	Sand left side parting line	14	2
12	Set bumper on rack	4	2
	Total	107	28

Finished bumpers
Finished bumpers
Bumper trim nest
Machine control
Bumper mold (tilts out)
Bumper machine

Standard work-in-process Quality check Safety Page 1 of 1

Figure 7–1. Standardized worksheet for bumper-molding operation

actually perform the work. This is where the ability to break down a job using the Job Instruction method is beneficial. The Job Instruction method concentrates on what is important to successfully complete the task. We suggest that you define the work requirements to a basic level, as we have demonstrated here, and then study the job breakdown method discussed in Chapters 8 through 10 to learn more about identifying the critical details of the work. The progression will move from defining the basic work pattern, to details of how to perform the work, to teaching the precise method.

How to Approach Nonroutine and Ancillary Tasks

A large portion of our bumper-molding operator's job is made up of nonroutine work and ancillary tasks—work that is necessary to support the completion of the core task. In this case, the individual tasks do repeat in a fairly consistent pattern, but there are multiple variations of patterns. For nonroutine work the repeatability or pattern of the work is not as important as it is for routine work. Ancillary work is more random in nature and takes place when it is needed. For the purpose of analysis, it is more relevant to review the work as individual pieces or in common groupings. These common groupings may be related to the type of task, location where the task occurs, frequency, duration, or another category.

For the bumper-molding operation the tasks fit nicely into categories according to machine functions, preparation of molding tooling, quality-related tasks, and then leftover miscellaneous tasks. Our groupings are also related to the frequency of occurrence and repeatability of the task itself. The groupings of nonroutine and ancillary tasks for this job are as follows:

1. Operation of the machine (variable frequency, repeatable work).
2. Tasks related to tending the machine (variable frequency, repeatable work).
3. Quality-related tasks (variable frequency, repeatable work).
4. Miscellaneous tasks (variable work, some repeatability).

We continue by breaking down the basic elements of the job into detailed elements. Each of these elements will again be broken down, and the detailed levels are beginning to be the basis for the defined standard method for that *portion* of the task. We have the standardized worksheet for the routine core portion of the job, and we have defined methods for each nonroutine and ancillary task that is detailed in operator instruction and job breakdown sheets and used to train employees.[1]

The following list shows the breakdown of each category related to each of the associated individual tasks that must be taught to the operators.

1. Machine operation activities
   a. Machine start-up
   b. Machine controls
   c. Machine cycling
   d. Mold change
   e. Machine shutdown
2. Job tasks related to tending the machine
   a. Spray mold release (every 10 cycles)
   b. Mold release touch-up spray (every cycle and part of standardized work)
   c. Full mold cleaning (every 120 cycles)
   d. Partial mold cleaning (every 40 cycles)
   e. Mold preparation after cleaning (every 120 cycles)
   f. Buffing mold surface (to correct defects, random occurrence)
3. Quality-related tasks
   a. Partial inspection (every cycle)
   b. Full part inspection (every hour)
      i. Visual inspection
      ii. Weight confirmation

[1] Within the Toyota Production System there are few hard and fast rules. The core principles (eliminate waste, create flow, etc.) are consistent rules, but the method of implementing them and how the tools are used vary. All the tools mentioned here are under the broad umbrella of standardized work. We are referring to the tool (document) used to capture the essence of the value-adding work on paper—the standardized worksheet.

4. Miscellaneous tasks
    a. Safety gear and requirements
    b. Using hand tools
    c. Completing data collection sheets
    d. Completing production data boards
    e. Adjusting spray gun

We continue to break each piece down into smaller details. An example of one of the subentries from the machine start-up task (one of the machine operation tasks) is as follows:

1. Machine start-up
    a. Power on machine
    b. Manual release of mold cores
    c. Open platen
    d. Tilt out platens
    e. Extend upper platen
    f. Retract upper platen
    g. Start dry-cycle operation

Now we are getting close. This list shows the steps necessary to start up the machine, but we still have a way to go before the complete process is delineated. From this point it is possible to begin to define how to do each of these steps. Some of the steps are fairly simple and need little definition. Some are complex or have a safety concern involved and need more details. Any time a machine is operated, the safety key points must be clearly identified as we will show in Chapter 9.

We have seen that one of the most basic ancillary tasks of a machine operator (starting the machine) is actually quite detailed. Each of the detailed tasks must be taught to every new operator. We can see then that teaching the job can be a complex assignment. Some of these individual tasks are less complex and will not take a great deal of time to teach. Some are more complex and may take days or weeks to teach. Developing talent in employees is a much bigger task than we often think. Make sure you break down every job into details so that people will develop the highest skill level.

To prevent "analysis paralysis" and getting bogged down in superfluous details, we use a method of further categorizing the work tasks according to their importance. Some of the tasks are critical in nature and must be very carefully defined. Others are less important or have a wide range of acceptability and do not need such detailed analysis. We discuss this idea later in this chapter.

Let's go back to the issue of job task type and the documentation method for the standardized work process. We have shown the standardized worksheet (Figure 7–1) for the routine core task. What documents are used for the routine ancillary work? There is an element of "it depends" here, but Figure 7–2 shows the breakdown of tasks for the bumper-molding operation and the associated written forms used for the purpose of documenting the defined method (also see Table 6–1). The Job Instruction method is used for the transfer of knowledge for all types of tasks regardless of the documentation used to record the actual job.

Routine ancillary tasks with a consistent procedure but a variable and random sequence are captured on work instruction sheets (also called *operator instruction sheets*). Other information related to policies and work practices may be captured on operator instruction sheets for tasks such as handling waste material. Information related to policies and procedures is contained in standard policy documents.

Often we find people who are just learning lean want to make sure they have found the "ideal" or "perfect" solution. The philosophy of continuous improvement begins with the assumption that there is no perfect solution, nor is it desirable to spend excessive time trying to find one. The essential method of Toyota is to first identify the need (i.e., increased output), study the work method looking for waste, identify what improvements can be made in short order (a few days at most), get busy making the improvements, and at the same time plan and implement longer-term items. Then repeat the steps again to make further improvements. This is the plan-do-check-act cycle.

<table>
<tr><th colspan="6">Rear Bumper Molding Operator</th></tr>
<tr><th colspan="2">Routine in-cycle tasks</th><th colspan="2">Out-of-cycle ancillary tasks</th><th colspan="2">Policies and judgment-based work</th></tr>
<tr><td rowspan="12">Consistent repetitive cycle
Consistent repetitive sequence</td><td>De-mold bumper</td><td rowspan="12">Consistent work procedure
Inconsistent random sequence</td><td>Machine start-up</td><td rowspan="12">No cycle
No sequence</td><td>Safety procedures</td></tr>
<tr><td>Set bumper in trimming nest</td><td>Machine cycling</td><td>Environmental procedures</td></tr>
<tr><td>Mold release touch-up spray</td><td>Mold change</td><td>Quality standards</td></tr>
<tr><td>Retract platen</td><td>Machine shutdown</td><td>Machine controls and programming</td></tr>
<tr><td>Trim flash</td><td>Spray mold release</td><td></td></tr>
<tr><td>Sand parting lines</td><td>Mold release touch-up spray</td><td></td></tr>
<tr><td>Inspect</td><td>Full mold cleaning</td><td></td></tr>
<tr><td>Load on rack</td><td>Partial mold cleaning</td><td></td></tr>
<tr><td></td><td>Mold preparation after cleaning</td><td></td></tr>
<tr><td></td><td>Buffing mold surface</td><td></td></tr>
<tr><td></td><td>Quality-related tasks</td><td></td></tr>
<tr><td></td><td>Miscellaneous</td><td></td></tr>
<tr><th colspan="2">Standardized work</th><th colspan="2">Standard written procedures and work methods</th><th colspan="2">Defined policies, procedures, and standards</th></tr>
<tr><th colspan="6">Develop talent using Job Instruction method</th></tr>
</table>

Figure 7–2. Documentation used for various work tasks and knowledge development

Analyzing a Complex Job from the Health Care Field

In health care, defining effective methods for things as simple as washing hands can mean the difference between life and death. The rate of patient mortality due to infections contracted within the hospital is staggering. In the United States alone, over 2 million patients get infections or diseases in the hospital, and 100,000 of them die every year from infections introduced within the hospital. One person dies every 5 minutes from a hospital-induced infection!

In one case when the physicians were questioned about their adherence to the defined hand-washing standard, they all reported that they were completely compliant. Actual observation in the workplace however, indicated a compliance rate of only 32 percent.[2] The study found that in some cases hand washing was skipped all together, and in many cases there was not a consistent method used by everyone.

As another example, a major cause of infection is intravenous catheters, which are placed in blood vessels leading to the heart so they can more easily administer IV fluids. Estimates are that 250,000 patients per year suffer infection from this procedure, with some 15 percent or more leading to deaths. Despite general guidelines from the Centers for Disease Control and Prevention there is tremendous variation in this procedure. In one hospital, by studying the root causes of infections, standardizing the process, using visual signals, and training nurses, the incidence of infections was reduced from 37 deaths in one year to 6 in the following year. Associated deaths were reduced from 19 to 1.[3]

This problem of inconsistent compliance or variation of method is of course not unique to health care. We see it all the time in other industries. We believe the root cause to be the same in all cases—a failure to drill down into the details of the work, to identify the items of a critical nature, to define a specific method to do the task, to diligently teach everyone the correct method, and then to continually follow up

---

[2] L. Savary and C. Crawford-Mason, *The Nun and the Bureaucrat: How They Found an Unlikely Cure for America's Sick Hospitals*, CC-M Productions, 2006.

[3] S. Spear, "Fixing Healthcare from the Inside, Today," *Harvard Business Review*, September, 2005.

to ensure the method is being used by everyone (and using specific measurement indicators, such as the number of infections, as an overall verification that the process is in control).

For our analysis we look at typical duties for a nurse in a busy hospital. Of course there are a variety of nurses, each performing different work in all areas of the hospital. Remember to start with the broad view first. The work of most nurses in a hospital will be aligned closely with craft or technician-type work. This type of work will most likely not have a routine core task (although some might, in which case refer to the previous section). The ancillary tasks, however, may be very routine and definable in nature. The nursing job also includes some fundamental skills that are covered in nursing school, extensive policy knowledge, and judgment learned on the job.

When we observe work of a typical nurse, what we would see is a series of events that occur randomly. The nurse may be attending to a patient and get a request for something (say another pillow). As he is heading to get the pillow, a call comes from another room. Off he goes to attend to the new issue. After attending to the call, he is stopped by a doctor requesting special attention for a patient. Then he's off to administer medication to the patients. An hour later he remembers the pillow and heads off to get it. On the way he is stopped by another nurse with a request to assist with moving a patient to another bed, and on and on. If we follow the nurse all day, we would feel like a pinball bouncing around and shooting to and fro. How then is it possible to standardize this seemingly random process?

The "real world" of the nurse's job requires flexibility and the ability to respond to the ever-changing situation. We hear this same objection in manufacturing or other fields where the work appears to be highly variable. It is assumed that the nurse's job must be made routine like an assembly line job. Herein lies the mistake. It is not the intent of standardized work to make all work highly repetitive; it is the intent to define the best methods and to reduce variation in the *work method* as much as possible.

By studying the nurse's job carefully to identify common or repeating tasks rather than focusing only on the differences, we would begin to see some patterns emerge. We would see individual tasks that are the same, but that do not follow a consistent pattern. The routine portion of an assembly line job has the same tasks following the same pattern—completely repetitive. The nurse has some repeating tasks following a consistent pattern at times and an inconsistent pattern at other times. These are sprinkled with random events occurring here and there—quite a hodgepodge of activity.

Using an approach similar to the one used in the bumper-molding job reviewed earlier in the chapter, we begin by breaking down the nurse's total job into individual pieces, looking for the common definable elements as shown in Table 7–2. A portion of the total job is routine in nature and will follow some pattern. Rounds may be conducted every hour for example, and during the rounds the nurse will follow a standardized method of checking patient vital signs, administering medications, verifying the proper operation and delivery of IV fluids, and so forth. During the rounds, but also at other random times, the nurse may be required to perform other tasks such as drawing blood. The task itself is defined and routine, but it does not follow a repeating sequence.

There are many other definable tasks performed, but they follow no particular patterns. They are "on demand." There is an element of miscellaneous and uncategorizable content that is also made up of individually definable elements.

Clearly we can see that the tasks within health care and many other fields are quite complex in their entirety, but if we take the time to view them from the perspective of finding commonality, we would see a good percentage of the tasks are made up of simple, definable, and teachable elements. This must be the focus. The goal is not to try to create a perfectly repeatable and consistent process when the reality is otherwise, but to always work toward reducing the causes of variation within the tasks.

Remember our objective at this stage is not to detail every single element of the job. We are attempting to identify those tasks that make up the bulk of the work, or at least a good part of the total job. If we identify the most important and frequently occurring tasks and begin the breakdown process with them, our effort will be most

Table 7–2. Separation of hospital nurse's job into task categories

Hospital Nurse		
Routine core tasks	**Nonroutine core tasks**	**Ancillary tasks**
Routine rounds	Start IV fluids	Charting and records
Check vital signs	Defibrillate patient	Admissions records
Administer medications	Draw blood samples	Stock supplies
Verify medication delivery	Admissions processing	Check equipment
		Dispose biowaste
		Assist physicians
		Assist patients
		Miscellaneous

beneficial overall. When the major tasks have all been defined and taught to all nurses, it would make sense to go back and begin to analyze the smaller details of the work in order of importance.

As is usually the case (just like with the bumper-molding operator), some of these tasks are easier to define and detail than others. Begin with the most repeatable tasks and those that are easier to define. We have been fortunate to have some examples provided from the field. Dr. Richard F. Kunkle, currently with the Kennametal Center for Operational Excellence, provided us with the detailed steps of the task of starting an intravenous line (IV) in a peripheral vein. Note that this is a subset of the nurse's task of administering IV fluids.

Dr. Kunkle detailed all steps necessary to complete the task and organized them in groups as shown below:

Primary Job Tasks

1. Identify an appropriate site.
2. Select the appropriate size and type of IV device.
3. Ensure that the device is in proper order.
4. Decontaminate the IV insertion site.
5. Puncture the vein.
6. Remove the needle.
7. Safely dispose of the needle.
8. Stabilize the catheter.

Ancillary Tasks

1. Obtain the IV start basket.
2. Resupply the basket to standard.
3. Determine if there's a latex allergy.
4. Pre-tear the tape to length.
5. Open the "micropore" catheter restraining device.
6. Determine and obtain the correct IV solution.
7. Determine the correct type of IV tubing to use.
8. Insert tubing into bag.
9. Prime the line with fluid.

Policy and Judgment Tasks

1. "Sharps" (needle use and disposal) safety policies and procedures.
2. Infection prevention and control policies and procedures.
3. Infectious waste management policies and procedures.
4. Latex allergy policies and procedures.
5. Documentation requirements for chart.
6. Documentation requirements for IV site.

This small portion of the overall job involves many detailed steps, and these steps need to be broken down into even greater detail for training purposes. In Figure 7–3 we take the liberty of reorganizing the IV insertion tasks (and a few additional ones) into groupings that will facilitate training and also identify the individual tasks that need to be standardized.

We made the decisions regarding how to separate the tasks based on the logical groupings for training purposes. We begin by identifying the core value-adding portion of the task. The core task should be taught first because it is the most critical value-adding portion. In this case the core task is the actual insertion of the IV.

Next, look for any portion of the task that is repeated but is not included with the core task because it does not repeat on the same frequency or is actually performed as a separate event from the core task. In the example in Figure 7–3 the repeating noncore tasks are then grouped according to whether they occur prior to or after the core task. These repeating tasks are generally some type of preparation for, or finish-up required for the core task (like cleaning the kitchen after cooking).

Here we felt that the pretasks and posttasks should be performed separately from the actual patient contact. It would not be wise to have the patient sit and wait while the preparation is being done. This is analogous to a machine waiting for a setup change while tooling is prepared. There may be an exception in this case for the preparation of the materials (IV bag and tube) because of possible contamination if this is done ahead of time. It may be necessary to do this task just before the actual insertion of the IV. If the materials must be prepared each time the core task is performed, this portion of the task would also be considered part of the core task, but for training purposes we would still separate the two tasks into individual training sessions. These repeating tasks would be the next level of importance for training purposes. Because these tasks repeat frequently, there is high value in having people trained to perform them.

Finally, we considered the remainder of tasks that did not repeat, or are repeated at a low frequency (once per day). Again, these were divided into pretask and posttask groups. As we continue to divide the various tasks into groupings, we are attempting to organize them according to training events and to priority of the training events. Minor miscellaneous or infrequent tasks should be taught after the more important core tasks and repeating tasks.

We have also included necessary supporting information such as policies and decision-making tools (training aids) that can be used to assist the student when being taught tasks that require decision making or would require additional education.

Thus far we have identified a variety of job tasks and broken one down into moderate detail, but we have yet to actually define and standardize any *methods*. Here's the rub—we need to break down each detailed task for Job Instruction so we can find the best method and standardize it. Thus far, we have identified the *steps* of the tasks. These steps are the foundation of a standardized process and define *what* is being done. The job breakdown for training will take the process one step further and identify the key points of the work. Key points

Last priority	Third priority	Fourth priority	Second priority	First priority	Fifth priority	Last priority
Nonrepeating pretask	**Repeating pretask: Patient interview (requires decision)**	**Repeating pretask: Obtain materials (based on decision)**	**Repeating pretask: Prepare materials**	**Repeating core task: Insert IV**	**Repeating posttask**	**Nonrepeating posttask**
• Resupply the basket to standard • Order supplies	• Verify medical history to select admin site • Determine the size and type IV device • Determine if latex allergy	• Select appropriate size & type IV device • Obtain IV start basket • Determine IV tubing • Determine & get correct IV solution	• Pre-tear tape to length • Open "micropore" catheter restrainer • Insert tubing into bag • Prime line with fluid • Assure device is in proper order	• Decontaminate IV insertion site • Puncture vein • Remove needle • Dispose of needle • Stabilize catheter	• Clean up • Dispose of waste • Process documentation	• End of day cleanup • 5'S activity
Policies and judgment	**Policies and judgment**	**Policies and judgment**	**Policies and judgment**	**Policies and judgment**	**Policies and judgment**	**Policies and judgment**
• Purchasing procedure • Stocking procedure (kanban)	• Latex allergy procedures • Documentation on chart			• Sharps safety procedures • Infection prevention & control procedures	• Sharps safety procedures • Infectious waste management • Documentation on chart • Documentation for IV site	• 5'S procedures
	Decision-making tool	**Decision-making tool**				**Decision-making tool**
	• Use patient interview sheet	• Decision matrix for tubing selection • Decision matrix for solution selection				• 5'S check • Use patient sheet

Figure 7–3. IV insertion tasks grouped by training events and knowledge required

specify *how* to best perform the steps. We will explore the identification of key points in Chapter 9.

Before we leave this example, let's back up a bit with standardized work. On the last several pages, we describe how to look at the individual details of the work and organize them into categories so specific methods of performing the tasks could be defined. Remember though that standardized work is primarily intended to analyze work for the purpose of identifying and eliminating waste. In the next section we throw in a little twist. At Toyota each work task is not blindly analyzed in isolation. Before digging into details, it is best to step back even further and expand your view from a single operation and to consider the entire process.

Evaluate the Entire Process

When evaluating standardized work, it is important to remember a key difference between Toyota and traditional cost accounting–based companies. Toyota focuses on *total system efficiency* rather than on individual efficiency. It is important to look beyond the individual's work during the evaluation of standardized work and to examine the total picture in the workplace.

If we examine the case of the nurse above and expand our view to include all nurses within the department or on the floor, we will likely see several nurses, each running to and fro and being distracted from their primary value-adding function—to make rounds and administer to the patients. One key principle we discussed in *The Toyota Way Fieldbook* is the isolation of variation within the work processes. If variation occurs, it is best to isolate it to as few people as possible so that its effect is contained. Toyota has a structure in place to allow the value-adding team associates to focus on their tasks and not be distracted by other issues.

Just suppose for example there were five nurses within a department and each was doing the same thing—attempting to get his or her work done amid numerous distractions and calls. Now suppose we separate the consistent work (the value-adding work) from the inconsistent work (perhaps value-adding, but random) and find that if three nurses could focus on only the consistent work (the rounds) without distraction, they could successfully complete the consistent portion of the work previously done by five nurses (with random activities included). This is when we use the principle of consolidating the waste activities of many people into one person's responsibility and in the process gain some efficiency. We often find that when several people all have distractions in their work, the cumulative effect is larger because each person is repeating similar wasteful activities. If these activities are consolidated, some efficiency is gained and the total labor requirement is reduced.

Now suppose one of the other two remaining nurses could be responsible for responding to the unplanned calls and needs of the patients with no responsibility for the rounds. Perhaps a call system (andon) would be necessary for the three nurses to contact the support nurse when needed. That leaves us with the fifth nurse as "extra."

We suggest you take a continuous improvement perspective when deciding what to do with the "free" labor. Perhaps the remaining nurse is not needed to complete the regular work but can be more effectively utilized for other tasks. Maybe there is a need for specialized nursing care or additional administrative activities. The fifth nurse could be utilized as a trainer or be involved in additional continuous improvement activities. There are numerous possibilities, and in many cases hospitals are faced with critical nursing shortages, and any nurses who are removed from the daily tasks may be redeployed to other areas. Consider the long-term potential of utilizing people fully rather than the short-term cost reduction possibility of letting a person go.

Determine What Items Are Critical and Ensure They Are Performed Flawlessly

When we ask leaders and workers to estimate the percentage of the total work that is critical we usually get a very high number—often 90 percent or more. This is a common misunderstanding regarding the definition of "critical." All of the work steps are *necessary* for the successful completion of the task, but they are not all critical. By definition a critical work step is one that must be followed with a high degree of accuracy. If the step is not followed precisely a "defect" will occur (any result that does not meet the expected standard). Critical aspects of the work also tend to have a very narrow range of acceptability and, thus, must be monitored carefully.

In most cases the critical aspects of any work equal about 15 to 20 percent of the total work. Beyond the critical steps are those steps of high importance descending to lower levels of importance. The key to successfully developing talent is to identify the small portion of the work that is critical and very important and to take special care to define the best standard method and train everyone to follow the prescribed method consistently.[4] All aspects of the work are not equally important, and extra effort should be applied where it will yield the greatest benefit. In addition the critical items must be monitored closely.

Leaders should focus their attention on the most crucial tasks and stress them to the associates. If leaders attempt to place equal importance on all details, they will likely get limited results. It is not practical to closely monitor every detail in the workplace. Achieving the desired results requires the ability to differentiate between items of critical nature, high importance, and little or no importance.

Insist that every person follow the critical steps exactly. Allow work methods within defined ranges for less critical work when they do not negatively affect performance. In some cases the way the work is performed has little or no significance and requires limited follow-up and monitoring.

We use the bumper-molding job as an example to provide an idea of the detailed and critical portion of the work. Every work step or procedure has a tolerance range of performance. Some tolerance ranges are fairly narrow and must have a high degree of conformance. Others have a wider range, but it is still necessary to perform them carefully with a specific method. Finally there is a portion of nearly every job that allows a greater degree of variability, and differences in technique will have little impact on the final outcome. Table 7–3 provides a

[4] Thanks to our colleague Tim Szymcek for his input on this topic.

Table 7–3. Breakdown of work tasks by level of importance

Percentage of total work	Importance	Effect on work
15–20%	Critical—work must be highly consistent	Definite effect on results if performed out of range
60%	Important—work must be consistent within a slightly wider range	Probable effect on results if performed out of range
20%	Low importance—work method may be variable	Not likely to effect results regardless of method

guideline for the approximate content of most work. Of course the exact percentages in each category will vary according to the work, but the basic idea is consistent; there will be some degree of variation in every work situation.

As a general rule, spend 80 percent of your time focusing on the 20 percent of items that are most critical. These are the items that allow very little variance in their operating parameters. For these items there is no acceptable deviation from the defined method. Team members are not allowed to "freelance" with their own preferred style. In many cases we see leaders who mistakenly place equal importance on all aspects of the work. In some cases critical elements are reduced to a general level of importance, and the disregard for the critical nature of these tasks leads to safety and quality issues. On the other end of the spectrum, we see items of low importance that are stressed inappropriately. If you attempt to put a high level of importance on the entire job, it will be necessary to insist that the work be performed exactly as defined—no deviation is permissible. Placing the highest level of importance on the entire job is a sure way to annoy the workers and to drive yourself crazy by trying to have everyone perform all of the work at critical levels.

What we typically see as a primary difference between Toyota and other companies is the degree to which Toyota clarifies the importance of the various aspects of the work. Most other companies consider the work to be fairly general in nature and don't often distinguish the importance of the aspects of the work, and there is a fair amount of disagreement about the "best way" of doing the work. At Toyota it is clear to everyone what the critical aspects of the work are, and the importance of doing them in the specified way. Failure to do so would lead to undesired results and most likely have an impact on the entire system. On the assembly line Toyota will post signs to indicate which jobs include critical safety or quality steps. These signs are easily visible above the work area.

In referring back to the bumper-molding operation, we see that the task requires the team member to de-mold the bumper manually, and also to trim and sand excess flash from the parting lines. Only a small portion of the total job is critical in nature. The actual hand trimming of the flash from the parting lines is the most critical part of the job. The trimming knife must be held perpendicular to the surface, and the trimming line must be followed to within 2 millimeters. If the trim knife is angled just a few degrees off, the resulting cut is unacceptable because it is a visible finished surface. Also the trim line at the injection gate adjoins another surface and must be extremely straight. For these tasks the technique is very precise, and workers performing this task are carefully trained and monitored. It is unacceptable to have any variation of method or experimentation with individual preferences for these steps.

The major portion of the bumper-molding work is important but has a fairly wide tolerance range. For example, when the bumper end is pulled from the mold, it must be pulled out from the mold between 2 and 5 inches and at the same time pulled down a few inches. Pulling the bumper much more than 5 inches is likely to crease the side of the bumper. Notice we say likely to cause a crease. In reality if the bumper is pulled down at a sharp angle beyond 7 inches, the likelihood of a defect increases to a certainty, so operators are taught a technique to de-mold the bumper between 2 and 5 inches, thus ensuring a good quality product. Teaching and performing a work technique with acceptable variation of 3 inches is much easier than a technique requiring precision of 2 millimeters. The possibility for error is lower as the acceptable work range increases, and it is not necessary to focus training efforts on following a method as precisely as with a critical step. If a crease on the side of the bumper is discovered at a later point in the process, the team leader would immediately verify the operator's de-molding technique, but this is an infrequent issue and would not require constant vigilance. The critical steps require close monitoring.

Spraying the mold surface with release agent is important, but still has a tolerance range of an inch or two, and the spray angle may vary by several degrees. The setting and calibration of the spray gun is important, and the fan pattern is verified and the amount of release agent is captured in a vial once per day and measured to calibrate the spray amount. The operator is taught to hold the spray gun a specific distance from the surface of the mold, at the proper angle, and also with the correct orientation of the fan (the spray gun may be held in a vertical, horizontal, or angled position, accordingly). In addition the distance from the mold surface, the pattern, and the number of times the spray gun trigger is pulled are specified.

We can see within this portion of the task there are many items specified and standardized, but there are also some items that allow for minimal variation within the task. If the spray gun is held too close to the surface, the spray will build up on the surface and create a defect on the bumper surface if the mold is not polished. Holding the spray gun too far away will cause a "dry spray" on the mold surface, and the bumper will not release properly, causing a defect. The range between too far away and too close to the surface is about 3 or 4 inches. It is better to err on the side of being too close to the mold surface because the resulting defect is less likely to occur and can be repaired effectively. When training, more emphasis is placed on keeping the spray gun closer to the surface to prevent this problem.

The bumper-molding operator job also requires the accumulation of specific know-how because each mold and machine has an individual "personality." Operators have to learn to "read" the mold surface and make minor adjustments according to the current conditions. The best operators learn to be sensitive to the sights and sounds of each machine. The mold will make a distinctive popping sound when the mold release spray is light, and excessive spray is detected as a hazy surface on the bumper. As Bill Marriott noted, it is not always possible to completely standardize every aspect of the work. This is a primary value of humans over automation (robots). People are adaptable and can make necessary adjustments to the work technique as required (although the adjustment is also predetermined and loosely standardized—standardized deviation if you will).

Very little of this task is actually of low importance. Operators have a preference for how many sheets of sandpaper they hold in their hand, and how to fold it (although how to use the sand paper is important because the edge of the paper could scratch the bumper, causing a defect). The rest of the job is considered to be either critical or important, and there is a specified method that is followed.

It is probably worth noting that David Meier, as a group leader at Toyota's Georgetown plant, was responsible for this bumper-molding operation and had to understand all the above and more at a great level of detail. He was responsible for training the workers as well as auditing them regularly to ensure that they were following the standardized work—in the broad sense including all of the key points. Any quality problem could generally be traced back to failure to follow the standardized work or, if the work was not properly defined, led to a revision to the standardized work. Notice the degree of detail goes well beyond what is on a standardized worksheet. Also notice that traditional supervisors are rarely trained to this level of detail, so they cannot teach or coach others.

Success Is in the Details

Unfortunately the development of standardized work and defined methods does not follow a linear path. We would like to be able to say, "This is the way to do standardized work step by step," but it does not work that way. We have focused primarily on the process of analyzing jobs and defining the steps and critical aspects of the work for the purpose of supporting training. There are many other facets of the standardized work process we have not touched on. As with the analysis of jobs, when broken down to the single details, any one detail by itself is not complex. When hundreds or thousands of individual details are combined, the process becomes very complex. In our case here, we are attempting to think about work in terms of definable and teachable bits.

Seemingly random and nonstandardized work activities can in fact be made more standardized by simply changing your vantage point. It is easy to assume it is not possible to standardize work in certain situations. Be careful about assuming what is possible and what is not. The truth is these principles can be applied in any situation to some extent. The goal is to apply the principles as much as possible. As you take steps in the direction of standardizing, you will begin to see additional steps are possible. This is the nature of continuous improvement. If you allow yourself to realize there will always be another possibility and your current activities are never going to be the "ultimate" solution, you will be on the right track.

As we have already said, it is our belief that most companies outside of Toyota do not evaluate work tasks in enough detail. Definition of work methods is often superficial, and the correct method is left in question. Toyota is able to produce consistently high performance because the work is carefully analyzed in great detail and because great effort is made to teach every employee the correct way to do the work.

It is crucial to the success of your improvement efforts to learn to carefully analyze work, break down each element into detail, identify the critical aspects, and rigorously teach others to follow the defined steps. Remember this is a continuously improving process. You should learn more each time you analyze and break down a job. Teach others the analysis process so everyone is capable of understanding what is most important about every job.

If you spend the majority of your time and effort on the most critical parts, you will have greater success. We don't think the devil is in the details; we know success is! When you think you have enough detail, look again. If you master the tiniest item of the highest importance, you will achieve greater results.

Chapter 8

Breaking a Job Down into Pieces for Teaching

Breaking Down the Job for Training Is Different

In Chapter 6 we reviewed a method for breaking down a job for the purpose of developing standardized work. There is a direct connection between the development of standardized work and the job breakdown used for Job Instruction, and it is impossible to separate one from the other. Defining the job for the purpose of standardizing the work provides the framework for how the job is to be done—and thus taught to others. It is extremely difficult to teach a job that is not standardized and does not have a defined method for performing the work.

The steps defined in the standardized method, however, are not necessarily the same as the steps in the job breakdown, which are used for teaching purposes. The steps of the standard method may be broader and might need to be divided into smaller pieces for effective learning. Students are learning to do the work as it is supposed to be done according to the standardized method, but they are learning in a way that is more conducive to the learning process. The purpose for breaking down the job now shifts from defining the method to transferring the critical information about the work and necessary skills to others. Breaking down a job into manageable "training pieces" is necessary to effectively teach others.

For example, the standardized method may describe the work step as, "Install the radiator," but for training purposes this step may be broken down into three smaller steps in order to simplify the training process as follows:

1. Position radiator on mounting studs.
2. Route the hoses.
3. Install the nuts.

The end objective is the same for both processes—well-defined jobs that are performed flawlessly by the team members. This discrepancy between the steps identified for the standard method and those for Job Instruction does cause some confusion for people attempting to duplicate Toyota's system who somehow learned that the standardized worksheet is also the training sheet. To achieve maximum results from the training process, it is necessary to break jobs down into small pieces that can be effectively learned. If the work is not detailed enough, many of the critical elements of the work will be lost. One caveat is worth mentioning. Some companies have chosen to include key points on the standard worksheet and use it for Job Instruction. While we do not normally recommend that, it can be done effectively.

Slice and Dice the Task into Small Details

In *The Toyota Way Fieldbook* we introduced the idea of "slicing and dicing" (page 161) when analyzing product mix. The idea is to take a large complex situation with high variation and break it into smaller pieces, first by slicing into the individual groups and then by dicing each group into the subgroups. For the purpose of job breakdown, the idea is to slice the entire job into individual tasks grouped according to their characteristics (as discussed in Chapter 7). Then each task is diced into steps that are diced again into detailed elements suitable for training as shown in Figure 8–1.

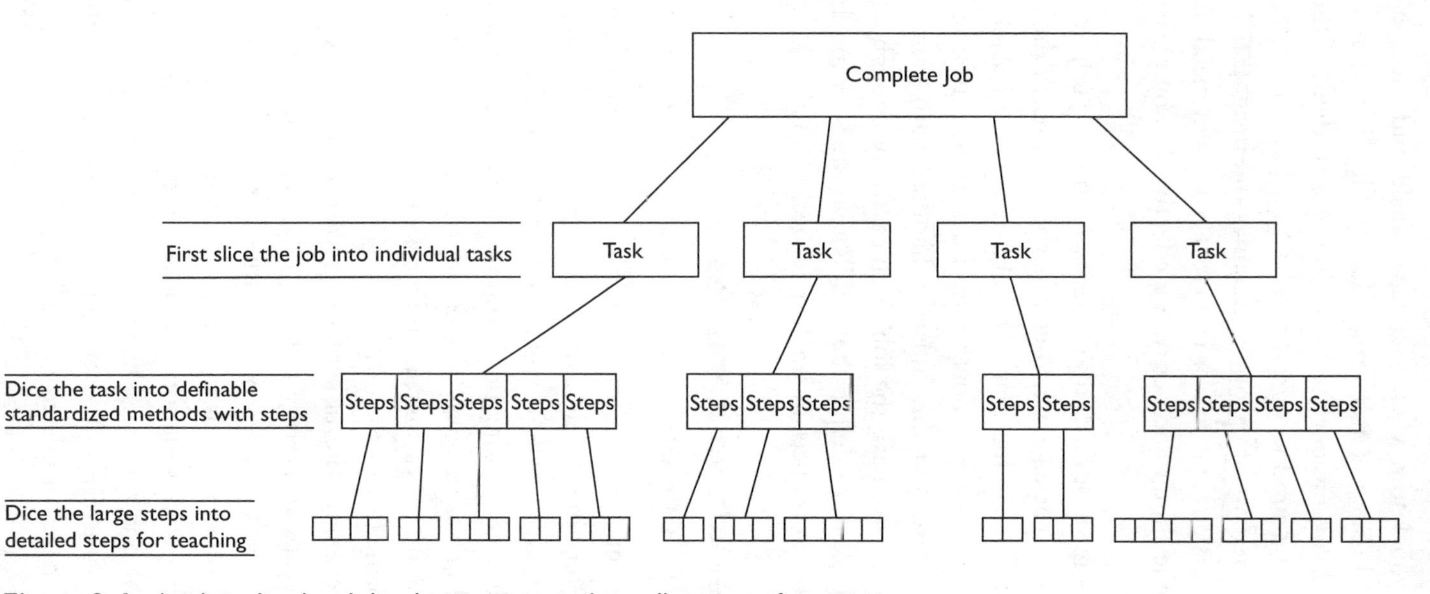

Figure 8–1. A job is sliced and diced into successively smaller pieces for training

How do you know when you have sliced and diced a job into sufficient detail, but not too much detail? The final evaluation will not come until you present the operation to a student. If the student learns quickly and produces great results, you have effectively broken down the job. Here we offer some guidelines and insights to help make your process easier, but to some extent you will need to experiment with some things and verify the effectiveness by measuring the final result.

One of the greatest mistakes we see is attempting to put too much together into one package, whether it is trying to teach the entire job in one session or lumping many important details of a job into one general task. Breaking jobs down five times as effectively is a crucial part of the process, and this must be handled with great diligence. When you think you have the job detailed finely enough, remember that Toyota is likely to define the details five times as much! Present the information to trainees in small manageable bits.

A Job Breakdown Requires Careful Reflection

One problem encountered when breaking down a job to define the task and to determine how it is done is people who are familiar with a task no longer "think" about what they do or how they do it. Their actions have become automatic. If training were attempted without a complete and critical analysis of the work beforehand, many important aspects of the work task would possibly be overlooked because they are performed subconsciously.

Take for example the task of tying your shoes. It is a task you have done perhaps an average of once a day for many years—let's say 25 years—or nearly 10,000 times (times two shoes). You can most likely tie your shoes without even looking at them. Now let's make a comparison to a work situation. Suppose someone does a job that has a cycle time of one minute. Doing the job for an entire day would result in approximately 400 repetitions of the task. In just 50 days the worker would have completed the task 20,000 times!

In only 50 days on the job, the "body experience" is acquired, and the task can be performed without active thought.[1] Of course the employee is still thinking—he just no longer needs to think about each step of the job, or about what to do when, or about mastering a special technique. His motions now are more fluid, more automatic.

Unfortunately it is extremely difficult to train people without first taking the time to break down the job so the important aspects of the work are "remembered." Those of us who have struggled with teaching our children how to tie shoes quickly realize it is necessary to stop and think about the many complex tasks required and the little knacks we naturally use without conscious thought. The job breakdown process requires a careful analysis of exactly what is being done to complete the task successfully and is necessary prior to actually training a team member.

Try this simple experiment using our shoe-tying example—a task that is routine and very familiar to you (so you should remember how to do it). Teach someone else how to tie a shoe without analyzing the task or thinking about the best way to teach the job ahead of time. Don't write down the method or think through the steps—just wing it (as if you had to train someone unexpectedly). What happened? Were you able to identify for the student how many steps there were in the task prior to beginning (to implant an expectation in the student's mind)? Did you have to stop and think about what to do next? Did you find a better way to describe what you were doing as you went along? (Restating how to do the same tasks several different ways leads to confusion.) Did you identify all the critical aspects of the work? (Yes, even a task as simple as tying a shoe has critical aspects!) Most likely your test was flawed unless you found someone who did not

[1] This is a phenomenon known as *muscle memory*, and it is what allows sports greats like Tiger Woods to be consistent with his golf swing. He does not consciously think about all the mechanics to create the perfect swing each time he plays. Part of his mind is on automatic pilot governing routine body movements, and his swing is habitual. Unfortunately, when poor work habits are developed they become ingrained in muscle memory and are difficult to change.

already know how to tie a shoe, but it simply demonstrates the need to carefully study and record the job elements and critical points prior to launching into a training session.[2]

Present No More Than Can Be Mastered at One Time

The Job Instruction method stresses that the student should not be presented with more than he or she can master at one time. One of the challenges is every student has a different learning capacity and the trainer must evaluate the situation during the training activity and adjust accordingly. As a rule of thumb each training session should last approximately 30 minutes or less, after which the student is allowed to absorb the learning and practice the technique before moving to another training event.

Another rule of thumb for repetitive manual tasks is work that takes about 15 seconds to perform will take approximately 30 minutes to teach (but longer for the student to master). This is just a guideline and varies according to the complexity of the task and the techniques required. The 30-minute guideline is only the time required to present the operation and allow the student a few opportunities to practice. Mastery of the task may require days or weeks and perhaps several thousand repetitions.

Let's put the effort required for effective training into perspective. Using our rules of thumb as a guide, if 15 seconds of work requires about 30 minutes for presenting the operation, and a job has 30 individual tasks and the tasks range from 1 minute to 3 minutes (average 2, which may require 8 separate training events) in duration, the total time investment to train one person would be:

$$[(30 \text{ tasks} \times 8 \text{ increments (of 15 seconds each)})] \times 30 \text{ minutes} = 7200 \text{ minutes or } 120 \text{ hours}$$

[2] If you attempt to teach someone to do a job they already know how to do, and if you have not clearly specified a method, the student will revert to their own method. We believe this is the cause of the complaint about people doing the work "their own way." It is critical that you specify the correct method for people to follow.

Perhaps this level of commitment required is why so many trainers attempt to cover all the details at one time and shortcut the process. Again we remind you the potential payoff is great, but the investment is significant as well. It is little wonder that many managers and employees feel as though they have been inadequately trained for the work they do. We often hear supervisors say they have "told that person how to do the job," and yet the employee "won't do the job the correct way." We see, however, that most often information was dumped on the student in excessive amounts, preventing the student from completely understanding. People tend to make every effort to fill in the blanks, and in the absence of effective training, people will find a way to get the job done—correctly or incorrectly. They are doing the best they can with what has been provided.

Determine How the Job Will Be Presented

Many trainers mistakenly assume the best way to teach someone an entire job is in a sequential manner as the work is actually performed. In reality, the best way to teach the entire job is one portion at a time in a defined sequence (but not necessarily in the order in which the steps are performed). This requires forethought from the trainer and the ability to define the individual training events from the slicing and dicing of the total job.

Here is a hypothetical training event that demonstrates this point. This is based on an actual training session we witnessed. We have added some commentary in italics to explain what the problem is from a training perspective.

Trainer: Hi John, my name is Ed. I am going to show you how to do the center column welding operation today. Here is the welder and your equipment. First, we need to go get the parts for the job. *(Although the parts are necessary to complete the core routine task, the retrieval of parts is an ancillary task and should be taught as a separate event. The trainer switched tasks. The parts should have been gathered as part of the preparation so the core task could be taught without interruption.)*

We have to go to the computer to order the parts. *(They walk to the computer breaking the flow of training.)*

Now, you need to get into the computer and get to this screen. Did you get an ID code for the computer? *(If this were a separate training event, this detail should be verified before training—part of preparation. Once again the training session will be interrupted.)*

No? Ok, well I'll take you up to the office in a minute to get one. *(Which will be another diversion in the process.)* For now we can use mine. *(This will not be an accurate representation of this task and may create confusion if it is not demonstrating the actual process).*

You need to check the drawing to verify the part numbers. *(The task is ordering parts and should concentrate on the ordering process. Verifying parts to the drawing is job knowledge and is best shown in a separate training session.)*

Ok, let's see, what is the part number? Hmm, it looks like the new revision did not get made on these parts. This is the old part number. We need to go up to the engineer's office to get the new number. *(This is another diversion from the original training task, which was to weld, but now they are chasing part numbers. At this point it is unclear what the actual work is.)*

While we are here we can stop in to get your computer ID code. *(Stopping into an office, they find that the person who issues computer codes is in a meeting. They will need to return later. When they arrive in the engineer's office to request the part information, the engineer sorts through several files to find the information regarding the parts. She is not sure what the new part number is and explains that she will let them know later. Meanwhile the trainer returns to the computer to resume the parts ordering task. Do we have any idea what is actually being taught here?)*

So here we are, 30 minutes or so into "training," and thus far nothing has been taught. The training flow has forked several times. At the end the student will have seen a variety of things but will lack a clear vision of how the work is to be done. The trainer tried to cover it all at one time and in the end accomplished very little other than to frustrate the employee.

You may see some familiar situations in this example and be asking yourself, "How is it possible to do the training differently?" "He needs to order the parts, doesn't he?" "He needs to know how to verify part numbers, doesn't he?" The answer is yes, but the training does not need to proceed in this way. If the welding portion of the job is to be taught (a good place to start), all of the parts, materials, tools, and equipment should be *ready* prior to the beginning of the training. Then the trainer can concentrate on teaching the task of welding. The tasks of ordering parts should be taught at another time, and the task might be broken into two separate parts for training purposes—one involving collecting and verifying part number information and the second involving the task of entering this information into the computer.

The problem with this training event started well before the actual training began. The trainer did not take the time to break down the job and to divide it into individual parts—each part being a separate training event. Learning is more effective when tasks, events, and knowledge are compartmentalized. We have a limited retention rate and can multitask only to a point. When information is jumbled, crosses categories, and has no clear distinction between individual tasks, confusion increases and retention will be reduced.

Table 8–1 shows how to break the job down to determine the best way to present each element of the total task. The welding portion of the job may need to be presented in three separate training events depending on the complexity of the task. From our dialogue we have seen that it would be best to teach the verification of part numbers and the placement of the order as separate events. This decision is based on the differences in how the individual tasks are performed. Because they are different in nature (verification requires judgment, and the training will include numerous details), it is best not to mix

Table 8–1. Breakdown of welding operation showing individual training events

Job	**Welding Operation**						
Task	Welding			Gather parts for job		Equipment operation	
Training event	Part 1	Part 2	Part 3	Verify part numbers	Place order	Start and stop	Set parameters

them when teaching. It will not take any more time to teach these events separately unless your intent is to dump the entire task onto the trainee at one time and move on to other things (in which case the effort to retrain and correct problems later will result in significantly more total time).

Breaking Down the Job—Part One

The job breakdown includes three main parts: the steps of the job, the important information regarding how to perform the steps (known as *key points*), and reasons why the key points are important. We have focused thus far on breaking down a job into tasks, and now we need to go to the next level of detail—to identify the actual steps that will be taught. Identification of key points is the most important part of the entire job breakdown, and we devote the next chapter to this activity.

Identify Major Steps

Every job task consists of a series of activities that are completed in a specific order and way. Training Within Industry (TWI) refers to these activities as *important steps*, and Toyota refers to them as *major steps*. The reference to steps is a natural one because people tend to think of work tasks sequentially. During training we often hear the trainer say, "The first thing you do is . . .," "The second thing you do is . . .," and so forth. A major step describes *what* is done in terms that are neither too broad nor too specific (like Goldilocks's porridge, they are just right and are best determined after some experimentation). Major steps do not include details of *how* the work is done—how to perform the steps is explained with key points.

We have seen that the steps identified for standardized work are not necessarily the same steps as identified in the breakdown for training. The standardized work step is a general description of the work being performed, and the Job Instruction work step is more detailed to simplify the learning process, or to place more emphasis on some portions of the work. More complex or critical steps may be broken down into smaller pieces.

There are no hard and fast rules on how to define the proper amount of work for a major step; however, there are some tips that may be used. It is always best to break down a job while watching the work being performed by a skilled operator.[3] We provide an example in Chapter 10, Figures 10–2 and 10–3, for analyzing the work. The original TWI material suggested stopping the operator as the work is performed and asking the question, "What did you do?" If the answer to the question is, "I did this *and* that," it is likely that there are two steps. Have the operator repeat the procedure, and this time stop her after completing the first item. Again ask, "What did you do?" and record the response.

After the response, TWI suggested the question, "Does it advance the job?" This question is similar to a question regarding the addition of value to the task. For example, a major step may be to "Pick up the parts," but "Carry parts to machine" would not be considered a major step unless there is something special that occurs during the journey to the machine. Simply carrying parts does not advance the job task, and if there is nothing specific about how the parts are to be carried (key points), listing this activity as a major step would be unnecessary.

Certain portions of any job are "obvious" and need no explanation and thus should not be listed as a major step. If you are showing someone how to tighten a bolt, for example, it is not necessary to tell the student to pick up the tool; it is obvious, and the student can learn how to do it simply by observing. However, as always, be careful with assumptions. What is obvious to you may not always be obvious to others.

One notable exception (there is always an exception!) is when parts are oriented or subassembled while being carried. In the relentless pursuit of waste elimination, Toyota makes every effort to include some value-adding activity during necessary waste steps.

---

[3] If the breakdown is for a new product or process, you will use a similar method as described here. Ask someone to demonstrate the proposed method while you question them to determine the steps and key points to create a job breakdown. When introducing a new work process remember the new work method will be refined as people gain experience with the nuances of the job.

In this case the steps would be:

1. Pick up parts (key points include specifics on how to orient parts).
2. Assemble part A to part B (while walking).
3. Load subassembly into machine.

The following list provides examples of typical major steps from both manufacturing and health care jobs. The action of the major step is described using a verb and object combination. Notice that major steps are written as simple statements rather than lengthy sentences or paragraphs. The idea is to state what is being done as simply as possible.

- Install the headlight.
- Assemble the fan housing.
- Tighten the set screws.
- Remove the label.
- Insert the washer.
- Load/unload the machine.
- Inspect the part.
- Pick up/set down the fitting.
- Press the button.
- Check patient temperature.
- Apply conductive paste to paddles.
- Enter the data.
- Collate the documents.
- Decontaminate the IV insertion site.

The original TWI documents provide guidelines for breaking down the job into steps. The TWI questions are subjective in nature and do not provide an absolute guide. For your first job breakdown, we recommend that you try out your results in an actual training situation. The best way to find out if your steps are too broad or too narrow is to get feedback from a student. We explain this in Chapter 13, but for now the following items help to determine the amount of work to include in one major step:

1. The degree of difficulty or complexity of the action taken. A more difficult task should be divided into multiple steps so smaller portions can be easily mastered.

2. If the activities take place in different locations, which requires the movement of the hands or feet, it is best to identify them as separate steps.
3. Similarly, if the task requires using different tools or parts, a separate step is indicated.
4. The total cycle time of the job can be used as a guide. For example, if the entire job can be completed within 60 seconds, each step would not likely be over 5 or 10 seconds of work time.
5. If a step has many associated key points, it is best to divide the step into multiple smaller steps for ease of teaching. This decision is related to the complexity of the task. You will need to get to the next step of identifying key points to determine how many key points each step has. We find it necessary at times to go back and forth between the identification of major steps and key points and to make adjustments to the major steps as needed.

Major Steps Are Important, but Key Points Are Critical

With experience you will learn to identify an appropriate amount of work for each major step. Keep in mind that each training event will be unique and adjustments will be necessary. The capability of the student and the time available for the training will vary, and the trainer will need to adapt accordingly—including modifying the amount of work content defined in a major step. The student's ability to perform the task as demonstrated provides feedback for the trainer as to how effectively the major steps have been defined. You must develop skill in interpreting the nonverbal feedback you get from the student.

There is in fact little risk to the results of training if the major steps are not identified perfectly. Defining steps properly is important to the overall success, but it is not as critical as the identification of key points. Some minor misjudgments in the content of major steps will not likely have a great impact on the training result. Adjustments to the steps are relatively easy and can be made during the training event if the trainer realizes a mistake. In many cases it is possible for the student to pick up the major steps simply from observing while the task is being done—without any explanation from the trainer at all. Of course, if you omit a step completely, it is a larger problem, but it will be detected quickly during the training event.

Chapter 9

Identify Key Points and Reasons

Breaking Down the Job—Part Two

The identification and presentation of key points is the single most important aspect of the training process. Key points are items that ensure the safety of the worker, the quality of the product, the productivity rate, and the control of costs. They are the special techniques that help to achieve one of these criteria. The major steps define *what* is being done while the key points describe *how* to perform the major steps.

In most cases when students observe a job task being performed, they will be able to identify the correct sequence of work even if the major steps are not well defined. It is easy to see *what* is being done. It is much more difficult to see and understand *how* to do the task if it is not carefully demonstrated. This often leads to the incorrect assumption by the trainer that if the student is following the steps correctly, the key points are also being done properly. Key points tend to be subtle and are not easily picked up by the student from observation only and must be carefully taught if they are to be performed as required. Mastering the ability to identify and teach key points will greatly improve the training results.

Effective Identification of Key Points Is Critical

We have said it is necessary to identify the most critical part of any task and to focus the bulk of the effort on it. The effective identification of key points is the most critical part of the process. There are a few techniques and guidelines you should use when identifying key points. This process gets easier with practice and reflection after the training event. The follow-up phase of the training requires evaluation of the student's performance to determine the effectiveness of the presentation of key points. If there are any lingering issues with poor performance, the work method must be carefully analyzed to determine if additional key points must be identified.

In Chapter 8, we explained the method of observing the work and questioning the operator about what was being done. This is how we identified the major steps. After the major step has been identified we would continue the questioning of the operator by asking, "Is there anything important about how you did that step?" We dig deeper and explore the process completely by asking, "Is there anything you must do to ensure the quality of the work?" "What about safety? Is there anything important to watch out for when doing that step?" We also might query, "I noticed when you did that step you use a special motion to insert the part in the machine. Can you explain to me how you do that?" During the identification of key points, it is important to ask numerous questions until every detail is revealed. The following criteria will provide a framework for determining critical aspects of the work.

If It Is *Critical* to the Success of the Job, It Is a Key Point

In a sense everything that is done to complete the task is *necessary,* but a few things are *critical.* These items must be done correctly or the task will not be performed properly. These items are the most important part of the training process. The secret is to correctly identify the critical elements and not to overwhelm the student with superfluous details. Because key points are critical to the success of the job, they are not optional. Team members must not deviate from the defined method without first reviewing any new methods with the supervisor.

Any item that is easily distinguishable by observation alone need not be included as a key point. For example, the job task may require that a certain part be picked up with the right hand while a tool is picked up in the left. This simultaneous activity may help with achieving the productivity requirement, but it is easily observed and learned by watching the trainer perform the work, so it need not be added as a key point. Also the layout of the work area will make this point obvious (the part will be located on the right side and the tool on the left).

While these items are a necessary part of the work, the specifics of technique are not critical to the success of the work. Many trainers make the mistake of trying to teach every detail of the job. It is only necessary to emphasize those items for which there is a critical method or specific technique. The student must learn to perform the work in the correct manner, but in this case it is not necessary to stress which hand to use as a key point. As we said, there is always an exception (which is what makes training so challenging). If for some reason a student attempts to do the work incorrectly, the trainer should "add" the key point and stress the importance during the training (the trainer must always make adjustments during the training as needed). You want the student to know and understand all key points extremely well, so it is important to stress only the most critical aspects of the work as key points. If too many items are stressed as key points, the critical ones will get lost in the crowd. It is best to reserve key points only for items that are critical.

Let Experience Be Your Guide

The best way to identify key points is to use your past experience, which will let you know where problems have occurred previously. An understanding of potential quality problems and how they occur is used to identify the remedy—the proper way to perform the work to prevent the defect. Without an in-depth understanding of the things that you are trying to prevent, it is not possible to identify the remedy. This is why a trainer must have good knowledge of the job.

This logic can be applied in reverse as well. If a problem occurs and the cause is understood (the problem happens when work is performed in a certain way), it is possible to develop a key point that prevents the defect. When a problem occurs, evaluate it to determine whether there was a key point previously identified that would prevent the problem. If so, verify that it is being followed correctly. If not, determine the correct way to perform the task, and teach everyone the new method (continuous improvement).

As we have stated, Toyota employees relentlessly pursue factual information regarding what really matters for every job. This may include verification of the effectiveness of key points through testing and experimentation. Confirming customer expectations directly with the customer also provides guidance for determining what is most important to the customer. Verification with the customer can also lead to a reduction in overprocessing waste that is often performed because everyone thinks the customer expects the extra processing work.

Experience helps a trainer develop an understanding of "knacks"—special techniques to make the task simpler or other ways to "know" when the task is done properly. For example, if a quality problem involves loose screws on an assembly, the key point would pertain to knowing how to tell when the screw is completely installed. This may include how it should feel, look, or sound when the step is completed correctly. These are the aspects of the work that are more of the "art" rather than the "science," but they can be explained. During the actual training, the trainer can demonstrate to the student how the sound, look, and feel would change if done incorrectly and provide examples of quality defects that occur if the key points are not followed. One word of caution regarding "experience." We prefer to think of experience as being an accumulation of knowledge and mastery of skill with time. This means it is necessary to continuously reflect on the outcome and learn from the process. Often it seems people stop learning after the first year and then simply repeat the way they learned for 29 more years.

State Key Points in Positive Terms

It is best to state key points in positive "how to" terms rather than negative "don't do" terms. For example, if the desire is to prevent injury from a potential pinch point, the key point should be stated as, "Hold the work piece here and here" (pointing to the location of hand placement). Refrain from key points such as, "Don't put your fingers here." It is always preferable to state instruction in terms of the proper way to do something (which is what we want people to do) rather than telling them what you don't want them to do. Accidents happen by accident. If you tell people not to put their finger in a pinch point rather than telling them how to correctly hold the work piece, and thus keeping their fingers out of harm's way, they may unintentionally move their hands into the danger zone because they hold the work in random locations. Learning to always keep their hands in the same safe location will minimize the possibility of a random accident.

There have been studies done with small infants regarding the use of positive requests versus negative requests. If children are told, "Don't touch the glass," they apparently respond to "touch the glass" because they are drawn to the glass (anyone who has had children can attest to this). The human brain is not able to process the concept of "don't." Try this little experiment: Don't think about a banana split. Don't think about the bananas or the ice cream or the chocolate sauce. What happened? It is not possible to not think about a banana split without thinking about a banana split!

Instead it is preferable to explain to people what you do want them to do. This is challenging because we have been conditioned to think in term of "don't do."[1] Think about that for a moment. What would you tell children to do so they would not touch the glass? Perhaps you would try, "Please stay over here," or "Play with this toy." Reflect on how often you tell employees *not to do* something versus how often you ask them *to do* something. Make an effort to change your approach.

During the explanation of reasons, it is important to let people know what they are avoiding if necessary. It is acceptable to tell someone, "The reason you keep your hands here and here is to avoid getting

---

[1] We can assure you of the difficulty of this as we made every effort to explain things in the "how to" rather than the "don't do" mode. It takes practice to stay away from the "don't do" version.

your hand in the pinch point." Explaining the specific reason to do something a certain way may include giving information about the avoidance of injury or defects.

Identify Safety Key Points

Safety key points tend to be related to injury avoidance or specific things done to reduce the likelihood of repetitive stress injuries (ergonomic focus). People tend to understand the obvious injury potential in a situation, but they may not intuitively understand the effects of cumulative stress on their muscles and joints. A trainer should have a thorough understanding of ergonomics and good application of body mechanics so effective key points can be identified and so poor habits can be recognized and corrected during the tryout phase of the training. The following are typical examples of safety key points for manufacturing, health care, and service type jobs:

- The correct body posture for lifting (bend the knees, back straight).
- Correct placement of hands to prevent injury.
- Cutting away from the body when using a razor knife.
- Using the correct grip on an air tool to avoid hyperextension of the wrist.
- Correct procedure for handling hazardous chemicals.
- Maintaining clearance from patient when using defibrillator.
- Maintaining correct body posture while working (keeping work close to the body, using the feet to activate foot pedals, etc.).
- Length of time and procedure for a hospital staff member to wash hands to prevent the spread of disease.
- Proper height and positioning of the keyboard and screen when using a computer.

Note that required personal protective equipment (PPE) is not stated as a safety key point unless a specific PPE item is required for one step only. It is best to have the PPE worn during the entire task to prevent the likelihood of "forgetting" it during the critical step, but there are exceptions when the PPE is too cumbersome for the entire job. Overall use of PPE is very important, and the correct usage should be a separate training activity that includes when, where, and how the protective equipment is to be used.

Identify Quality Key Points

Quality key points are intended to provide specific instructions on how to perform a task without making mistakes that cause defects. Again the preferred presentation is in the positive terms—"how to," instead of "don't do." Your intention is to teach team members how to do the job correctly, rather than teaching them how to avoid mistakes. The quality key points, then, are related to understanding when the major step is completed properly. Following are typical examples of key points for quality:

- The correct placement or orientation of the part in the machine or fixture.
- The proper alignment of parts (correct side up, edges aligned, holes aligned, etc.).
- The correct distance or length (leaving 1/2-inch overhang).
- The proper sequence of part installation.
- The placement of defibrillator paddles for most effective use.
- Ensuring the correct quantity of an item.
- The proper thickness, depth, or other critical measurement.
- The correct amount or degree—as in cleanliness.
- The sound, feel, or appearance of an item that is completed correctly.

Note that inspection criteria (types of defects or levels of acceptability) are not included in the key points for the job task. Recall that key points are intended to explain *how to do* a specific task. Identifying defects and acquiring judgment are separate from how to actually perform the task. If the trainer attempts to include judgment and decision-making information in the task portion of the presentation, the training will get off track. We cover these issues in Chapter 14.

Identify Productivity Key Points

Productivity key points explain certain techniques, which are used to ensure the job is performed within the correct amount of time.

In many cases the work can't be completed within the required time without utilizing the key points. In these situations the key points are critical to the success of the job. In other cases productivity key points aid the worker by reducing the burden and simplifying the task. Following are typical examples of key points for improving productivity for various types of jobs:

- Utilizing both hands simultaneously.
- Performing a subassembly operation while carrying parts.
- A technique for holding screws and the screw gun to ease insertion.
- Movement of the hands smoothly from point to point without pausing in between.
- Specific movement of operation to minimize wasted motion (for example, polishing a surface in a specific pattern).
- Rhythmic and fluid movement of the body.
- Method to support customer productivity. For example, a hospital pharmacist places medications in the correct orientation for the customer (administering nurse).
- Using draft mode when printing documents of low importance.
- Using shortcut keys on the computer for common tasks.

Identify Special Technique Key Points

There are certain aspects of almost every job that require special finesse. These items are often subtle and not easily seen through simple observation (a person trained to identify these special techniques can often see them, but they may not understand how to do them). If you observe a skilled operator, you will see fluid motions and simultaneous activities. There may be a subtle rotating of a part during transport or a slight angling when inserting it into a machine. Also, if you observe an operator struggling with a task, it is likely he or she has not learned a special technique key point or a technique needs to be developed (it may also indicate a change has occurred in the process itself and must be evaluated). Following are typical examples of key points for special techniques:

- A sweeping motion used for spray-painting, especially for a contoured shape. This key point would include the position of the feet and movement of the body trunk, arm, and wrist.
- The ability to "read" the surface when spray-painting to determine if the coverage is correct and to prevent thin spots or paint sags.
- How to orient a part for ease of assembly with another part.
- The correct speed and pause time, such as that involving swiping a credit card or a hotel room key.
- The proper technique for stretching the skin to make the insertion of an IV needle easier and more accurate.
- The striking of an arc when welding with an electrode requires a flick of the wrist, a lengthening of the arc, and then a movement closer to the workpiece to shorten the arc to the proper length.
- The distinctive sound similar to frying bacon when the welding machine is set properly.
- The feel or distinctive sound of parts as they are assembled.
- Description of the action necessary to drive a standard shift car—the gradual release of the clutch while simultaneously depressing the gas pedal.

Special technique key points are the most difficult to express in words. The actual training session will include the use of gestures and exaggerated movements to help show the special technique. Toyota trainers from Japan who spoke broken English were forced to use gestures and movements to show special techniques, and this turned out to be quite effective. It is also possible to guide the student's hand through the motion so he or she understands the motion. (See Chapter 14 for further discussion on teaching special techniques.)

Identify Cost Control Key Points

Cost control key points refer to methods that are necessary to maintain the standard cost of products. Typically they refer to the quantity of raw materials or consumable items such as sanding paper, grinding wheels, gloves, adhesives, and utilities used to complete a task. The misuse of materials will not typically affect the quality of the product or the safety of the operator (unless they are used incorrectly or not used at all), but the proper use of all material is important for cost control. The excessive use of materials may cost a few pennies or several dollars extra. These small excesses add up over time, particularly in high-volume processes, and cumulatively they have a real impact on profitability. Employees at Toyota are taught to be conscious of the waste of even small amounts of materials. Following are typical examples of key points for cost control:

- The proper number and size of staples used to fasten a cabinet side (also quality-related).
- Using the black ink cartridge when printing text-only or black-and-white-only documents.
- Printing less important documents in the draft mode (also a productivity key point).
- The number of products to finish between exchanges of the sanding disc.
- The amount of paint to apply to ensure correct quality but not excessive cost.
- The correct number of cleaning rags to be used for cleaning a bumper mold.
- The correct amount of tape used for packaging boxes (also quality).
- The correct amount of packaging material used in packaging finished goods.

Cost control key points are often overlooked. The Toyota complex in Georgetown, Kentucky, produces nearly 400,000 vehicles per year. An extra cost of only 5 cents per vehicle equals $20,000 per year. If one percent of the employees (70 people) were each adding only 5 cents per vehicle, the total additional cost would be 1.4 million dollars per year! It is important to consider even the smallest cost, especially when multiplied by high volume!

Confirm the Reasons for the Key Points

One way to know whether a key point is essential rather than a preference is to ask, "What is its purpose?" All valid key points must have a sound reason that meets one of the criteria—safety, quality, productivity, special technique, or cost control. In a sense the reasons for key points come before the identification of the key point itself. As we said, the identification of key points is based on personal experience and understanding of potential problems. If you know a problem is caused when an important technique is not used, you have both the key point (use the technique) and the reason (if it is not done, the problem will occur).

The key points are the most important part of the job task, and the reasons for them should provide a sound rationale that encourages people to want to use them. Suppose a quality key point specifies leaving 1/2 inch of fabric beyond the edge of the part when trimming the fabric. If you tell students the reason is "to ensure quality," they will not have a complete understanding of the importance, and without this understanding, they are not likely to take the key point seriously. A more specific reason for leaving 1/2 inch of material must be given.

Suppose the successful completion of the key point affects the following operation where the material is stapled into place. If the material is too short, there will be an insufficient amount for stapling and the part will be scrap, at a cost of $25 per part (high importance). If the length of material is too long the excess material may protrude and create a bulge in the finished product (a defect for the customer—very high importance). If people understand the full implications of their actions (or inactions), they are much more likely to "do the right thing."

If a weak reason is provided that does not indicate the critical nature of the key point, the student may decide it does not matter and deviate from the defined method. Later the frustrated trainer will comment, "I told him to do it the right way, but he didn't listen." This is why we must always remember the Job Instruction motto: "If the student hasn't learned, the instructor hasn't taught." The trainer must ensure students have a full understanding of the importance of each key point.

Beware of Urban Legends

We all have heard some things are done a certain way because, "That's the way we've always done them." This is exactly what we are trying to avoid. In some cases we hear a reason that a key point is necessary and it sounds like it might be true, but clearly people are not certain. There is hesitancy in the explanation; there is disagreement among the workforce about whether the key point is necessary or not. Perhaps long ago someone told someone else that certain things had to be done in a specific way because that is the way she was taught or figured out how to get the job done. We call these items "urban legends." A typical dialogue goes something like this:

"Why do you do it that way?"

"Because it is important. If you don't do it, there will be a problem."

"Really? What kind of problem?"

"Well, if this isn't done, there will be a quality problem."

"What is the quality problem? Have you confirmed it?"

"Well, I am not totally sure. Maybe you should ask the supervisor."

"You don't know what would happen if you changed the method?"

"Not really, but someone told me to do it that way."

At Toyota everything that is considered important should be verified. This allows people to demonstrate why things are important and what will happen if the correct method is not followed. This is not to say that some urban legends don't still exist at Toyota, or there isn't some disagreement over the best method. But there is diligent effort to confirm all aspects of the work and communicate the best method to all employees.

Key Points Are Key

The key points are not simply helpful tips to be considered as advisory. Key points actually represent the majority of what you need to teach the trainees so they can consistently perform the job at a high level of performance. The description of the step itself is fairly plain and tells the trainee what to do, but the key points tell the trainee how to do it to be safe, to be productive, and to ensure high quality. The reasons for the key points help to motivate the trainee to take them seriously. Anything else the trainer can do to reinforce the importance of the key points will only help get to the desired result—highly competent team associates who can reliably perform the work.

Another powerful motivational tool is to let the team associates see for themselves the impact of their work. It is helpful during the training to take students to subsequent operations (their customer) to see firsthand how what they do affects others and how their work fits into the overall picture of the organization. This provides a sense of importance and meaning. The widespread practice of *genchi genbutsu*, going to the actual place, is often intended for this purpose. For example, an engineer learning how to design a part will be taken to the line where the part is used to understand why designing it a certain way for ease of assembly is important.

Now that you have the basic concepts of breaking the job down into individual pieces and identifying key points, you are ready to put this information together into the job breakdown sheet, which summarizes the major steps, key points, and the reasons for the key points. In the next chapter we walk you through this process with examples from a variety of different types of jobs, including cases where the job is not routine.

Chapter 10

Job Breakdown Examples

Putting It All Together

In the last four chapters we have provided the fundamentals for breaking jobs down into manageable training-sized bits. We are following one of the concepts of Job Instruction by presenting the information a little at a time and by repeating the key points to enhance learning. In this chapter we show a variety of job breakdown examples and provide an evaluation of some of the common mistakes made when people break down jobs.

When jobs are broken down into small training pieces, they will have a similar format on the job breakdown sheet no matter what category of work is being detailed (routine, technician, craft, or non-routine work). As we have said, when you drill down into the details of each type of work, you end up with some portion of the work that is definable step-by-step work. This is the content that goes on a job breakdown sheet. It does not matter what the broad category of work is. We are now dealing with specific definable tasks.

The Job Breakdown Sheet for Bumper Molding

We pick up with the bumper-molding job we introduced in Chapter 5. The job has been sliced and diced into small training bits as shown in Figure 10–1. Each task becomes a training event, and the detailed steps make up the individual job breakdown sheets.

Figure 10–2 shows the job breakdown for the de-molding and placement of the bumper in the trimming fixture.[1] The placement of the bumper into the trimming fixture is a relatively simple one-step operation, and it is part of the work flow for the de-molding operation, so both tasks are combined into one job breakdown and training event.

Notice the description of the major steps, key points, and reasons for the key points are very brief. The descriptions are not intended to be fully detailed Job Instructions. They are only for the trainer to use as a reference during training. The trainer will be demonstrating the method while explaining it, so there is no need for detailed written instruction sheets. Also, simple brief statements are more easily conveyed by the trainer and understood by the student. Excessive verbiage may overload the student and diminish his or her ability to remember the important content. Note that this amount of information is about right for one training session.

Each part of the routine core task is broken down individually on a job breakdown sheet. Figure 10–3 shows a job breakdown for the trimming portion of the bumper-molding job. This portion of the job is the most critical (and difficult), so for training purposes each step may be taught separately—one at a time—with several repetitions of practice before the student learns the next step.

Previously we estimated the amount of time required to conduct the actual training. Now imagine the time required to break down and detail each of the individual tasks. The good news is the work done to break down a job does not need to be repeated each time a new student is trained. Now let's look at how to actually define the steps and key points for nonrepeating jobs.

---

[1] A blank form is available for download at www.thetoyotaway.org.

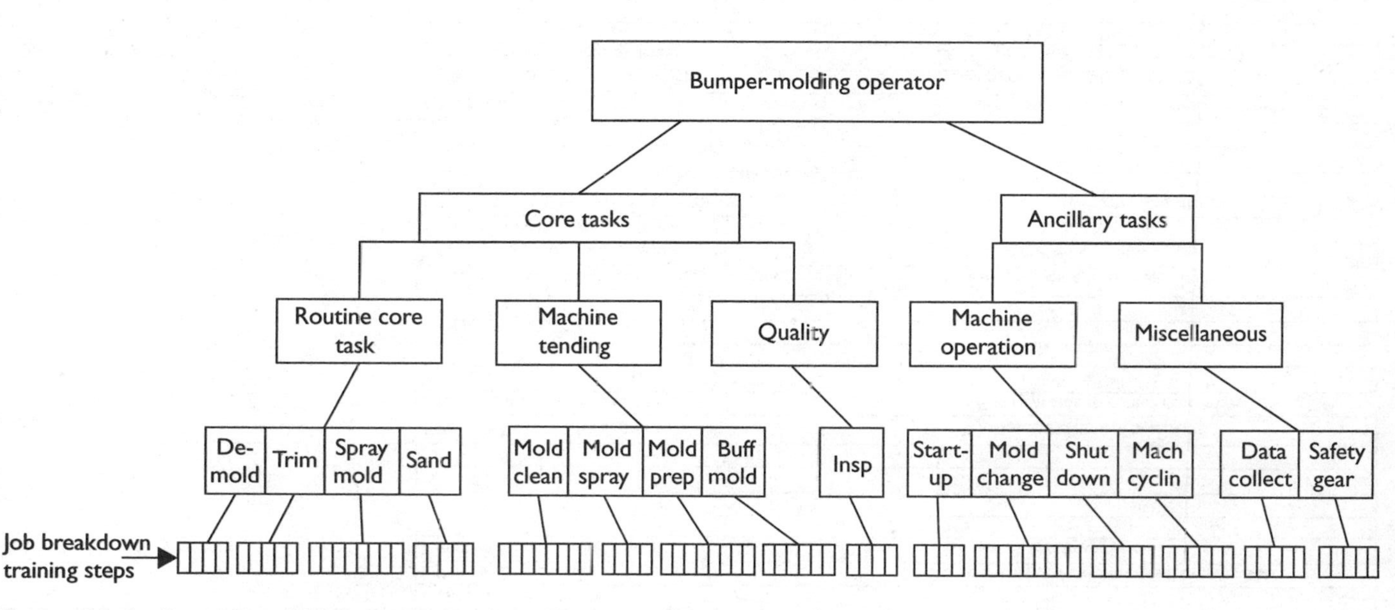

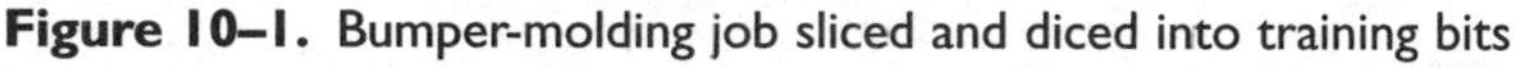

Figure 10–1. Bumper-molding job sliced and diced into training bits

JOB BREAKDOWN SHEET DATE: 8/24/20___		Steve Morgan Team Leader	Pete Desoto Supervisor
AREA: Bumper molding	JOB: Rear bumper molding operator—de-mold	WRITTEN BY: D. Williard	

MAJOR STEPS	KEYPOINTS **SAFETY:** Injury avoidance, ergonomics, danger points **QUALITY:** Defect avoidance, check points, standards **TECHNIQUE:** Efficient movement, special method **COST:** Proper use of materials	REASONS FOR KEYPOINTS
Step # 1 De-mold right side of bumper	1. Grasp at top and back	1. Easy to get hand hold
	2. Pull out 2 to 5 inches	2. Less will not work, more will cause crease
	3. Pull down after pulling out	3. Releases side from the mold
Step # 2 De-mold center of bumper	1. Push down with left hand in the middle	1. Releases the center of bumper
	2. Keep right arm extended	2. Pulling right side to center causes crease
Step # 3 De-mold left side of bumper	1. Use left thumb to push along edge of bumper	1. Peeling movement to release bumper
	2. Place pressure in the crease of thumb	2. Pressure on tip will cause injury
	3. Push toward left side away from mold	3. Releases left side of bumper
	4. Grasp top edge when bumper is released	4. To hold correctly, preventing defects
Step # 4 Place in trimming fixture	1. Keep arms spread	1. Bringing arms together will crease bumper
	2. Make sure gate is not folded under	2. Gate will distort causing scrap
	3. Trim nest must be free of debris	3. Any debris will cause a dent and scrap

Figure 10–2. Job breakdown sheet for de-molding task

JOB BREAKDOWN SHEET		Robert Peters	Tom Cummins
DATE: 7/20/20__		Team Leader	Supervisor
AREA: Bumper molding	JOB: Rear bumper molding operator—trimming	WRITTEN BY: Greg Hancock	

MAJOR STEPS	KEYPOINTS **SAFETY:** Injury avoidance, ergonomics, danger points **QUALITY:** Defect avoidance, check points, standards **TECHNIQUE:** Efficient movement, special method **COST:** Proper use of materials	REASONS FOR KEYPOINTS
Step # 1 Trim flash ball on left side	1. Hold flash straight up and tight	1. Makes trimming easier
	2. Trim away from body and arm	2. Prevents injury—cuts
	3. Blade flush with top surface	3. Visible surface, flash line 1 mm max
Step # 2 Trim left side core flash	1. Start on trim line—1 mm variation	1. Visible surface—quality specifications
	2. Blade must be perpendicular	2. Angled cut not acceptable
	3. Follow trim line—1 mm variation	3. Visible surface—quality specifications
	4. Curving motion while trimming	4. Technique to make trimming easier
Step # 3 Trim gate flash	1. Hold gate up horizontally	1. Prevents twisting of bumper during cut
	2. Rest blade on bumper edge horizontally	2. Helps make cut horizontal and straight
	3. Angle knife handle back (blade is horizontal)	3. Cut is easier
	4. One continuous movement	4. Stopping will cause a jagged cut
Step # 4 Trim flash ball on right side	1. Hold flash straight up and tight	1. Makes trimming easier
	2. Trim away from body and arm	2. Prevents injury—cuts
	3. Blade flush with top surface	3. Visible surface, flash line 1 mm max
Step # 5 Trim right side core flash	1. Start on trim line—1 mm variation	1. Visible surface—quality specifications
	2. Blade must be perpendicular	2. Angled cut not acceptable
	3. Follow trim line—1 mm variation	3. Visible surface—quality specifications
	4. Curving motion while trimming	4. Technique to make trimming easier

Figure 10–3. Job breakdown for hand trimming a rear bumper

Job Breakdown Examples for Nonrepeating Core Tasks

The world is full of jobs that do not fit the traditional manufacturing model of repeating a core task over—and—over. Very few jobs actually follow the cyclical core task model. In fact, many jobs in manufacturing involve continuous operations that are not repetitive in nature or operations that change from cycle to cycle because of product variation or other variation within the task.

Because of their nonrepeating nature, these jobs tend to be difficult to capture in a standardized pattern. One manufacturing job of this type is the tending of continuously operating machines—feeding materials, making adjustments, monitoring conditions, and so forth. This task could easily be correlated to a nurse in a hospital making rounds and tending to the various needs of patients.

On the surface the pattern of the job appears to be completely variable and unpredictable. The individual core tasks do not repeat. The needs of equipment vary from moment to moment. In some cases employees are tending multiple machines simultaneously—just like a nurse tends several patients and takes instruction from numerous doctors. In this case the sequence of the job task varies even more.

For highly automated, continuous-process operations, there is no routine cyclical task as part of the job. Examples of this type of work include the processing of plastic resins, metal, rubber extrusion, paper making, float glass, chemical processing, and book printing to name a few. The entire job is tending the machine, and each individual task occurs at a different frequency depending on what is needed with the machine at any given time. It is not possible to define a standardized sequence of steps for the entire job (a standardized worksheet); however, it is possible to standardize the method used to perform each nonroutine core task.

Table 10–1 shows the various nonroutine core tasks and ancillary tasks for a continuous operation (not a Toyota example). None of the tasks is performed with any specific frequency because product variations cause the timing to change. For these types of operations, there

Table 10–1. Separation of machine-tending job into task categories

Continuous-operation Machine-tending	
Nonroutine core tasks	**Ancillary tasks**
Change reels	Machine start-up
Change layer stock	Machine process checks
Change tube	Recording data
Verify wire pitch	Machine shut down
Check wire cast	Machine adjustment
Wire changeover	Miscellaneous
Correct wire break	

needs to be some type of andon (visual and audible signaling method) so the operator is alerted prior to the need to perform the specific machine-tending task. This also allows time for preparing tools and materials that are necessary for the task.

The example in Figure 10–4 is a small task that is required as part of a machine-tending operation. This particular task takes only a minute to complete. Another task on this machine (a changeover) may require up to four hours to complete. Clearly, that operation cannot be detailed in a single job breakdown sheet but must be further broken down into several smaller pieces (and training will be conducted during several separate events).

One training challenge for this type of work is knowing when to perform each of the individual tasks. This knowledge is gained over time through experience. The trainer must work side-by-side with the student providing direction until the knowledge is gained.

Nonrepeating Core Task Example from Health Care

We often hear that health care is completely different from manufacturing. It might be argued there are no repetitive jobs in health care like those we would see on a moving assembly line. The argument that health care is different from manufacturing is true, and if we were attempting to apply some other tools and concepts of the Toyota Production System (TPS), we might need to make some modifications.

JOB BREAKDOWN SHEET DATE: 4/10/20___		Rick Lusk Team Leader	Steve Preston Supervisor
AREA: Flex Braider	JOB: Braider Operator—Change layer stock		WRITTEN BY: Di Bartels

MAJOR STEPS	KEYPOINTS **SAFETY:** Injury avoidance, ergonomics, danger points **QUALITY:** Defect avoidance, check points, standards **TECHNIQUE:** Efficient movement, special method **COST:** Proper use of materials	REASONS FOR KEYPOINTS
Step # 1 Remove empty layer stock core	1. Disconnect safety interlock	1. Keeps machine from operating—safety
Step # 2 Install new layer stock core	1. Thread over top roller and under shutoff bar 2. Overlap old layer stock about 5 inches	1. Keeps the layer stock even and aligned 2. To be able to make angled cut
Step # 3 Cut layer stock	1. Cut at approximately 45-degree angle	1. Angle allows layer stock to wrap around the hose at the correct angle without making a bulge (collar)
Step # 4 Glue spliced ends together	1. Apply glue to both surfaces about 1 inch 2. Overlap ends between 3/8 and 1/2 inch	1. Enough to ensure proper overlap (3/8) 2. Overlap over 1/2 inch will cause large Outer Diameter (OD); overlap under 3/8 may pull apart
Step # 5 Adjust tension on reel	1. Remove slack from layer stock 2. Set tension for slight pull	1. Slack will cause improper wrapping 2. If no tension, layer stock will get "floppy" causing a jam

Figure 10–4. Job breakdown for small task of changing material on a machine

In the case of talent development however, the differences between health care and manufacturing have little relevance.

Many of the jobs in health care are not repetitive, but there is a defined set of core and ancillary tasks. It is possible to use the same method to break down the job and define the individual tasks that can be taught using Job Instruction. There is a fair amount of policy knowledge and accumulated know-how that might be learned in a classroom or on the job with a mentor, but the basic core tasks will be taught just as they would be at Toyota or any other workplace.

We have been using the work of a nurse as an example from health care. Using the same breakdown model as we used for the bumper-molding operation, we broke down the job of a typical nurse, as shown in Figure 10–5.[2]

Figure 10–6 is a job breakdown for starting an IV in a peripheral vein. As we showed in Figure 7–3, there are other parts of this task that would be taught during separate training sessions. This portion is the core content of the task; it is the repeatable portion. Other portions of the task may repeat, or may repeat on a differing frequency from the central task. Because of the differing repeatability, they should be taught separately. We have shown that attempting to teach multiple tasks, each with different repeating frequencies, during a single training session, will lead to confusion during training.

You can see the health care job breakdown example is really not very different from a manufacturing example. Both the health care task and a manufacturing task have defined steps indicating what is done. Both have key points explaining what is important about how the step is done, and both provide supporting reasons why the key points are important. At this level of detail, we are not focused on how this task fits with all other tasks or whether it is repetitive or not. It is a portion of the total work, and it is definable and teachable. This is the key—a basic job breakdown applies to any defined task regardless of the industry or job type.

[2] The tasks listed are a compilation from several different nurses working in different areas of a hospital. It is not a complete list and is only meant to provide an example.

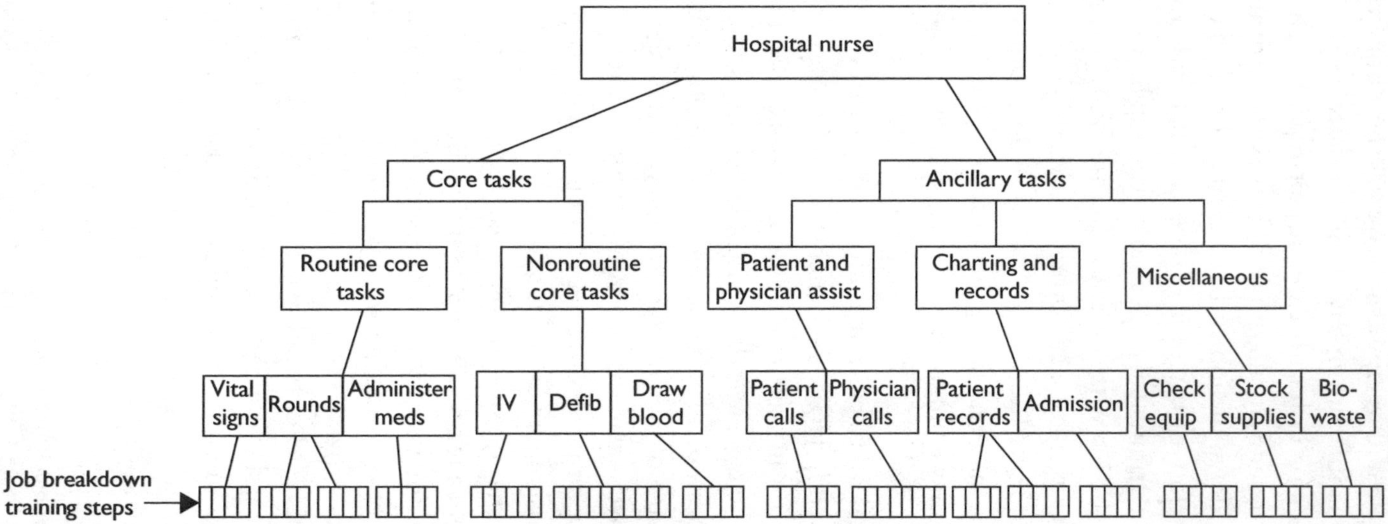

Figure 10–5. Hypothetical hospital nurse's job sliced and diced into training bits

JOB BREAKDOWN SHEET DATE: 7/20/20___	M. Warren Team Leader	P. Kenrick Supervisor
AREA: ER	JOB: Starting IV in peripheral vein	WRITTEN BY: R. F. Kunkle

MAJOR STEPS	KEYPOINTS **SAFETY:** Injury avoidance, ergonomics, danger points **QUALITY:** Defect avoidance, check points, standards **TECHNIQUE:** Efficient movement, special method **COST:** Proper use of materials	REASONS FOR KEYPOINTS
Step # 1 Stabilize vein	1. Stretch skin tight over vein	1. Keeps vein from rolling
	2. Use thumb and index finger of nondominant hand	2. Keeps dominant hand free to guide catheter
Step # 2 Place tip of needle against skin	1. Needle bevel up	1. Easier and more accurate to enter skin
	2. Needle slightly angled up from skin (5 degrees)	2. Correct angle for entering skin
Step # 3 Depress skin with needle	1. Indent skin 1–2 mm	1. Pushes vein up in front of needle
	2. Maintain angle of needle	2. Greater angle may push through vein
Step # 4 Puncture skin with needle	1. Push needle forward paralel to needle angle	1. Overcomes skin resistance and perforates skin
	2. Continue forward motion until slight "pop" is felt along with a decrease in resistance	2. Indicates you are through vein wall
	3. Push slowly	3. To prevent inserting through vein
Step # 5 Change needle angle	1. Lift tip (lower back of needle)	1. Moves needle bevel to top of vein preventing puncture of opposite side of vein
	2. Needle parallel to skin	2. Aligns needle with bore of vein making advancement of needle easier
Step # 6 Advance the catheter	1. Insert completely up to the "band"	1. Band indicates proper depth for each type of catheter. Insufficient depth may dislodge

Figure 10–6. Job breakdown for IV insertion in peripheral vein

Dr. Kunkle was kind enough to provide additional examples from health care, and we configured an additional task into the job breakdown format. Figure 10–7 shows the job breakdown for the use of a ventricular defibrillator. This may not be part of a nurse's responsibility, but it is a wonderful example of an important task.

Note that this task is a little longer than some of the others we have shown. There is no set limit to define the appropriate amount of work per training session. This task would probably take around 30 minutes to teach and is an appropriate amount of work for one training session. Another consideration is there is no natural break point in the task that would facilitate separation into two training sessions. Natural break points occur when the task has smaller segments that "complete" a portion of the overall task. The bumper-molding job is an example. The operator is able to de-mold the bumper and set it in the trimming fixture, and the remainder of the task can be completed by the trainer while the student observes. It would be difficult (and perhaps life threatening) to hand off the defibrillator paddles in the middle of the task!

Correcting Common Job Breakdown Errors

Initial attempts at breaking down a job may result in some common mistakes. Figure 10–8 is an example of a job breakdown that was turned in during a Job Instruction trainer certification class. We would like to comment on some of the errors that regularly occur when people are first learning to break down jobs. This is not intended to be critical of the individual who did the breakdown. An essential part of the Job Instruction method and talent development is the willingness to reflect on any situation and to accept coaching. Trainers must work closely with students, and they have the responsibility to correct any errors as they occur. This applies also when developing trainers in the Job Instruction method.

The trainee was allowed to use the breakdown as written in Figure 10–8 during the training demonstration in class to find out firsthand what the effects of the errors would be. Sometimes it is best to try out the breakdown in a real situation and then pay close attention to the outcome. In this case, the mistakes in the breakdown led to

JOB BREAKDOWN SHEET DATE: 9/4/20___		Michael Adam Team Leader	Matthew Aaron Supervisor
AREA: ER	JOB: Use of ventricular defibrillator, page 1	WRITTEN BY: R. F. Kunkle	

MAJOR STEPS	KEYPOINTS **SAFETY:** Injury avoidance, ergonomics, danger points **QUALITY:** Defect avoidance, check points, standards **TECHNIQUE:** Efficient movement, special method **COST:** Proper use of materials	REASONS FOR KEYPOINTS
Step # 1 Turn on defibrillator	1. Depress red switch labeled "power" on front of defibrillator	1. Defibrillator will not function with power off
Step # 2 Select "nonsynchronized" mode	1. Depress yellow switch labeled "synch" untill yellow synchronized light is extinguished	1. Defibrillator will not "fire" in a fibrillating patient unless "synch mode" is disabled
Step # 3 Pick up sternal paddle	1. In left hand 2. Sternal paddle is marked "sternum" 3. Graphic of midsternal location on handle of paddle	1. Current must flow from sternal side to lateral side and will prevent you from misapplying paddles and from crossing arms and leaning over patient which could cause you to be shocked
Step # 4 Pick up lateral paddle	1. In right hand 2. Lateral paddle marked "lateral" 3. Graphic of lateral location on handle of paddle	1. Current must flow from sternal side to lateral side and will prevent you from misapplying paddles and from crossing arms and leaning over patient which could cause you to be shocked
Step # 5 Apply conductive paste to surface of paddles	1. Squeeze 1 inch of paste on the left paddle 2. Evenly distribute over both paddle electrodes 3. Rub together in circle 2–3 times	1. Patient will receive a significant skin burn if insufficient conductive paste is applied, and if too much is applied, the current can arc between the paddles and no current will transit the heart
Step # 6 Place paddles in position	1. Sternal paddle over midsternum 2. Lateral paddle over midaxillary line 3. Paddles at level of fourth intercostal space	1. The locations that will allow for maximum current flow across the heart

Figure 10–7. Job breakdown for use of a ventricular defibrillator *(Continues)*

JOB BREAKDOWN SHEET

DATE: 9/4/20___

Michael Adam	Matthew Aaron
Team Leader	Supervisor

AREA: ER   JOB: Use of ventricular defibrillator, page 2   WRITTEN BY: R. F. Kunkle

MAJOR STEPS	KEYPOINTS **SAFETY:** Injury avoidance, ergonomics, danger points **QUALITY:** Defect avoidance, check points, standards **TECHNIQUE:** Efficient movement, special method **COST:** Proper use of materials	REASONS FOR KEYPOINTS
Step # 7 Apply force to each paddle	1. Lean lightly on sternal paddle to apply about 20 lb of force 2. Apply force with lateral paddle until strain in bicep	1. This amount of force will assure good contact with the skin and maximal current flow
Step # 8 Alert team you are about to defibrillate the patient	1. Call out, "All clear" 2. Speak loudly	1. To prevent accidental shock to other caregivers or yourself 2. So all in the treatment area can hear and respond by removing any contact with patient or bed
Step # 9 Repeat alert to team	1. Call out, "All clear" again	Same as above
Step # 10 Defibrillate patient	1. Depress red buttons on both paddles simultaneously 2. Maintain pressure on paddles 3. Maintain clearance from patient and bed	1. To maximize current flow to the patient 2. Same as above 3. Prevent injury (electrical shock) to self and others
Step #		
Step #		

Figure 10–7. Job breakdown for use of a ventricular defibrillator *(Continued)*

JOB BREAKDOWN SHEET

DATE: 3/8/20___

Phil Posey	David Sullivan
Team Leader	Supervisor

AREA: Glass room JOB: Screw and glue insulated glass WRITTEN BY: Lana Waters

MAJOR STEPS	KEYPOINTS **SAFETY:** Injury avoidance, ergonomics, danger points **QUALITY:** Defect avoidance, check points, standards **TECHNIQUE:** Efficient movement, special method **COST:** Proper use of materials	REASONS FOR KEYPOINTS
Step # 1 Safety	1. Always have PPE on	1. Safety first
Step # 2 Turn on machine	1. Make sure temperature is where it needs to be 2. Screw gun needs to be on	1. So glue is hot enough to spread properly 2. Won't drive screws
Step # 3 Install screws	1. Need to put screw in straight	1. Needs to be straight so it looks nice
Step # 4 Glue the panel	1. Glue the panel so it seals the glass	1. If glass is not sealed, it will fog up
Step # 5 Wipe the corners	1. Push the extra glue to spread the extra glue to seal the top	1. Helps to complete the process. Glue needs to be below the glass or it will get on the frames.

Figure 10–8. Common mistakes made when breaking down a job

confusion for the student and inability to perform the task in the correct manner.

Step 1 is simply listed as "Safety" and the key point states, "Always have PPE on." Our first comment is that explanations regarding the use of PPE (personal protective equipment) are best handled as a separate training event because of their importance and because it is not an actual job task—it is a requirement for the job. That being said, we would also add that the major step "safety" does not tell the student *what to do*. The key point does not really state how to do the step (because there is no step). If we were teaching the correct use of PPE, the job breakdown would state an action (a verb), such as, "Put on the Kevlar sleeves," and the key point would be, "Attach clip to shirt sleeve—fully covering arm." While it is true that we want the employee to always wear the PPE, it should be instructed prior to the task-training event while preparing the student for the job task because it is not part of the repeating cyclical task. In this case the training should focus on the actual task of installing screws and gluing panels. During training, remember to separate the core-repeating task from other nonrepeating requirements for the job.

Step 2 states, "Turn on machine." Unless a machine needs to be turned on each and every cycle of the job (making it a cyclical event), this step is part of the start-up operation and is not part of the repeating task. Starting equipment and confirming process parameters (temperatures, pressures, etc.) should be a separate training session. There will be no great harm if this step is left in place, but as the trainee is asked to repeat the operation to confirm understanding, the machine will already be on.

We omit this step from our revised breakdown, but let's look at the key point for learning purposes. Does the key point specify how to turn on the machine? No. It says, "Make sure temperature is where it needs to be." What does that sound like? Let's change the wording a bit to, "Verify temperature setting." Verify is a verb, so this is really a major step. As we have stated earlier, it is best to separate the noncyclical portion of the task from the routine cyclical part. Turning on the machine or verifying the correct temperature would be done prior to starting the actual routine task.

The second key point for step 2 states, "Screw gun needs to be on." Is this really a key point? Does it describe how to do a specific action? No. It tells us what needs to be done—a major step, but again this is not a cyclical activity and is best taught as part of a start-up training session. We omit this key point from the cyclical task training.

Let's skip to step 4, "Glue the panel." This step is okay as it is, but we might state the major step as, "Apply glue to panel," because the glue is being applied to the surface. The panel is not being glued together. This is a minor difference, but your objective is to have instruction that specifically describes what is being done. What about the key point? This key point tells us what we are trying to achieve (sealing the glass, which is a reason), but it does not specify the correct method to use. To find out the correct procedure, we went to the workplace to observe the work being performed. Upon observation of the actual job, we discovered there are some specific techniques used. They are listed in our revised breakdown shown in Figure 10–9. Do the key points listed in Figure 10–9 help to clarify how the task of applying the glue is performed?

Step 5 is similar to step 4. The major step is fine, but the key point is vague regarding the actual technique. An objective (reason for key point) is stated, "Spread the extra glue *to seal the top*," but the actual technique for spreading the glue is missing. This is a crucial point to understand—the key points are not designed to tell what we want; they are designed to tell us how to get what we want. If we want the glue to be spread evenly and for the top to be sealed, we need to tell the student *how* to do that.

To more fully understand the correct method and improve the breakdown, we observed the actual job (always go to the actual workplace to see firsthand). Figure 10–9 shows a revised version of the job breakdown that was completed after the review of the actual work. Using the questioning method described in Chapters 8 and 9, we were able to determine the major steps and key points. It was easy to pick up the steps of the job while watching the operator perform the task. We needed to dig

JOB BREAKDOWN SHEET

DATE: 3/8/20___

J. Hanson	D. Picknell
Team Leader	Supervisor

AREA: Glass room JOB: Screw and glue insulated glass WRITTEN BY: G. Hager

MAJOR STEPS	KEYPOINTS **SAFETY:** Injury avoidance, ergonomics, danger points **QUALITY:** Defect avoidance, check points, standards **TECHNIQUE:** Efficient movement, special method **COST:** Proper use of materials	REASONS FOR KEYPOINTS
Step # 1 Insert screws in panels	1. Hold screw gun horizontally	1. Screws must be straight
	2. Screw head flush with panel	2. If screw sticks up, it will interfere with the frame
Step # 2 Apply glue to panels	1. No more than five panels at a time	1. More than five panels and glue will cool and will not seal properly
	2. Start at top edge 1 inch from corner	2. One inch to make sure sealed properly
	3. Pull down over corner 1 inch past corner	3. Motion is easier than from bottom to top
	4. Keep nozzle flush with panel	4. Excess glue will squeeze out if not flush
	5. Apply just enough glue to fill space between glass	5. Too much glue will need to be removed; not enough will not seal properly and panel will fog up
Step # 3 Smooth glue over corner	1. Hold fingers on top edge	1. To steady your hand
	2. Sweep thumb from bottom to top	2. Easier motion
	3. Push thumb just below edge of panels	3. Glue must be concave a little to prevent glue from interfering with the frames
Step # 4		
Step # 5		

Figure 10–9. Revised job breakdown after reviewing the actual job

deeper to find out critical details about how he was doing the task and what was important for the proper completion of the task.

We could see the operator installing the screws in the panels. We asked him, "Is there anything important about how you put the screws in?" He indicated the screws needed to be straight. We asked, "How do you make sure they are straight?" to which he replied, "I have to hold the screw gun horizontally." In this case the need to put screws in straight is the objective—it is not a "how to" instruction. It is necessary for the success of the job. In our revised breakdown the straightness of the screws is listed as the reason and holding the screw gun horizontally is the actual key point. We can pursue this further and ask, "Why do the screws need to be straight?" to get a deeper understanding of the reason.

We continued, asking, "Is there anything else important about how you put the screws in?" He indicated the screws need to be seated completely. "How do you make sure they are seated completely?" we asked. He replied, "The screw gun makes a sound when the screw is completely inserted." "So you listen for the sound?" we asked. "Yes, you can hear it," he replied. "Is it possible to tell by looking also?" we asked. "Well, yes. The screw head needs to be flush with the panel." "Why do the screws need to be seated completely?" we asked. "Because if they are not, the head of the screw will bind in the window sash frame."

The team member proceeded to apply the glue to the panel. We asked if there was anything important about how the glue was applied. We found it was important to glue only five panels at a time before spreading the glue. If more panels are glued, the glue begins to set and will not spread and seal properly. Also, it is important to keep the glue nozzle flush with the edges of the panel to help spread the glue and to keep excess glue from squeezing out. Any excess glue requires extra work to remove and adds a small cost (excess time and material). We proceeded to ask about how the glue was applied and found that starting on the top of the panel and sweeping down and over the corner was the easiest motion. This motion allowed the glue to be pulled along and pressed into the panel more easily. We also found out there were other items of importance, and they are listed as key points. For example, when wiping the glue, it is helpful to rest the fingers on the top edge of the panel and use them as a steady support and for leverage when wiping glue up and over the edge of the panel.

We continued probing and asking questions until all key points had been identified and the correct method was fully understood. Additional questions we asked were, "Why do you do it that way?" and "What would happen if you did it another way?"

It is also a valuable learning experience to try the job for yourself. This helps you get a "feel" for the task and a deeper understanding of how and why things are done a certain way. It is an important confirmation stage. Toyota's philosophy is to always verify understanding for yourself. By the end of the questioning and development of the job breakdowns, we were actually "trained" in the correct technique. With a little practice we could master the job!

Effectively breaking down jobs is a critical part of the talent development process. It is important to be fairly strict in the process. Job breakdowns with poorly defined steps and key points will yield a poor result. It is best if major steps and key points are expressed in simple statements. The major steps tell *what* to do, and the key points tell *how* to do the steps. Nonrepetitive and repetitive tasks should not be mixed in the same training event. Master the breakdown of jobs, and your results will improve. The greatest training presentation in the world will not produce good results if the material being presented is not complete.

Is It Possible to Standardize Complex Engineering Tasks?

Toyota has a standard process for developing new cars. Over the years it has been removing waste and reducing the lead time from 4 years in the mid–1980s to about 15–18 months today. The engineers know quite clearly what they need to do and by when. There are many standard parts in the car and many standard manufacturing processes to design to.[3] A great deal of know-how has been documented in engineering checklists that are now in a "know-how database." Yet any

[3] See James M. Morgan and Jeffrey K. Liker, *The Toyota Product Development System: Integrating People, Process, and Technology* (New York: Productivity Press, 2006).

Toyota engineer will tell you that following standards and checking off boxes in the know-how database do not make a high-quality engineer. It is creativity and deep understanding of the engineering specialty that comes from years of on-the-job training by experienced mentors. When asked how they learned to be engineers, they will not describe the coursework or what they learned in university, but rather what they learned from certain experienced engineers who they worked with side by side (see Chapter 16 for further discussion of how Toyota engineers are developed).

Having said that, the Toyota Technical Center in Ann Arbor, Michigan, has been rapidly expanding and bringing on new engineers. To meet this challenge, Toyota is working hard to develop a detailed understanding of the standard skill set of an engineer and to standardize the training and even standardize how the team leaders train young engineers.

Toyota has already done a good job in product engineering of breaking down the job and identifying the categories of knowledge and skills engineers need to learn over their careers. In Japan most of the learning by engineers was similar to craftspeople of old. It involved quite a bit of on-the-job training, and little was documented. What was documented very rigorously was referred to as the "engineering checklist."

Each engineering specialty was responsible for keeping its own engineering checklist. Senior engineers in that specialty maintained and added to the checklists. There were binders with hundreds of pages of specific things to consider in developing the design. Engineers were required, for a specific program, to actually take a copy of the notebook and to check off each item and get their supervisor to also check off each item.

The checklists represent accumulated knowledge of what is good practice and bad practice. They give standards. They have sketches of good and bad conditions. They have curves that indicate acceptable and unacceptable regions. In a sense, this is the formally accumulated knowledge base for this engineering specialty at Toyota.

But isn't a manual checklist very primitive? Shouldn't this all be computerized? Toyota's view is that if you cannot do it manually, you cannot do it on the computer. But the real answer is that there are some advantages to using computers, and information has been gradually moved to computerized databases over many years at Toyota. Now it is a "know-how database." It still works like the old manual checklist. The engineers need to check that they have considered each item when working on a particular design, and their supervisors have to check off that an item has been completed, but now that is done on the computer. Because it is on the computer, it is easier to find information by using a search engine. It is also easier to add more rich information like photographs of parts and 3-D images that are connected through hyperlinks. But the function is still the same, and the database is only as good as the engineers who add information to it and rigorously use it as part of the design process.

We can look at the know-how database as the "key points" of each engineering specialty. They are not listed by step in the design process as they are in the job breakdown sheets. But they are key points nonetheless. And the engineer is taught these key points by the team leader using the database as a visual training aid in much the same way as the Job Instruction training is conducted.

The Toyota Technical Center in Ann Arbor was not satisfied with just checking off key points. There have been a lot of new hires in a short period of time, and there is more turnover of engineers in the United States than there is in Japan. So Toyota managers decided they needed to add richer information to the know-how database, including some of the reasons for the key points. For example, there might be a good example of a part showing a competitor's vehicle and a bad example of another competitive vehicle to understand why a particular way of designing is important. There may be some history of what happened on a past vehicle so the engineer understands why a particular point was added to the database. In terms of the job breakdown, this is equivalent to adding the "reasons" for the key points.

There are many things contained in the database. For example, body engineers need to know there must be a minimum of a 10-mm clearance from a wire harness to a steel panel. Also safety standards are in the database. Table 10–2 lists key points associated with the

Table 10–2. Example of engineering checklist items for passenger air bag warning

Design key points for passenger air bag warning label (to warn of dangers for small passengers)		
Steps	**Key points**	**Check if OK**
1. Assess if warning label is needed	A. Not needed if no passenger air bag here).	____
	B. Not needed if it is a *smart* passenger air bag (senses passenger weight) meeting standard.	____
	C. If manufacturer recommends periodic maintenance or replacement of air bag, must label with recommended schedule specified by month and year or in vehicle mileage.	____
2. Develop location for label	A. Permanently affix to either side of sun visor, at manufacturer's option, at each front outboard seating position equipped with air bag.	____
	B. No other information shall appear on same side of the sun visor to which warning label is affixed.	____
3. Design warning label	A. Letter in English in block capital and numerals not less than three thirty-seconds of an inch high.	____
	B. The label shall conform in content to the label shown in either Figure 6a or 6b of the standard (not shown here).	____
	C. The heading area shall be yellow with the word "WARNING" and the alert symbol in black.	____
	D. The message area shall be white with black text. The message area shall be no less than 30 square cm and 4.7 square inches.	____
	E. The pictogram shall be black with a red circle and slash on a white background.	____
	F. The pictogram shall be no less than 30 mm (1.2 in) in diameter.	____
	G. If the vehicle does not have a back seat, the label may be modified by omitting the statement: "The BACK SEAT is the SAFEST place for children."	____

Note: The data for this example came from the U.S. government's federal motor vehicle safety standards Web site. It is a summary and not the full standard.

labeling requirements for a passenger air bag that are based on the U.S. federal motor vehicle safety standards. These are publicly available on the Internet, but Toyota does not want its engineers to constantly have to search for all the relevant databases each time they do a design, and it also wants engineers to systematically check off that their designs meet the requirements. In this case the air bag engineer also has to design the label and its placement, and to design the correct labeling for every country in which Toyota will be selling vehicles (of course with help when it involves another language).

The warning label example is based on public data, and including it in the know-how database is a matter of ensuring the standard is followed. Most of the data are the accumulated technical know-how of Toyota that has been developed over decades, and it is treated as very proprietary. Toyota guards it mightily and considers it a competitive advantage. It is guarded to the point that engineers do not even have access to the know-how databases of other specialties. Toyota knows that engineers leave, and the company does not want them taking copies of the databases with them. One departing engineer tried to take complete hard copies of a database to a competitor when he left. Toyota discovered this and was able to prevent it. However, the experience has lead to more intense security measures. Not only is technical know-how guarded for security, but the content is also closely controlled. The databases are specific to an engineering specialty, and only *senior* engineers in that specialty are authorized to modify it.

Toyota engineers emphasize that learning how to use the know-how database does not make a good engineer. It is a tool to provide guidelines and to ensure the engineer does not forget key points. It is helpful in training young engineers. But the database is simply presenting constraints on possible design solutions. The engineer will know not to exceed some limit or to keep something at some minimum. But that does not tell the engineer what the specification should be. And the engineer can even exceed the limit if there is a particular reason. From past experience, the engineers have found that exceeding the limit (a warning) may cause a problem, and so the engineer must now do extra testing or field studies to prove it is okay to exceed the limit. The real engineering is still the creative thinking to solve the problem or provide the function to the customer, while treating these standards as constraints. Toyota places a great emphasis on developing know-how over time by doing the work under the guidance of a mentor because it is the only way to develop the real creative power of the engineer. We discuss this further in the final chapter of this book.

Job Breakdown: The Critical Step

Aside from the training itself, the job breakdown is arguably the most critical step in the Job Instruction process. It is when you identify the what, how, and why of the job. It is closely connected to the standardized worksheet, but as we explained, it is not the standardized worksheet. It is another level of analysis and detail. The standardized worksheet tells us the steps to follow as well as how much time each step should take and how the task time relates to the takt time (customer demand rate). But as we break down the job further and identify the key points, we are developing a more detailed understanding of the standardized approach needed to do the job right for safety, quality, productivity, and cost control. If we did not get to this level, we would not have complete standardized work.

We do not post the job breakdown at the work site. We post the standardized worksheet at the job site. In reality the standardized worksheet is not for the workers to refer to as they do the job because referring to it would prevent them from doing the job fluidly. They should have learned to perform the job flawlessly during the training period. The standard worksheet is a reference mainly for supervisors to audit the job. The job breakdown can also be a useful reference for the supervisor who wishes to audit the standardized work, particularly if there is a problem, such as a worker not being able to keep up, or if there are quality or safety problems. As more is learned over time, the job breakdown should be revised to reflect changes made during the kaizen process. This will help in documenting the current best way of doing the job and in updateing what will be taught to new team associates.

In the following chapters we begin to describe the actual training process. Before attempting to transfer knowledge to others, it is crucial that the correct information be identified. Earlier we noted that Abraham Lincoln said that if given six hours to chop down a tree, he would spend four hours sharpening the ax. We recommend that you spend the time thoroughly breaking down jobs into great detail. Dig deeply to find out what matters most in every task. Focus your effort on the critical aspects present in every job. Achieving great results will require great effort. There is no shortcut. This is the "make-or-break" part of the process. Do your best!

Part Three

Transfer Knowledge to Others

For the things we have to learn before we can do them, we learn by doing them.

Aristotle

Chapter 11

Prepare for Training

The Job Instruction Method Requires Thorough Preparation

You have probably noticed by now there is quite a bit to do to prepare for training. In Chapter 4 we reviewed the organizational preparation necessary, such as selecting and training the trainers as well as assessing the overall needs of the company. We have looked extensively at the analysis and breakdown of jobs into the detail necessary for effective training. All these things need to be done prior to the actual training. But we are not quite done preparing. There are a few more things to think about.

When we think about training in the classroom, we often expect there will be a certain degree of preparation required. You need to select the teachers, design the curriculum, put together the training materials and handouts, invite the students, arrange the logistics, and design the course evaluations. This type of preparation all seems to go out the window when we are training on the job. The typical new hire, be it an engineer, shop floor worker, nurse, supervisor, or even manager, might receive well-prepared and well-presented classroom training, but then he or she is thrown into the job to sink or swim. Fortunately for the workers our performance assessment methods are generally superficial enough that even if they are sinking, they can get away with minimal performance. On-the-job training typically means you start to work and ask questions when you are struggling, and over time you will find some way to get the work done.

Think about the following situation if you were asked to teach a three-day training course. Students show up the first morning, and you are in front of the room. You arrived a little early and threw together some training materials. You give the class a quick introduction to the topic, and you suddenly realize you want to show them some stuff but there is no computer projector or overhead projector, so you ask them to start looking over the handouts and tell them you will be back later. In a couple of hours you show up with an overhead projector and ask them how things are going and begin to present some material. Then you ask if there are any questions. When there are none you say, "Good," and they can look over the materials some more and talk among themselves if they want to. You will be back in a few hours—and oh yes, there is a cafeteria in the building if they get hungry. Now you may say you have been to a course like this, and you may have paid good money for it, but all would agree it would be an abomination and the students should be in an uproar. Yet, do you do on-the-job training in a way that is even this organized?

If you first think about the preparation that is required for a top-notch training program in a classroom and translate it into on-the-job training, you will be off to a good start. We typically know a lot about how to prepare for classroom training and would be highly embarrassed if we did no preparation and were stuck in front of the classroom with nothing prepared. The Job Instruction (JI) method is a highly refined training process that should be as organized as any top-notch training program. And the exciting thing is it is all learning by doing. We often knock ourselves out in the classroom to find good exercises that are "realistic simulations," and on-the-job training is even better—it is the actual job.

Creating a Multifunction Worker Training Plan

The development of employee talent is too important to leave to chance. Planning for the development process not only increases the likelihood of success, it also demonstrates the importance of development to the individuals of the team and lets them know the leaders place high importance on talent development.

Learning the skills necessary to perform the work for which a person was hired should be the first priority of every leader. This is the value-adding work. The development of the training plan to learn the work is based on the premise of "how much, by when." In other words, how many tasks must a person learn and in what period of time? If a person was hired for a routine manufacturing operation, a typical expectation would be for that person to become proficient in the first job within a few weeks (depending on the complexity) and to be capable of performing three jobs within three months.

Toyota has discovered the value of having employees capable of performing multiple jobs. Gone are the days of one person working on one machine who has done a single job for 35 years. Creating multifunctional workers not only increases flexibility and helps support the system, but it also allows team members to have some variety in their work, to rotate jobs for ergonomic benefit, and to learn and grow in talent and capability. We often hear of supervisors who are struggling because they are unable to complete a critical task or staff a position by moving people to vacant positions because of the lack of necessary skills among other employees. Developing a multifunctional workforce should be at the top of every leader's priority list.

Toyota adapted the training plan development process initially introduced by Training Within Industry (TWI) and created what it refers to as the Multifunction Worker Training Timetable (called a training timetable by TWI). This plan is designed to show the skill levels needed to support the work area and the skill development of each worker. Figure 11–1 shows an example of a completed Multifunction Worker Training Timetable (MFWTT). (All forms in this

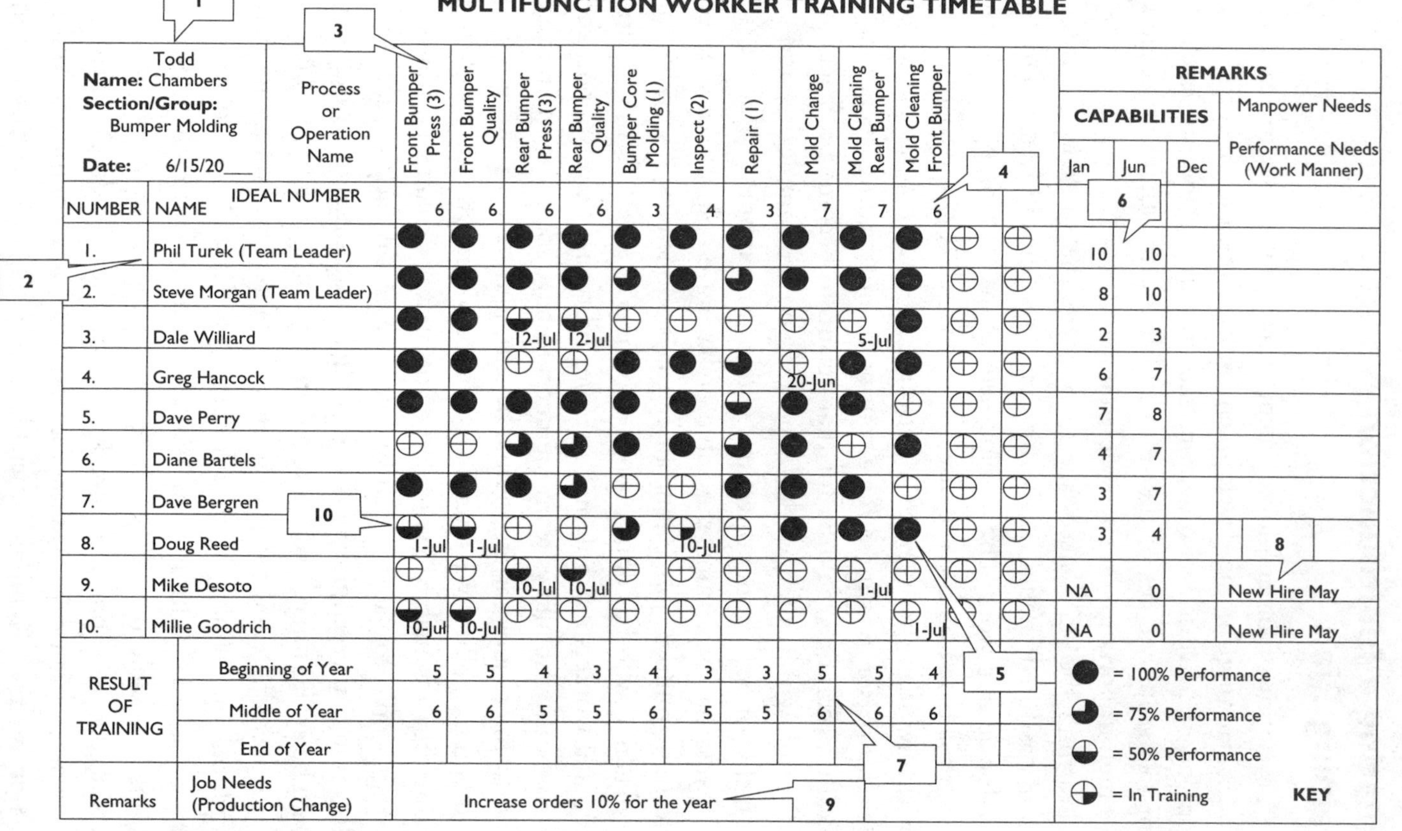

Figure 11–1. Example of completed Multifunction Worker Training Timetable

book may be downloaded from our Web site—www.thetoyotaway.org.) Conceptually it is very simple. Identify the job tasks in the work area, list the people in the work area, evaluate each person's capability for each job, identify the gaps in skill levels between the current level and the desired level, and set a time frame for developing the necessary people to close the gaps. Keep it simple by focusing on your intended outcome—exceptionally talented people producing great results!

The MFWTT also provides a visual indicator of the status of skill development within the team or group, which can be posted in the team meeting area. With brief study anyone can see the status of skill development for all employees. This is a reflection of the importance of talent development by the leadership and should be taken very seriously. Management has the responsibility for ensuring that every leader is making efforts to fully develop the talents of all members of the team.

On occasion a leader attempts to make the current condition look better than it actually is by overstating the competency of the team members. Management must confirm by verifying the performance indicators of the work team. If the safety, quality, or productivity results for the team are low, it is likely the skill level is not as high as portrayed. Specific deficiencies can be pinpointed if the performance indicators decline when certain individuals do certain tasks. The intent is not to find poor performers and single them out; the intent is to recognize deficiencies and to correct them.

In Chapter 1 we discussed the fact that the Toyota system creates a need for highly skilled people. Any weakness in skill levels will be indicated by an inability to meet the production demands. We recommend you take actual skill levels seriously when filling out the MFWTT. Overstating performance to make individuals or the leader look good will not benefit anyone in the long run. As part of the auditing process, leaders should always confirm the development process results by verifying performance.

The following instructions explain how to complete the MFWTT shown in Figure 11-1. Each item number from the list corresponds to the numbered balloons in Figure 11-1.

1. The supervisor completes this section with his or her name, the group or area, and the date. A training plan is generally created every year at the beginning of the year. If you are just starting the process midyear, your initial plan may be completed at any time and reevaluated at the beginning of the next year.
2. List the names of all employees within the team or work group. If there are more than 10 people use additional sheets. In most cases at Toyota, one sheet is completed for each team, which normally has about four to seven people.
3. List the names of all the jobs or job tasks in the area. Chapters 6 and 7 provide detailed information on defining job tasks. Remember that in our bumper-molding example some tasks (mold change and mold clean) are not truly separate jobs, but they are important aspects of the primary job of the bumper-molding operator. In this case the leader also wants to track the skill levels on those crucial parts of the job and has listed them individually.
4. The "ideal number" represents the minimum number of people who should be trained on each job in order to ensure the job position can always be filled when absences occur. This is more than the minimum number of trained people needed to perform the work at any particular time. For example, if there are three identical operations (and three operators are required at all times), it will be necessary to have more than three people trained so that any absences may be covered adequately. The ideal number in this case may be five people trained. Having two additional people trained (as a minimum) will allow for the loss of a skilled person either on a short-term basis (vacation) or as a permanent loss (job transfer). Preferably every person within the team will ultimately be trained for all positions.

This often confuses leaders who decide they want everyone trained, and therefore the ideal number must be "everyone." While this may in fact be "ideal," what is important is any shortages between the current state and the desired level. If the ideal number is stated as the total in the group (everyone), an immediate training need will always be indicated unless everyone is trained on every job. The ideal number defines the minimum number of trained people necessary for coverage of the work and helps to identify immediate training needs (gaps). Toyota leaders are not satisfied with achieving the minimum, which is just an indication that the process will function in the event of a loss of employees for whatever reasons. The supervisor is responsible for determining the ideal number of people trained for each job and uses the following criteria for guidance:

a. Jobs or tasks that are more difficult to master should have a greater number of people trained to perform them. For example, if it takes six months to master a certain task, it would be prudent to have "extra" people trained for that task in case one of the skilled workers leaves unexpectedly.
b. If there are multiple and identical jobs or tasks, the ideal number of trained workers should be increased accordingly. In the example there are three front and three rear bumper-molding machines. This task also has a long learning curve, so it would be wise to have a minimum of six people trained for each position. Note that there are currently five workers skilled in the rear bumper-molding job. This does not indicate an actual current shortage (the job only requires three), but it indicates a potential problem, and there is a plan in place to train additional workers.
c. Future staffing changes, such as promotions, transfers, leaves of absence, and the like, will affect the ideal number of trained employees desired. If such changes are anticipated, the ideal number should be adjusted accordingly.

5. The circle with four quadrants is used to visually depict each person's skill for a particular job. Color in the portions of each circle for every member and task according to the individual skill level. The following descriptions should be used as a guide to determine the appropriate skill level of each individual.

a. An *empty circle* indicates that no training has been started.
b. *One-quarter of the shaded circle* indicates a person who has just begun the training process and has a competency level of approximately 25 percent (a beginner). This person should never be left alone on the job, because he or she does not completely understand the safety and quality requirements, nor is he or she capable of maintaining the proper pace.
c. *One-half of the circle is colored in* to represent a person who is able to perform the task on his or her own for brief periods or with close monitoring and support. Generally it is best not to have a person with this level of ability working without close supervision, but in a pinch such a person may fill a vacancy. This person may be too slow to work completely alone, and the quality of work should be monitored closely.
d. *Three-quarters of the circle is colored in* to represent a worker who is very capable of performing the job and needs little supervision. A person with this skill level can work alone most of the time and fulfills the requirements necessary for the "ideal number" of skilled workers because he or she has enough capability to work without assistance from a trainer. At this stage the only thing remaining to learn is the accumulated know-how that is acquired over time. This student knows to stop and ask a question if he or she runs into an unusual situation.
e. A *fully colored circle* represents a person who is completely trained and needs little or no supervision. Such a person is completely knowledgeable of the safety and quality rules and can maintain the required pace. Normally the full circle is reserved for a trainee who has worked at least a few months (or more) on the job accumulating the necessary know-how. The fully trained person would be considered an "expert," and this person's knowledge and skill should be exceptional.

In some cases we have seen the fourth quadrant of the circle used to designate individuals who are capable of training others (certified

Job Instruction trainers). We prefer to designate training capability in another way (such as with an asterisk next to a name) and to reserve the full circle as a designation of exceptional capability with the job task. We agree that fully trained people should have the job knowledge to teach others, but this does not mean they will necessarily make good trainers. These are two different skill sets.

The certified trainer and supervisor collectively evaluate the progress and skill level of each individual (note that the supervisor should be a certified trainer as well). Some trainers and trainees view the progress as a "score" and feel inadequate with anything less than completely filled in circles. It should be stressed that the training process is not a competition and there is no benefit to the leader in attempting to make the evaluations appear better than they actually are.

We are often asked how Toyota rewards people and motivates them to learn multiple skills. It is part of the job expectation from the beginning. All production employees have the same job classification and pay (based on length of service). As a minimum, everyone is expected to learn all jobs within the team. Team members may choose to learn more and are encouraged to do so. There is no reward or bonus system for learning additional skills.

Other companies use various pay-for-knowledge schemes, but Toyota does not use these. Any motivation or incentive other than self-motivation is likely to lead to problems and limitations. Everyone is expected to meet the minimum requirement (which is high), and many opportunities are provided to develop greater talents.

At Toyota poor job skills are reflected in other performance measures such as quality and productivity, and the trainer and leader will continually struggle with problems if they do not have exceptionally skilled people. Shortcutting the training process will not provide the long-term benefits desired, and students may feel pressure to perform to a level they are not capable of. It is a sure way to create a "bad attitude."

6. The total number of circles colored in to at least the three-quarter level are totaled for each employee and placed in the column at the end of the employee's row. The supervisor will

make an assessment at the beginning, middle, and end of each year to determine individual and overall training needs and will evaluate whether the training plan has been achieved. This allows the supervisor to track progress of each individual and to develop plans for the development of each person. This number is updated midyear and at year-end to verify progress.

7. The number of people fully trained for each job is totaled and recorded at the bottom of the sheet. This allows the supervisor to monitor progress toward achieving the ideal number of trained people for each job. As with the individual progress, this total is evaluated midyear and at year-end to ensure progress. We see in our example that the rear bumper operation is below the ideal number as is mold changing and mold cleaning for the rear bumper. Note that target dates have been established for rectifying these deficiencies.
8. Any special development needs are noted in this space. Most often these are related to specific techniques that have not been mastered. The lack of skill may cause an increase of defects or may slow the work pace. Comments may relate to any items necessary to move from a three-quarter circle to a full circle, or as in this example, indicates that members were hired recently and need special attention to bring their skill level up to the minimum.
9. Note any future production changes in this space. For example, if production will increase, or perhaps a key person will be out on leave, it is noted here. This serves as a reminder that the ideal number of trained workers needs to be adjusted or additional people need to be trained.
10. When the need for training is identified based on a deficiency in the number of trained workers or in an individual's capability, a plan is made, and the target dates are penciled in. The dates serve as a target to begin the training process, or to complete the training necessary to advance to the next stage. Immediate needs should be considered first, and long-term development is planned for future dates.

When completed, the MFWTT is posted in the work area where all workers and managers can monitor progress and identify any development needs. As noted, the supervisor and Job Instruction trainer will review progress throughout the year, update the status of workers, and make new plans. Unfortunately we often see the development plans posted in work areas, and then they are forgotten as if completing the form was the assignment and now the assignment is complete. The development plan is a plan that now must be executed. It is also a dynamic process and must be reevaluated regularly. The responsibility for training ends.

Developing a Training Plan for Other Types of Jobs: Lean Facilitator Example

You can develop the equivalent of multifunction training plans for many different types of jobs. For example, Toyota has developed highly visual graphical displays for all engineers in product development to review the status of their skill development. We developed a training program for internal lean facilitators by breaking down the job into fundamental skills and using something like the training plan matrix to keep track of progress. Figure 11–2 shows the training plan for lean facilitators. It starts with a basic orientation in the classroom. It continues with more classroom training covering a variety of lean tools, including simulated exercises and experiencing a one-week kaizen workshop. Individual tools appropriate for the particular company had to be mastered so the lean facilitator could effectively lead kaizen workshops for these individual tools. The skill sets required are listed in Figure 11–3, and the training approach is similar to the JI approach in which students participate in a facilitated event using the tool and then lead parts of subsequent events until they can lead an event unsupported.

In the last stages of training, they participate in a system kaizen to create a lean value stream using a set of tools and then ultimately lead a team of people to develop and implement a system kaizen (significant part of a value stream) in an area of the operation. Progress for

Required Training for Lean Certification					
Certification level	Key leader training (2-day basics)	Facilitator training (1-week lean tools + RIW)	Participation in RIW as team leader or coleader	Supervised facilitation of 3 or more RIW	Unsupervised system kaizen project utilizing multiple lean tools
Lean practitioner	REQUIRED	REQUIRED	REQUIRED	REQUIRED	REQUIRED
RIW* facilitator (by specialty†)	REQUIRED	REQUIRED	REQUIRED	REQUIRED	
Lean yellow belt	REQUIRED	REQUIRED	REQUIRED		

* RIW = rapid improvement workshop (kaizen workshop)

† Areas of specialty: Flow/pull system, value stream mapping, TPM, standard operations/work, 5S, business process kaizen

Certified RIW facilitators will focus on at least two specialties. The first specialty would require participation in three workshops (observing, coleading, leading). Subsequent specialties could be abbreviated (e.g., one or two workshops) as there is carry over.

Lean practitioners would be advised to colead and lead workshops in several different areas. The plans are more customized to the individuals based on their backgrounds and skill levels. An unsupervised system-level project is also required.

Key leader training description: Two-day lean tools course

Facilitator training description: One-week course including deeper technical understanding of lean tools plus facilitation and problem-solving skills. Also includes participation in one RIW.

Figure 11–2. Curricula for certification of an internal lean facilitator

	Basics		Successfully led RIW						System		
NAME	Key Leader Training	Facilitator Training	Flow/Pull	VSM	TPM	Standard Work	5S/Visual Management	Business Process	System Kaizen Member	System Kaizen Leader	**REMARKS**
	⊕	⊕	⊕	⊕	⊕	⊕	⊕	⊕	⊕	⊕	
	⊕	⊕	⊕	⊕	⊕	⊕	⊕	⊕	⊕	⊕	
	⊕	⊕	⊕	⊕	⊕	⊕	⊕	⊕	⊕	⊕	
	⊕	⊕	⊕	⊕	⊕	⊕	⊕	⊕	⊕	⊕	
	⊕	⊕	⊕	⊕	⊕	⊕	⊕	⊕	⊕	⊕	
	⊕	⊕	⊕	⊕	⊕	⊕	⊕	⊕	⊕	⊕	

Figure 11–3. Example of training timetable for internal lean facilitator

individuals is tracked on a skill development matrix similar to the multifunction training plan (see Figure 11–3).

Set Behavioral Expectations from the Beginning

We often hear managers and supervisors complain about the "bad attitudes" of their employees. We hear, "Young people don't have the work ethic the older workers have," and "You'll never get these people to put forth extra effort." Or perhaps older employees "resist learning new skills." Employees generally begin a new job with enthusiasm, full of hope for a bright future. It takes effort for us to turn these high hopes into feelings of apathy, despair, frustration, cynicism, disgust, or outright rebellion. Much of this attitudinal shift occurs at the very moment when a new hire is introduced to the work area. Behavioral expectations are communicated to employees from the very first moment and especially during training events. You will demonstrate the behavior that is expected by your own attitude before, during, and after the training.

Consider the following example that is all too common in reality. Linda starts a new job as a production operator, and Joe is assigned to teach Linda the job. Linda has gone through a one-day orientation, mostly covering company policies as well as safety procedures. Linda is happy to have this high-paying job and is eager to learn. She is sent to her work area to learn her assigned job. She approaches it and sees a sloppily dressed man working in an equally sloppy work area. The area is a mess, littered with a newspaper on the floor and empty soda cans. Joe introduces himself and assures Linda, "These jobs are simple; any moron can do them. Don't worry. You will learn in no time." Joe demonstrates the job to Linda over a few cycles and lets Linda try a few times, while helping her a little (but not too much—after all, she needs to learn sometime). Part way through the training a buddy of Joe's stops by, and they chat about the upcoming game this weekend. After 20 minutes Linda can keep up reasonably well, and Joe says, "You are a natural. You can handle this fine. If you don't mind, I'm going to take a break." It is clear to Linda that she is on her own and the training is done.

What impression does Linda now have of her trainer and the job? The work area is a mess and conveys a sense that no one cares about the sloppiness. Joe obviously thinks the job is so simple that it can be done by anyone. Why would Linda feel a sense of accomplishment in learning the job? Joe has done nothing to prepare for training Linda. Will this help Linda to feel like a valued member of the team?

What about the important parts of the job? Apparently Joe does not think there are any key points worth noting. Clearly either quality does not matter, or perhaps any way of doing the job will produce satisfactory quality. Joe clearly does not place a high priority on his role as a trainer because at his first chance he takes off on a break. Is Linda supposed to develop an attitude that this work is important based on Joe's nonchalance?

There is an old saying that, "You only have one chance to make a first impression." This is especially true when a person is first introduced into the work area. There is one chance to convey the importance of caring about the work, the customer, and fellow employees. If you are not willing to show people you care by making time, focusing on their success, and helping them to learn and to grow, how do you expect them to develop a positive attitude?

There are a few key steps the leader and trainer must follow prior to beginning the training event.

1. Meet with each person, review his or her previous experience, and determine any specific development needs.
2. Create an overall development plan and review it with him or her (explained in the next section). Clearly explain your goals in terms of what the employee will be trained for and by what date. Ensure he or she understands the importance of their development to you.
3. Prepare the work area so it reflects caring and attention:
   a. It must be as neat and organized as you expect it to be kept.
   b. Have the necessary tools and equipment (including any necessary safety gear) ready *before* the trainee arrives.
4. Make sure adequate time will be available to complete the intended training without disruption. Make sure your job responsibilities are covered while you are training. Remind others that you do not wish to be disturbed during the training unless there is an emergency.
5. Prepare a job breakdown, and understand the critical points of the work so good explanations can be provided when questions are asked.

During the training there are a few things the trainer must do to convey the proper attitude:

1. Be enthusiastic about the work and its importance.
2. Convey to the trainee the importance of his or her work to the customer. If possible show them or explain how the customer uses the product or service. In manufacturing the person running the next operation is considered the customer. Demonstrate how the work affects the next operator, and make sure the trainee understands the importance of satisfying the customer.
3. Demonstrate patience, and continue to support the students until they are capable of performing the work successfully.
4. Be encouraging. Recognize good performance, and suggest opportunities to improve performance.

5. Exude confidence in your ability as a knowledgeable trainer and in your belief that the student will become an outstanding employee on the job.
6. Assume responsibility for the outcome, and continue until the student is capable of performing flawlessly on his or her own.
7. The trainer is always responsible for safety and quality during the training and must make the student feel secure.

After the training there are also a few things that must be done to ensure poor attitudes do not develop later after the training is completed:

1. When you are confident the student is ready to perform the work, assign her or him a task. State clearly what she is expected to do (quantify how much, by when), and remind her you will be nearby for support.
2. Provide positive feedback when the student is performing well, and continue to work on areas that need improvement.
3. Remember to pay close attention to the verbal and nonverbal feedback regarding your training method. If you are overbearing, people will send you signals. If you are inattentive, they will also provide signs. Since every person has different needs, trainers must interpret the feedback during the training session and adjust their approach accordingly.

Develop Related Job Skills to Broaden Capability

Related job skills are not always required of employees, but they will help to maximize the contributions of workers as well as provide them with new challenges and opportunities to expand their horizons. There are numerous job-related skills including becoming a trainer, learning problem solving, participating in team improvement activities, becoming a continuous improvement facilitator, and expanding some skills such as computing or communications.

These skills are generally best developed over time. The first step may be for workers to attend a formal training session. The skill is developed and mastered through application in the workplace and with ongoing mentoring from someone skilled in the practice. Specific assignments should be made that will utilize the new skill and also provide opportunity for additional coaching. Remember the example of the team member who wanted to move to the maintenance area? The leader facilitated the team member's ambition by providing opportunities to develop new skills and to practice them while also benefiting the team and the company.

This planning and coaching requires extra effort on the part of the leader, and often the leader perceives it as less important than the actual job for which the person was hired. As we mention earlier in the book, all Toyota managers are expected to be teachers. It is the most important part of their role. Smart leaders understand that people who are pursuing personal growth are generally happier and more satisfied. They also know that by demonstrating care for the individual's personal desires, the team member will reciprocate. If the leader goes the extra mile for the team member, the team member will generally be willing to go an extra mile for the leader.

Leaders show their commitment by making a plan, scheduling regular follow-up sessions, and routinely providing guidance on specific goals for development. The leader's attitude should be, "What can I do to help you achieve your objectives?" The progress of the individual should align with the needs of the organization, and the leader must provide direction.

Prepare the Work Area

TWI suggests the work area be clean and orderly "just as you expect it to be maintained." It is amazing how quickly people become acclimated to their surroundings and no longer notice if the work area is cluttered and messy. If a new hire's first exposure to the work area shows a messy and disorganized place, he or she will become accustomed to that condition and will be inclined to keep it that way. Conversely, if people are acclimated to a neat work area and are expected to maintain it in that state, they will likely do so. Some people need more reminders than others, but with a defined expectation, it is easier to require people to follow a standard.

Our best advice is to seek the people with a natural talent for organization and neatness and to engage them in your effort to put the workplace in order. It is remarkably easy to maintain once it is established and people become acclimated to order rather than chaos. It is, however, easier to acclimate people when they are first exposed to a place and are creating new habits rather than trying to break bad habits after acclimation.

Fortune Favors the Prepared[1]

Preparation is the key to successful training. We would not embark on a cross-country journey without a map and a plan. Why would we begin a training process without the same level of preparation? There are times when we are in such a hurry to "get going" that we shortcut or bypass the preparation phase. Sometimes we claim we don't have time to do it properly. The trouble is that shortcutting this phase may lead to continual problems in the future. We will continue to pay for our lack of preparation with repeating problems time and again. Our lack of preparation for training sends a message to employees that their development and success are not important to us. Bad attitudes and apathy are sure to follow. Good preparation provides a positive model to the employees. They see how the workplace should be organized, understand expectations for keeping it up, and are aware that developing exceptional people is a high priority for management.

Time is the one resource that is limited for all of us. There is only so much time available, and it must be used wisely. The best use of time is when the time spent today returns much more time in the future. A well-trained workforce will have fewer problems and will require much less time and attention on a daily basis. People with a short-term focus will miss this important point. Time must be spent today for a payback tomorrow.

The investment in the development of people is similar to the investment in your financial future. The advice to, "Start early; invest

---

[1] Louis Pasteur said: "In the fields of observation, chance favors only the prepared mind." (Source: Lecture, University of Lille, December 7, 1854.)

often and consistently no matter how much," applies equally to the investment in people. Deep development occurs gradually over time, and the training process is a series of larger investments followed by numerous and frequent small contributions.

We often suggest to beleaguered leaders who complain of time constraints that if they have only 5 minutes to spare, they need to make it the best five minutes possible! It is entirely possible to conduct the bulk of your development process in 5- or 10-minute increments; in fact, smaller amounts of information are much easier for students to absorb and are more readily retained. Of course the total development will require numerous individual events of only 10 minutes. In Chapter 14 we provide additional suggestions for improving the training result when time is limited. But first, and not soon enough for many readers, we must get into the actual training session itself, which is covered in the next chapter.

Chapter 12

Present the Operation: The Training Session

Are We There Yet?

We have arrived at the part of the process that everyone looks forward to—the time when we actually get to train someone. This is it, the final test. Now we can find out how good we are as trainers. But wait. You may have noticed that this book has 16 chapters, and this is Chapter 12. Three-quarters of the book is behind us, and we are just getting to the actual presentation—the training event.

You will also notice that one chapter is devoted to the presentation, and a few are devoted to the events after the training, but eight chapters are focused on breaking down jobs and preparing for the training event. Why the disparity? Isn't the delivery of the information the important part? The truth is that good performance during every step in the process is necessary for success, but the breakdown of the job is critical, and the delivery is important. If the correct information is identified during the breakdown, all that is necessary after that is to convey it to someone else. And if you are able to perform the job and give the students the correct information, they can see what is being done and learn to do it properly.

The Toyota Way distinguishes between process orientation and results orientation. Let's face it, most people and companies are results oriented. We want to get busy on the task, get it done, and get the fruits of our labor. But then we learn how Toyota does thinking and planning and preparation, and it seems like an endless process.

From our experience, the correct information conveyed poorly will produce a better result than poor information conveyed perfectly. Developing exceptional talent is more about clarifying the correct information and then learning how to present it. A bountiful garden harvest comes only after much preparation and tending.

Without all this planning and preparing, you will do what countless others before you have done: hire the people, show them how to do the job, leave them on their own, and then "fight the fires" that ensue. You will *not* get exceptional people who can consistently deliver results. So like everything worth doing in life, preparation will make the doing much more successful.

You might notice the first step in the presentation is actually *more* preparation! Don't worry; this preparation is just a little warm-up to the training. The real preparation has already occurred. It is important before launching into the training to find out a little about the student and to make sure he is in the right frame of mind for receiving the information.

Training Within Industry (TWI) developed the four-step method for the actual teaching phase of the process (reviewed in Chapter 3). We have split up the four-step method into three chapters for ease of explanation. In this chapter, we start with the necessary preparation (step 1), and then, at last, we get to presenting the operation (step 2). Chapter 13 discusses trying out the performance (step 3), and Chapter 15 covers the follow-up needed (step 4) to ensure the learning is successful and is sustained.

Prepare the Student

After the training plan has been developed and the job has been analyzed and broken down into major steps, key points and reasons, you are almost ready to begin the actual training. But, before beginning the training event, there are just a few additional things that need to be handled.

First, make sure you have the time to devote to the training session. Make sure your job has been covered so you will not be disturbed and you will have time for follow-up after the training session. If time is limited, the scope of the training session may need to be adjusted to cover less material.

Second, the work area must be prepared *prior* to meeting with the student. You will send a poor message if the student is left to wait while you run off to get the necessary items together. This includes making sure the work area is clean and orderly, having all tools and equipment ready, and preparing all safety gear for the student.

Finally, let the other people around you know you will be conducting training, and instruct them of any changes they will need to make to their work during that time. For example, if you will be teaching only a portion of the complete job, make sure the normal operator completely understands which portion of the job you will be doing and which portion he or she needs to do. You may ask this person to also make a special effort to evaluate the portion of work your student will be performing to ensure perfect quality. See Figure 14–1 for an example of the positioning of the trainer and student each doing part of the work.

Step 1 of the four-step method is "prepare the student." This step is a warm-up and the initial assessment of the student and his or her capability by the trainer. During the actual training, the instructor must adjust the presentation based on the student's capability. If the student is a new hire and working with the trainer for the first time, additional time might be spent putting the student at ease and also explaining the importance of the work and its context within the organization. The trainer has no previous experience with the student and his or her abilities and learning capabilities, and so the trainer must proceed slowly while assessing the situation. In subsequent training sessions it will not be necessary to establish a relationship and develop rapport as this has already been done. The following items explain the preparation of the student for the training session.

Put the Student at Ease

The learning process can be a nerve-wracking experience, especially for a new member of the organization. New hires may be concerned that they will be unable to perform the work and as a result lose their job.

People have been conditioned to believe the training will be limited or they will be shown the job only one time. Students may believe if they don't learn the job the first time, they will be left to fend for themselves.

The training session should begin with introductions and general chitchat to allow the student time to relax. The trainer should explain what will be occurring during the training session and reassure the student that his or her success on the job is the foremost priority. This reassurance also includes a statement that the job will be presented and reviewed several times to ensure the student fully understands and will be 100 percent capable when the training is complete. The following sample dialogue provides an example of a conversation with a new hire prior to beginning the training.

Trainer: Hi. My name is Diane. I will be the trainer today. How are you today?
Student: Fine, thanks. I'm Bob.
Trainer: I'm here to make sure you learn everything and you're able to do a great job.
Student: That's good.
Trainer: Tell me a little bit about yourself.
Student: Well, I am married, and I have two kids, eight-year-old twin boys actually.
Trainer: Wow. That must be a handful!
Student: Yes, they keep me running . . . and staying fit.
Trainer: That's a positive. Bob, I am going to teach you the air-bag retainer assembly operation. We'll be going through this step by step so you can get comfortable with the job. I want you to know my main priority is to make sure you are successful. We will go over this several times, so just relax and do your best.

Tell the Student the Job Name

It may seem obvious, but it is important to tell the student the name of the job. We are amazed to find many people working at jobs who don't know what the job name is. It is difficult to develop a sense of "ownership" or caring about something when you don't even know what to call it! Keep in mind—you do not want people who are just *doing* work, you want people who *care* about the work they are doing.

Find Out What the Student Knows About the Job

This step is intended to help the trainer assess any potential skill gaps and possibly accelerate the training process, if the student has had previous experience with similar work. It may be necessary to slow down the training, or to review some fundamental skills such as the use of tools prior to beginning the training, if the student has little or no experience. If the student has prior experience, it may be possible to accelerate the training session.

A word of caution—people may have a tendency to embellish prior experience or their capability. New hires may feel pressured by the question regarding past work history and mistakenly believe they must have prior experience in order to get the job (or to keep it).

When Cockiness Can Blow Up in Your Face

The following story by David Meier exemplifies what can happen with a new hire.

When I was 18 I was hired as a welder's helper on a large farm in Florida. I had never worked as a welder before and was a bit apprehensive about taking the job. My only welding experience was the practice I'd had in high school shop class, which was rather limited. I could strike an arc and run a bead, but beyond that my skills were minimal. The farm's regular welder (Glenn) was smart enough to test my ability by having me weld a few pieces of metal, and I suppose I showed enough promise because I was offered the job.

On my first day Glenn asked me if I knew how to use an oxyacetylene cutting torch. Surely, this was a required skill for a welder-helper, and I was worried that if I did not know how to use the torch, I would lose the job. Besides, I reasoned, I had *seen* the teacher use one in school. How hard could it be? I said "sure" and was sent off to an out building to cut the axle from a wagon. After a few minutes (perhaps it was longer), I had the torch lit and began to remove the axle. What transpired was not really cutting; it was more melting the metal away slowly. I could see I was making a mess of the situation, but as I got deeper and deeper in trouble, admitting I had fudged the truth became more and more difficult. After perhaps an hour Glenn sauntered out to see what was taking so long. One look at the situation was all he needed to know the truth. He asked, "You've never used one of those before, have you?" in a remarkably calm tone. I knew my inexperience was obvious, so I came clean. "No," I replied. Glenn said, "Well you should have said something! The torch is dangerous. You could have killed yourself!" Full of the ignorance of youth, I thought he was exaggerating. "Acetylene is very explosive. Just a small amount makes a big explosion," he said. Still not fully convinced, I shrugged it off.

To prove a point Glenn suggested a little experiment. I was instructed to put a small amount of oxygen and acetylene into an overturned foam coffee cup that had a small hole in the bottom and then to put the flame over the hole to ignite it. As I prepared the cup, Glenn ran to the other side of the shop and hid behind a desk. I thought he was just adding to the hoax and was sure this small cup would do no more than make a little poof. I was not completely sure however, so I tentatively put the flame from the torch over the cup. BOOM! I was knocked completely over and lay on the floor, looking up, dumbfounded.

It was on that day I learned two important lessons. First, the explosive power in a small coffee cup is nothing in comparison to what is inside the entire tank, and second, it is okay not to know how to do something, and to ask for help. The important lesson for every trainer is to remember that the student may not make an accurate assessment of his or her own skill, and it is always the trainer's responsibility to verify the performance level of the student. Of course we would not recommend that the trainer allow the student to conduct dangerous experiments, such as the one described here. The trainer must never place the student in a potentially dangerous situation and must keep a close watch on the student during the performance of the work. In this example, the student should not have been allowed to work alone with hazardous equipment until the trainer had confirmed mastery of the use of the equipment.

In other cases it is difficult for people to admit they don't know how to do the job they were hired for. The trainer must always make the final assessment during the tryout phase of the training. If the student indicated previous experience, the trainer should continue questioning to understand the depth of the student's knowledge (or lack thereof).

We now pick up on the training dialogue where we left off.

Trainer: Have you ever done this type of work before?

Student: Well, not exactly, but I did do something like this at another company.

Trainer: Okay, it is best if I just review everything to make sure you get it all and we don't miss anything you did not do at your last company. If I am going too fast or too slow, we can make adjustments.

Student: That sounds good. It never hurts to hear something twice.

Trainer: I want to make sure you understand how important this job is, and I don't want to miss any of the important information. (Transition to the next phase.)

Get the Student Interested in the Job

People like to feel a sense of importance about what they do. National surveys indicate that having a sense of purpose or doing meaningful work ranks at the top of employees' priority lists (above pay). Work that has no meaning offers no fulfillment. All work has some meaning, we just need to give the question more thought to find it. Providing meaningful work is of course different from expressing appreciation for the work done by employees. As trainers we want to express both to our students—why the work is important and the fact that we appreciate them for doing it.

First consider the work being done from the customer's perspective. Why is it important to the customer (both internal and external customers)? How does the work we do support our customer? What would happen if we did not deliver to the customer on time?

Does the product or service affect others in a significant way? For example, you may produce products for the medical industry that help to save lives, or you may produce a critical component for customer safety such as vehicle air bags. If your task is service-related, how does the service you provide help people?

Why is the job task important to your company? Is the product or service a popular item and a significant source of income for the company? Is the expectation for quality exceptionally high? Is your product a market leader? It may be necessary to explain the importance of a portion of the product in the context of the complete item and how important it is for the final product to look nice.

One technique that may be used to develop interest in the work is to take students to customer operations so they can see how their work affects the customer, and so they can see a sample of the finished product. The best way to get others interested in something is to be interested in it yourself. If you do not give the student a real sense that you care, how can you expect the student to care?

Continuing our training dialogue:

Trainer: I want to make sure you understand how important this job is. I will be showing you how to install the air-bag retainer. I'm sure you know how important the air bag is for the safety of passengers in the car. The retainer holds the air bag in place and provides the seal. Without the seal the bag would not work properly and would not protect the passenger in an accident. This is one of our most critical operations, so I am going to take my time to make sure you learn it properly.

Student: Okay, I'll give it my best.

Trainer: Good. Now I'd like you to stand here on my right side so you can see what I am showing you. (Transition to the next step.)

Put the Student in the Correct Position

There are a few problems we want to avoid. First is a condition known as "mirroring." This occurs when the student is observing the training from the opposite side of the trainer, facing the trainer. The problem with this position is the student is watching the operation in reverse—similar to looking in a mirror. If the trainer performs an operation with the left hand, the student will see the opposite and try to do the operation with the right hand. It is the same thing that happens when you tell people they have something on their face. If you are facing them and point to the right side of your face, they will likely reach for the side of their face opposite yours (their left side)—the mirror image. The same problem would occur if you try to teach a child to tie her shoes while facing her. The best way to teach this task is while reaching around the child so she sees your hands perform the task in the same orientation as hers.

Second, the student needs to be able to see the hand motions of the trainer. The trainer must be careful not to obstruct the student's view while presenting the operation. The trainer may need to move to the side (out of the normal position) to allow the student to see certain parts of the operation. Always position the student so they are facing the work in the same orientation as the trainer.

Continuing the training dialogue:

Trainer: Bob, I want to make sure you can see what my hands are doing, so on a few steps I'll lean out of the way so you can have a clear view.

Student: Okay.

Trainer: If you stand right here, I think you'll be able to see everything. Let me know if there's anything you can't see.

Student: Okay.

Trainer: (Transitioning to the next phase). Bob, I'm going to show you this job several times, and by the end I hope most of your questions will be answered, so please just watch and listen right now. If you have questions when I'm finished, I'll go over them then. Okay?

Student: Sure.

Trainer: All right. Let's get started. This job has five major steps I'll show you. (See Figure 12–1 for the complete job breakdown.)

JOB BREAKDOWN SHEET DATE: 3/18/20___	Roger Johns Team Leader	Mike DeSoto Supervisor
AREA: Air Bag Retainer	JOB: Airbag flange assembly	WRITTEN BY: Roger Johns

MAJOR STEPS	KEYPOINTS **SAFETY:** Injury avoidance, ergonomics, danger points **QUALITY:** Defect avoidance, check points, standards **TECHNIQUE:** Efficient movement, special method **COST:** Proper use of materials	REASONS FOR KEYPOINTS
Step # 1 Pick up the mounting plate	1. Locating hole facing right	1. Save time prealigning the hole for next step
Step # 2 Load mounting plate in rivet machine	1. Place mounting hole over locating pin 2. Mounting plate completely seated (green light on)	1. Proper orientation prevents errors 2. If not seated, rivet will not seat properly causing defect
Step # 3 Apply sealant	1. Begin at mounting hole 2. Bead $\frac{1}{4}$-inch wide	1. Location for sealant bead overlap 2. Too little sealant may not seal, too much will squeeze out and need to be removed, also excess cost
Step # 4 Cycle machine	1. Must be off safety mat	1. Out of hazard zone, machine won't run
Step # 5 Inspect part	1. Four rivets in place 2. Sealant on edges	1. Machine may miss one 2. Excess needs to be removed and indicates too much applied in step 3

Figure 12–1. Job breakdown for training dialogue example

Present the Operation: Tell, Show, and Demonstrate the Job

Now we are moving into the heart of the training presentation—step 2 of the four-step method where the operation is presented to the student. As the title implies, in this step you will tell the students the major step, show them how it is performed, and later demonstrate the key points and explain the reason why each key point is important. We should note here that we are presenting the training method in the best possible way—as presented by the original TWI material; however, in the reality of the busy workplace, the trainer must adapt accordingly. It is not often that a trainer will be blessed with ideal conditions for training, but remember the best results will be achieved if you follow the method closely.

Present the Major Steps

The training is conducted in three consecutive repetitions (minimum), with the first being the major steps only. It may be necessary to repeat the presentation of the major steps additional times if the task is especially complicated, or if the trainer is working on the line while training (see difficult training situations in Chapter 14). Notice in the training dialogue the trainer prepared the student to concentrate on the major steps by stating, "This job has five major steps." This specifies for the student the number of steps in the job and forms a clear expectation in the student's mind regarding what to expect. This same technique is also used when presenting the key points for each major step. The process of stating the number of steps and key points is important to solidify the details of the work in the student's mind.

The major steps are presented in three stages. State the major step, perform the step, pause and point a finger at where the work was done, for reinforcement, and restate the major step again. This follows the common training practice of stating what will be taught, teaching it, and then telling the student what was taught. Repetition of this type helps to reinforce the learning. The training dialogue would be as follows:

Trainer: The first major step is to pick up the mounting plate. (Silently pick up the mounting plate and orient according to the key point. While holding the mounting plate in hand, pause and then repeat the major step.) The first major step is to pick up the mounting plate.

Student: (Watching and listening only.)

Trainer: The second major step is to load the mounting plate in the rivet machine [silently place the mounting plate in the machine—emphasize the motion of orienting the mounting plate correctly (a key point) and point at the locating pin]. (Then repeat.) The second major step is to load the mounting plate in the rivet machine.

Student: (Watching and listening only.)

Trainer: The third major step is to apply the sealant (stop talking and apply the sealant making sure to emphasize all key points with gestures). (Repeat.) The third major step is to apply the sealant.

Notice that during the delivery of the major steps the trainer does not explain other aspects of the work. She only states the major step while performing the work. The trainer would continue presenting and performing each major step until the job is complete. During the presentation of major steps, the trainer never explains how to do the key points, but she emphasizes them as they are performed. Note that the trainer states the major step and then stops talking and performs the step without talking. This is because the acts of listening and looking utilize different parts of the brain, and we don't want the signals to get crossed in either the students' or trainers' brains. First hear, then see, and then hear again. This will implant the verbal and visual information in the student's brain.

Clearly Explain the Key Points

The job is repeated, and the major steps are presented again, and this time the key points for each major step are explained and demonstrated.

The presentation of key points is the most crucial aspect of the training process. Give your best effort during the presentation of key points because this step of the process will have the greatest bearing on your overall results. The presentation follows this format: Tell the major step; tell how many key points there are for the major step; state the first key point, and demonstrate how it is done while emphasizing any motions or techniques; state the second key point (if there is one), and demonstrate how it is done. Repeat for all key points. The training dialogue would be as follows:

Trainer: Bob, I'm going to repeat the job again, and this time I want to explain some important key points that describe how to do the major steps.

Student: Okay.

Trainer: The first major step is to pick up the mounting plate. There is one key point for this step. The key point is to orient the mounting plate so the locating hole (pointing to the hole) is facing the right side (demonstrate the step and key point).

Student: (Watching and listening only.)

Trainer: The second major step is to load the mounting plate in the rivet machine. There are two key points for this major step. The first key point is to place the mounting plate with the locating hole on the locating pin (pointing while demonstrating). The second key point is to make sure the mounting plate is completely seated (emphasize the feel and sound of the mounting plate seating completely). The green indicator light comes on indicating that the mounting plate is completely seated (pointing to the indicator light).

Student: (Watching and listening only.)

Trainer: The third major step is to apply the sealant. There are two key points for this major step. The first key point is to begin the application at the locating hole (show by pausing and pointing). The second key point is to apply a bead approximately $^{1}/_{4}$-inch wide (hold fingers approximately $^{1}/_{4}$ of an inch apart to show bead width) all the way around the mounting plate.

Notice that during the presentation the trainer tells the student how many key points there are with each major step. This prepares the student for the key points and helps him remember the key points. The trainer also states the major step, states the key point, and then performs the key point without talking just as she did during the presentation of the major steps.

Key Points Are Not Optional

Key points are quite simply the most crucial part of the job. They are not just "good things to do." Key points must be considered mandatory items necessary for the successful completion of the job. There are numerous items in any job that are necessary, perhaps even important, or most important—critical. A skilled trainer must decide which to stress as key points. If too many key points are presented, the most important ones may get lost in the crowd.

When teaching any job, there will be some items that will be self-explanatory and will not need to be explained by a key point. If the correct action can be seen and learned without explanation and there are no critical or important elements of a task, a key point is not needed. In the previous training dialogue, the first key point was to "orient the mounting plate." This key point ranks at a low level of importance. The mounting plate will need to be oriented, but if the key point were omitted, the trainer could convey this information through demonstration. The operator will learn to orient the mounting plate during the walk to the machine but will not need to think of this action as critical—just necessary.

The decision to include or exclude this type of information as a key point is at the discretion of the trainer because the orientation of the part is not critical in nature. It is not possible to insert the part in the machine if it is not oriented properly so it must be oriented. If the trainer decides not to include the part orientation as a key point, the student will discover on his first attempt of the job that the proper orientation is necessary. At that time the information will become "self-evident." The student will learn that part orientation is necessary for the successful completion of the job.

A minor point here is that orienting the part while it is being transported is an efficiency-improving key point. It is our experience that most people will pick up on this on their own, but some people will not. We prefer to include this type of key point if there are no other more critical items to stress because it sets the stage in the student's mind regarding the desired efficiency of motion. We like to condition the students from the beginning to think about making every motion count, and to make the best of a non-value-adding step. This is one way Toyota squeezes out a little extra efficiency without any extra effort on the part of the team member!

The idea that the work method may vary seems like a contradiction to standardized work. A common misconception about standardized work is that it means everyone will perform the work in *exactly* the same way. Based on our discussion here, we see that the steps of the job *must* be performed in the same order, the key points *must* be followed, and there are some items that can be performed differently based on the individual. The great majority of the job is not optional and will be performed in the same way, but there are some minor examples of variation. Let's face it, people are not machines! People have variation, and the skilled trainer needs to know how to help each person be successful on the job.

One common question we hear when teaching standardized work or Job Instruction is, "Do we need to specify as a key point whether the tool is picked up with the right hand or the left hand?" The answer to the question is more questions: "Does it matter?" "Does the method used change the outcome or result?" Suppose the operator moves in a path in the work area and the layout presents the tool on the right side. It would not make sense to pick up the tool with the left hand reaching across the body. The student would be able to see the trainer doing the task with her right hand and from observation learn the correct method. If for some reason the student attempted to pick up the tool with the left hand, the trainer would stop him and point out that the tool should be picked up with the right hand because of its placement in the work area. This is another example of an item that may be self-evident and may not require specifying the method by using a key point.

Knack key points are an example of where some personal variation may be involved. *Knacks* are special techniques that could be used to make the job easier, but a specific method may not be mandatory. In many cases there are several possible techniques that could be used which will all achieve the same end result—completing the job with worker safety, a product that is free of defects, the lowest cost, and correct production rate. The techniques used by different people may vary based on things such as height, strength, handedness (left-handed or right-handed), or dexterity.

Repeat the Job Again While Explaining the Reasons for the Key Points

The job is repeated in the same manner—state the major steps, stress the key points, and this time through, explain the reason for each of the key points. This step appears to be one of the main modifications that Toyota made to the Job Instruction method. The original TWI material did not include the identification of reasons for the key points. We are not sure how Toyota came to add this portion of the training, but we believe it serves an important role in developing "operator ownership" in the job.

The reasons for the key points provide a rationale so the student can completely understand why the work must be performed as described. It is common for some people to do a job and discover "better" methods (the basis for continuous improvement). However, the "better" method may not actually be better. Typically, the key points are such that there is not a lot of room for modification. Lining up a hole to an orientation pin for example is crucial to the job, and it is not likely that an operator will find an improvement to accomplish this. Maintaining a 1/4-inch bead of sealant is important for product quality, cost control, and, most important, the safety of the customer. Reducing the quantity (to save time and improve productivity) will increase the likelihood of defects (a customer safety issue) and is unacceptable. Likewise, increasing the quantity of sealant will increase the cost, potentially create defects (excess sealant on parts), and also negatively affect productivity (it takes longer to apply more material). There may be many potential improvements to be made in any work area, but the core content—the key points—are rarely changed unless there is a process change (new machine, parts, or materials). One caveat—this is only true if the correct key points have been identified. If you have carefully analyzed the work, and specified the critical items necessary for successful completion of the work, it is not likely you will drop the requirement for that key point.

Key points are items that are necessary for the successful completion of the work, and the reason given for them should support their importance. It is unlikely you will provide a reason for the key point that is too compelling. It is more likely that you will provide a reason that is closer to a "just because" reason. This must be avoided! If you do not know the reason something is done, you must find out. The reasons also provide a deeper understanding for the students of why they do what they do, and the student will develop a better knowledge of the work from this understanding. Note that in the job breakdown the reasons for key points are not written in full detail. There is just enough detail to jog the trainer's memory of what she is going to say.

We believe the explanation of the reasons for the key points is one portion of the training process where it is desirable to provide greater detail. The key points are the most critical parts of your work. It is difficult to overexplain how important they are and why it is necessary for everyone to follow the key points diligently.

The training dialogue continues: (Note that it gets longer with each repetition. This is the reason the amount of material taught in one session must be limited. If the job task has too many steps, the student [and perhaps the trainer] will be overwhelmed with the amount of material to cover and learn.)

Trainer: Bob, I want to go over the job again, and this time I want to explain why the key points are important. They are really the most critical part of the job, and it's important that you understand why you must follow them.

Student: Oh, Okay. I'll try to remember them all.

Trainer: Good. It can be a lot to remember all at once, so I'll help you out if necessary.

Student: Thanks.

Trainer: No problem. I want to make sure you're successful on this job. Now, let me go through it again. The first major step was to pick up the mounting plate. (Pick up plate while doing the key point.) There was one key point for that step. The key point was to orient the mounting plate so the locating hole (pointing to the hole) is facing the right side (demonstrate the step and key point). The reason for this key point is to save time and have the part lined up for loading into the rivet machine. You can do it as you are walking to the machine. This will help you to keep up once you are doing the entire job.

The second major step is to load the mounting plate into the rivet machine. There are two key points for this step. The first key point is to place the mounting plate with the locating hole on the locating pin (pointing while demonstrating). The reason for this key point is to properly locate the mounting plate. Placing the mounting plate on the locating pin prevents errors with alignment.

The second key point is to make sure the mounting plate is completely seated (emphasize the feel and sound of the mounting plate seating completely). You can hear a "click" when it seats, and it will feel solid in the fixture. The green light confirms that it is mounted properly. The reason for this key point is to make sure the mounting plate is fully seated, which will allow the rivet to crimp completely. If it does not crimp completely, a defective product may get to the customer. That is a major problem, and we will have to rework the part, which is a waste of our time. (The trainer continues in this manner until all major steps, key points, and reasons for the key points have been explained.)

Do Your Best

Leaders at Toyota continually remind all team members to do their best. The same applies to trainers. They are faced with challenging situations and are rarely provided with optimal conditions for training.

The Job Instruction method—especially the presentation of the operation to the student—takes considerable time and practice. Trainers must be adaptable and modify their method based on the situation at hand—always with the same objective—to do the best possible job of training with the current conditions.

Trainers must learn to evaluate their own methods based on the performance of the student. We will learn in the next chapter how to interpret the results of the training event and how to identify weaknesses that occur in the preparation and presentation of the operation.

The training now transitions to step 3 of the four-step Job Instruction method—try out performance. It is time for the student to try the job and to recite the major steps, key points, and reasons while performing the work. In this crucial phase, the trainer gets the first glimpse of whether all the preparation for the training and the presentation of information were effective. It is proof of either success or of the need to regroup and try again.

Chapter 13

Try Out Performance

An Opportunity for Reflection

After presenting the operation to the students, the time comes for them to try the task. Training Within Industry (TWI) referred to the third step of the four-step method as "try out performance." This is a critical stage for the trainer. It is the moment he or she will receive feedback indicating how effective the preparation and presentation of the operation to the student was. It is a chance to see the results and to stop to reflect on ways to improve the process for future events. The bottom line is this—if the student performs the job correctly, the training was effective. If not, the trainer must reflect, make adjustments, and correct any problems.

This does not imply failure on the part of the trainer. It is simply recognition that the ultimate success of the student is the responsibility of the trainer, no matter the reason. This is a perfect opportunity to learn more about the process. We may believe we have done a great job with preparation and our presentation was flawless, but if the student struggles, this is an indication of the need to change our approach and to improve it.

Keen Observation Is Required

During this stage of training, keen observation ability is necessary. The trainer must pay particular attention to the execution of all the key points and ensure no details are omitted from the job. One common mistake trainers often make is to lose focus during the student tryout portion of the training. The trainer may believe the important part of presenting the task is complete, and, therefore, the student has learned. Nothing could be further from the truth. Showing and explaining how to do the work is only the beginning. Real learning comes from repeated practice with additional coaching from the trainer.

When the student is attempting the work for the first time, the trainer must pay close attention to every action and detail. Other people or activities occurring in the work area must not distract him or her. All attention must be on the actions of the student. This is necessary to prevent the development of poor work habits by the student and to provide the necessary assistance to ensure success.

We have on some occasions witnessed trainers looking off into the distance and not paying attention to the student during the initial tryout of the work. Perhaps, the trainer does not want to appear to be overbearing or too critical by looking over the student's shoulder. This is an incorrect perception. The trainer must demonstrate through his actions that what the student is doing is very important. To avoid seeming too critical the trainer should simply explain that he needs to pay close attention in order to provide the proper coaching and ensure the student's success (always place the success of the student as a top priority). Perhaps the trainer could state, "I really want to pay attention to what you are doing so I can help you learn and to avoid any mistakes. I want to make sure you are successful on this job."

Instant Feedback

One of the nice things about on-the-job training is the immediacy of the feedback. This allows instant recognition regarding any area of the training process that needs improvement. Any shortcoming in results may be related to the preparation of the job breakdown, readiness for the training session, or the presentation of the training itself. If the trainer is sensitive to the signals, he or she will be able to adjust and make instant corrections and modifications for future training efforts. In particular the trainer must pay attention to what the student struggles with. For example, if the student is completely confused when attempting the task for the first time, it may be an indication that too much material was presented and the student was overwhelmed and got "lost." It may also indicate the steps of the job were not explained clearly and completely.

Student Performs the Task without Verbalizing Any Information

When the student performs the task for the first time, the trainer will get an overall understanding of the effectiveness of the training. During this stage, the trainee will perform the physical task without verbally explaining the job. This is a stressful time for the student. Separating the verbal and physical portions of the task allows the student to concentrate on one thing at a time. If the trainee is able to perform the task with only minor struggle, the trainer knows *understanding* of the job tasks was transferred successfully (one-half of the battle). Most often the student is able to understand the job task but is not able to completely verbalize what he or she is doing and how it is done.

We continue the training dialogue from the last chapter:

Trainer: Bob, I'd like you to try what I just showed you. You only need to do the task. Don't worry about explaining what you're doing the first time. Just try to do what I showed you so I can see how I need to help you.

Student: Okay. (Starts the job.) Well, the first thing I do is…

Trainer: (Gently interrupting) For the first try I just want you to do the task. Don't worry about saying anything.

Student: Oh, sorry. (Begins the job.)

Trainer: No problem. (Trainer continues to watch the student's performance and corrects any errors or provides assistance.)

Notice that the trainer did not ask the student, "Do you think you are ready to try?" This places the responsibility for the decision on the student. The responsibility for all decisions is always on the trainer. The trainer should ask the student to do the task and then evaluate the student's performance capability. The trainer must pay close attention and assess the situation looking for problems and deciding what actions to take. The following examples describe some of the most frequent problems that occur during the tryout stage of the training process and possible corrective actions for them.

Possible outcome: Student is completely lost and unsure of how to begin.

Possible causes: Too much material was presented at one time, or the material was not presented consistently (each time the order was changed, or the trainer mixed up the steps).

Possible solutions: Help the student with the first step to get him going. Sometimes the pressure of trying to remember everything causes temporary confusion. If the student is able to continue with only minor help (minor struggles are normal), the training was effective.

If the student is unable to continue with the second and subsequent steps, it is best to stop and regroup. It may be necessary to repeat the training in smaller portions. Continuing with a student who is completely lost will frustrate both the trainer and the student. It is best to apologize (assume responsibility for the outcome) and suggest perhaps the training was not clear and you will repeat it again.

Repeat about one-half of the presentation. Ensure you present one step at a time and in the correct order. Slow down the presentation and emphasize the steps and key points with gestures. It may also be possible the major steps are too broad (multiple steps combined). If so, separate the steps into smaller portions, and present them again. Repeat this process until the student is successful.

Possible outcome: Student has some difficulty performing specific portions of the task.

Possible causes: This may be normal for particularly difficult tasks and techniques. With experience the trainer will be able to distinguish between usual and unusual struggles and make adjustments accordingly. It is possible the key points for a step were not demonstrated effectively or the student has a challenge with a specific key point (for example a student may be shorter than the trainer and therefore unable to perform a task in the same manner).

Possible solutions: Redemonstrate the specific technique that is causing the trouble, and allow the student to try it once more. If the student is not successful on the second attempt, consider demonstrating a slightly different technique (this is when the trainer must be creative and flexible in her approach). It may help to take the student's hand and guide him through the motions (always explain what you are going to do before grabbing someone's hand). Off-line simulations may be useful to allow the student to practice and develop skill without the pressure of performing the task in an actual work situation.

When the student is capable of performing the physical portion of the task with only minor struggle, it is time to move to the next step. The trainer may opt to have the student perform the task several more times without talking. This will allow the physical portion of the task to become ingrained prior to taxing the brain with the dual tasks of verbal and physical actions.

Student Performs the Task While Repeating the Major Steps

During the next stage, the student will perform the task again while stating the major steps. This will require the student to utilize both visual and verbal capabilities, and some mistakes in the verbal portion are considered normal. The student may not be able to repeat the major steps or key points exactly as stated. It is important that the student has a solid understanding of the task, but it is more important that he or she is able to perform it flawlessly. If the trainer attempts to correct the student too many times because the major steps and key points are stated incorrectly, the student may become frustrated and feel that the trainer is being overbearing.

A simple misstep by the student such as stating, "Put the parts together," when the major step was actually, "Assemble the parts," may be corrected by restating after the student, "Yes, the major step was to assemble the parts," as a reminder. It is always imperative to remember that responsibility for the final outcome is borne by the trainer. Being too picky with the verbal portion of the task will put people off, but it is also important that the student has a clear understanding of what to do and how to do it. It is a fine line the trainer must learn to walk.

Continuing the training dialogue: (Note: the trainer may decide to have the student perform the job silently a few more times before moving to the next step. The student should have a good grasp of the task before moving on. It is not a problem to do more repetitions.)

Trainer:	Bob, that was good. You had a few struggles with a step or two, but that is normal when you're learning a new skill. We'll keep working on them until you can do them without any problems. Now what I'd like you to do is repeat the job again. And this time tell me the major steps as you do the job.
Student:	Okay. Well, the first thing I did was to pick up this part.
Trainer:	(Gently interrupting) Yes, that's called the mounting plate.
Student:	Oh, right. Pick up the mounting plate.
Trainer:	(Encouraging) Good.
Student:	The second thing I did was put the mounting plate in the machine.
Trainer:	Ok, that's right. You loaded the mounting plate into the rivet machine.

Note that the trainer is correcting the terminology—from "part" to "mounting plate," and "machine" to "rivet machine." This also repeats the step again and reinforces it in the student's mind. There will be plenty of opportunity to coach terminology and develop deeper understanding during the follow-up phase.

We have listed some of the typical problems encountered during the tryout portion of the training and possible solutions to them. This is a challenging time for the trainer because she must be able to judge the difference between normal learning challenges and the student's inability resulting from poor training or even weak capability. If exactly the same training presentation were given to multiple students simultaneously (as we do in the classroom demonstration), there would be varying degrees of performance ability. The primary skill for the trainer to develop is the ability to coach students through to success. The following is a possible outcome and some suggestions for correcting any problems encountered during this stage of the training.

Possible outcome: Student can perform the job reasonably well, but can't verbally state the major steps.

Possible causes: This may be a normal block between the visual and auditory portions of the brain. Processing visual and verbal information simultaneously is challenging. The solution may be to help the student through the task a few times. If the student is completely unable to verbalize any of the steps, the training must be repeated. Try repeating only one step at a time.

This problem may also indicate the occurrence of extraneous conversation by the trainer during the presentation. Trainers often get sidetracked and tell the student nonrelated information about the job or workplace and explain the major steps and key points in a conversational style. If irrelevant information is presented during the training, it will overwhelm the student and limit their recall ability. Normally, if the steps are given succinctly, the student will not have trouble repeating them.

Another common cause of struggle at this stage is due to the trainer "blending" major steps, key points, and reasons during the presentation. It is a challenge for the trainer to state only the major steps during the first presentation, and to *do* the key point, but not to explain *how* to do it until the second presentation. The trainer must learn to resist the normal tendency to explain the entire job at one time.

Possible solutions: Major steps and key points should be presented as simple statements. Other information must not be introduced into the training presentation, and the trainer must "stay on task." For example, a trainer may be demonstrating a task and realize the student needs to "clock in" on the job. The training is interrupted and sidetracked while the clock-in procedure is explained.

During the clock-in procedure the trainer realizes he does not have the job number and must call to get it. Soon the presentation is a complete jumble in the student's mind. Again, we emphasize the importance of upfront preparation.

The presentation method is very specific. During the first presentation of the task, it is important to *only* present the major steps. When presenting the task the second time, the major steps are repeated and the key points are explained. The reasons for the key points are explained on the third presentation of the task. (Note: The trainer may decide to increase the number of repetitions for each step before proceeding to the next one, but the total number of repetitions should not be less than three.)

Student Performs the Task While Repeating the Major Steps and Key Points

Now the student is challenged with remembering and repeating some details of the work. It is normally relatively easy to state the major steps because it is only necessary to state in general terms what is being done. Stating the key points, however, requires a deeper understanding of the work, and they must be expressed in detail. The student is likely thinking, "What was that she told me to do and to pay attention to?" Three things are going on in the student's brain. The brain still needs to "tell" the body how to perform the task (muscle memory has not been achieved yet), the verbal portion of the brain must recall the content of what was said, and finally the student must put it all together in the correct words. The student will be intent on "getting it right" and may be worried about doing and stating the job correctly.

Consider the party game when a message is started at one end of the table and passed along to the other end. When the final message is repeated, it has little resemblance to the original message. It is extremely difficult to repeat exactly what has been stated, even if it is only a few sentences. In the case of an entire job, it is virtually impossible for the student to repeat all information precisely on the first attempt.

Also, the Job Instruction method is a new experience for people. They are not used to this much attention during a training session. In past experiences they were shown the job a few times and then asked to give it a try. The training was not so detailed, and the immediate expectation not so high. Remember to keep the students relaxed and to provide encouragement. Too much correcting may make them feel as though they are doing nothing right and may lead to frustration. The following is a possible outcome and some suggestions for correcting any problems encountered during this stage of the training.

Possible outcomes: Performs the job with the key points but can't repeat them back.

Possible causes: This may be a normal response, especially for complex jobs. If the trainer insufficiently stressed the key points during the training presentation, it may be difficult for the student to differentiate them from other conversation. In addition, the key points may have been omitted or blended together by the trainer.

Possible solutions: The most effective method for stressing the key points during the presentation is to "pause and point," or use accentuated body movement while stating the key point. The combined seeing and hearing helps to lock the key point into the student's brain. The trainer must state the key points clearly with a statement such as, "The key point is," followed by a short statement. Most students will need some reminders to help them remember the verbal portion of the key points. If the student is able to physically perform the key points while doing the task but is unable to verbalize them, additional coaching may be provided during the follow-up stage. It is possible to move to the next stage of the training provided the student is correctly performing the work.

Verify Understanding of the Reasons for Key Points

One modification to the Job Instruction method Toyota made was the inclusion of reasons for the key points. The reasons play an important role because they force the trainer to test the validity of what is critical to complete the task properly. They also provide the student with an understanding of why certain items are required. Providing a valid reason for key points will cause the student to want to follow them exactly as demonstrated rather than to deviate from them.

From experience however, we have concluded that verification of understanding of the reasons for key points is best done in small amounts over time. If a student is expected to remember all major steps, key points, and the reasons for key points, he or she will likely have some difficulty recalling every detail. We believe the most important aspect of the training is the student's ability to perform the job. Verbalizing the whats, hows, and whys is necessary to implant a thorough knowledge in the student's mind, but this knowledge may also be developed during the follow-up stage. Rather than badger a student to repeat all information during the initial tryout, we suggest gradual and repeated reminders over the first few weeks on the job until all the knowledge is attained.

As previously stated, if the student is able to develop muscle memory of the task, the brain is then free to concentrate on learning the verbal portion of the job. During follow-up coaching the trainer may ask simple questions such as, "Do you remember what the key points are for that step?" and "Can you remember why that key point is important?" If the student is unable to recall, the trainer may reemphasize the information. We have found in nearly all cases it is necessary to do some follow-up questioning regardless of how well the student recalled the information during the training. The day after the training event some of the information (and skill) may have been lost. Keep repeating the process until the task is completely memorized and performed without mistakes.

Correct Errors Immediately to Prevent Bad Habits

It is said, "You have one chance to make a first impression." We would add that you have one chance to prevent the development of bad work habits. Experts theorize it takes 21 days to break a habit. We theorize that those bad habits may be developed on the first attempt to perform a task! There is only one chance to get it right. This is why keen observation and providing support and correcting any errors immediately are so important. The trainer must be quick to act.

One challenge is to distinguish between normal difficulty in performing the task and an error. If the student is performing the task correctly but has not yet mastered the knacks, he may be allowed to continue with only additional suggestions for learning the knacks. If, however, the student is making an error—omitting a step or incorrectly performing a key point—he or she must be stopped and corrected immediately. Some students will react negatively to being "helped," so it is a fine line for the trainer. It is not acceptable to allow mistakes to occur. A trainer must not be afraid to challenge a student, but the trainer had better be certain of the correct method because a strong-willed student may challenge the trainer.

Assess Capability

Throughout the tryout stage the trainer is continually assessing capability and considering the ability of the student to work safely, without errors, and at the proper pace. The trainer must now make a crucial decision. She must decide when the student is ready to work independently. In most cases this will not be an all-or-nothing transition. The trainer may decide to share responsibility for the task with the student and to gradually relinquish more of the task over to the student. This is purely a judgment call by the trainer, but given the ultimate responsibility for the outcome, the trainer has a vested interest. If the trainer delays the full release of the student, she will have to maintain focus on the training (a distraction from other responsibilities). If the trainer releases the student prematurely, she increases exposure to potential problems later.

A possible alternative is to release the student under the watchful eye of another skilled person. We advise that the trainer request others in the work area (the next operation if applicable) to keep an eye out for potential safety and quality problems.

Give Students Responsibility, but Keep an Eye on Them

Every student must eventually be placed on the job and expected to work without direct supervision. This is similar to sending your children to school for the first time. You will be apprehensive, perhaps have some reservations, but you know it is time for them to go out on their own. Still, you will want to keep a close eye on the situation to make sure no problems develop.

We have used a repetitive manufacturing job as an example but we again want to point out this is only one example. The same principles of job breakdown, key points, preparation, and how to teach, apply to any type of job. For example, in our line of work we are often responsible for developing an internal "lean coordinator" who will carry on the company's transformation effort. Whether it is teaching how to develop standardized work, lead a set-up reduction activity, or do value stream mapping, the same four-step Job Instruction process applies. But how often does training happen with anywhere near the rigor we described for this relatively simple and repetitive manual job? Our experience is *rarely*. It is more likely that the lean consultant does the activity and then assigns it to the internal coordinator with encouraging words like "you will be fine." The internal coordinator may then work unsupervised and is asked to present what they did, after the fact, to the outside expert. The instruction and feedback while doing the work is notably absent.

In Chapter 15 we continue the four-step method with a discussion of step 4—the follow-up step. Students are not kicked out of the nest. They must be encouraged to take on more responsibility and be supported until they are capable of working on their own. But before we get to step 4 in Chapter 15, in Chapter 14 we examine some especially challenging training situations that may be encountered. Every training event will present some challenges, but there are a few situations that will challenge even the most experienced trainer.

Chapter 14

Handling Challenging Training Situations

No One Said It Was Going to Be Easy

We detailed the training process in Chapters 12 and 13. It obviously requires great discipline and is very time-consuming to do it all right. If all goes according to the textbook, it is a marvelous experience for everyone involved and leads to reliable and repeatable performance that drives quality managers to a state of nirvana. But it is not always straightforward, and we do not always have all the time needed to do it right. There is no "perfect world."

In this chapter we review some special training challenges that are often encountered. Training Within Industry (TWI) refers to them as "special instruction problems" and briefly discusses how to handle them in the Job Instruction class. Toyota places more emphasis on these situations because they have direct relevance to the work being done at Toyota. We believe that what TWI calls "special" problems are more the norm rather than the exception and, therefore, deserve additional comment.

Training people is one of the most challenging tasks because of the variation inherent in each situation. Every training session will vary because of the difficulty of the job, the learning capability of the student, or a number of other issues that may arise. A skilled trainer must be able to continuously adjust his or her method as challenges occur. Fortunately many of the challenges are similar in nature, and the trainer can master a few techniques that may be applied to a wide variety of situations.

In any training situation there is an "ideal situation" that will be best; however, it is not always possible to achieve the ideal condition because of extenuating circumstances. Always strive to use the best possible method, and only step down to a lesser method when there is no alternative. The following are some common training challenges that might be encountered. Learning how to handle these challenges may give you ideas on how to deal with other situations you will face.

Training at Line Speed

Training at line speed is a challenge in virtually every workplace. A person does not have to work on an assembly line for this to apply. (Remember that the original TWI material and terminology, which we are using here, was intended for use in manufacturing workplaces. We maintain the same terminology, but expand the *concept* to apply to all workplaces.) This situation refers to the fact that most tasks have a desired pace or time limit, and the work pace will not necessarily stop for training to take place. The work needs to be completed *while* the student learns and becomes proficient. Some jobs are not part of a connected flow like an assembly line and may have a greater degree of flexibility, but there are generally both a desired pace and an amount of work to be completed in a specific time period. In the case of salaried employees they may have to work additional hours if they do not learn to complete their work in the desired time frame. If an engineer does not meet the planned pace for designing a new product, the entire project may be delayed, and hundreds or thousands of others will be delayed as a result.

Training at line speed is especially challenging in an assembly line situation where the worker is connected via a conveyor belt to other workers or to machinery. At Toyota it is crucial to train team members while the line maintains a steady pace because of the connected nature of the entire operation to a shared takt time.

A classic example of how many people view training for an "assembly line" operation is the television show *I Love Lucy*, in which Lucy and Ethel go to work at the chocolate factory. The supervisor teaches them (a rather brief "training") to inspect the chocolates while the line is moving very slowly. Lucy and Ethel think the job will be a snap and settle in comfortably. Gradually, the line speed increases, and more chocolates begin to appear. Overwhelmed, Lucy and Ethel attempt every means of keeping up, beginning with working faster, and then eating chocolates, and finally stashing them in their clothes. The supervisor appears and sees that Lucy and Ethel are "keeping up" and shouts, "Speed it up!" which is of course, the punch line. Unfortunately, this view of life in a factory is commonly held and in many cases the experience of workers is just that—a very short training period followed by a quick toss into the fire.

When we are working with companies, we are surprised to see a person who is obviously struggling to keep up (often evidenced by others waiting, or by material piling up around the person). When we inquire about the situation, the supervisor or tour guide usually offers this explanation, "Oh, they are just learning that job, and it takes awhile before people can keep up. Usually they get the hang of it in a few weeks." This shocks us for two reasons. First, an important tenet of the Job Instruction method is that a student should never be left on his own unless he is capable of performing the work safely, with acceptable quality, and is able to maintain the correct pace. People left to struggle on their own prematurely will certainly feel as though they have been left to fend for themselves and that they are not cared for (and may begin to develop "bad attitudes"). This may also contribute to a high turnover rate among new hires. Not to mention the fact that in the training period they may create defects in the products.

Second, other workers may develop resentment toward the initiate if he does not progress quickly enough to satisfy their own individual expectations or the student's lack of ability affects their own pace.

A straight cost–benefit analysis will generally show it is cheaper in the long run to provide adequate support during the training period than the resulting cost of slowing the pace of the entire process. Of course everyone progresses at a different rate, but employees tend to judge the capability of others in comparison to their own ability. The judgment of capability is best left to the trainer who has the responsibility of helping the person master the skill and develop the correct work pace. In this way the trainer also has a vested interest. If trainers fail to adequately train the students, they will need to support them for a longer period and will take time away from their other responsibilities.

For this example we assume the job pace is fast and that stopping the line because of a slow operator is not acceptable. The techniques used here would not be necessary if the task is simple or if there is no risk to the safety of the student or the quality of the product. This is an example for handling a fast-paced work situation.

The student and the trainer would go to the workplace to observe the work being done by a skilled person. This will provide the student with an overall understanding of the work content and the necessary pace of the work. While observing (but not actually doing the work), the trainer is able to explain the major steps and key points to the student. The best method is to watch actual work, but if this is not possible or practical for some reason (see communication barriers later in the chapter), a videotape of the work may be used. This method is certainly not sufficient for actually learning the skill, but it is sufficient to convey the basic knowledge.

The next step involves an "off-line" simulation that allows the student to experience the work activity without doing the actual work. If the parts are relatively easy to move off-line for practice, a mock-up of the work area can be set up so the pressure of the line speed is removed from the student and risk to the student or product is minimized. At Toyota, new hires would not be handed a screw gun and placed on the line to install screws. They might first practice on a piece of wood or a test body until they were able to use the tool without damaging the vehicle (see more detailed explanation of off-line training in the description of the Global Production Center in Chapter 2).

This method is also useful in situations in which the job task is especially difficult or there are specific knacks that must be learned in order to maintain the correct pace and quality. The actual work may be simulated by using scrap parts as training aids. At Toyota, when a new vehicle model is launched, there are only a few parts to use for training during the early phases of production. In order to facilitate the training and increase the number of repetitions for the trainee, the parts are assembled, disassembled, and then reassembled again, over and over. (Of course these parts are scrapped—they are used for training purposes only.) In the paint department students would practice their spray-painting technique on steel panels so that they could develop the proper gun speed, distance from the part, and angle to hold the spray gun. If students were expected to learn the art of painting on the line during regular production, they would likely make many costly and time-consuming errors that are very difficult to correct.

A variation of this concept may be used when the work is not done in assembly line fashion or when there is only one station or machine on which to learn. The training may be conducted either before or after the shift. This allows the student time to master the skill without the pressure of the immediate production requirements.

After the basic skills are mastered off-line, the student and trainer would work in conjunction with the current operator if possible (see Figure 14–1). The trainer and student would position themselves between operations on the line and assume a portion of the operation from the regular operator (A). This must be communicated to the regular operator so he or she is able to modify the standardized work, and also the following operator (B) would be instructed to help check and verify that the trainer/student team did the work correctly (additional checks are important because the trainer is concentrating on the trainee and may overlook something). As the student progresses, the work will shift from the regular operator to the student, with the trainer continuing to observe and instruct, and the following operator double-checking the completed work.

In some situations it may not be practical to simulate the training off-line, and the only choice is to conduct the training on-line right in the thick of things. Depending on the situation at the time, the trainer

Figure 14–1. Placement of trainer and student between regular operators

may be presented with few options. If the line is fully staffed, the work-sharing method described in Figure 14–1 may be used. If there is a shortage of people, it may not be possible to use the work-sharing method. In this situation the trainer must assume full responsibility for the actual work *and* the training effort.

This is the least desirable situation because the trainer must divide her attention between teaching, observing the student, and completing the remaining work. This is particularly challenging because these activities each use different parts of the brain, and combining these activities is akin to patting your head while rubbing your stomach. It is possible, but it requires intense concentration!

This method is also challenging because the trainer must teach a portion of the job, and the student will perform it at a slower pace than is required to meet the line rate, so the trainer must make up the time loss on the remainder of the job. We often see a trainer patiently waiting for the student to complete the task (much slower than the required pace) while the work piles up. This is a mistake. Students will naturally be slower in the beginning, but the trainer must always make sure the overall work pace is maintained.

A skilled trainer may be able to perform the work at a faster pace for short periods and may need the student to step aside for a few minutes in order to catch up if they are falling behind the pace. This will increase the training duration, as small portions of the job are introduced bit by bit. When faced with this situation, the trainer must adjust and will only be able to give the student very small portions of the work at one time.

Teaching Longer or Complex Jobs

One key point of the Job Instruction method is the teacher should "present no more than the student can master" during any training

David Meier's Experience as a New Hire at Toyota

In 1987 I was fortunate to travel to Japan and to be trained for various jobs in Toyota's Plastics operation. The Plastics department is not tied directly to the main vehicle assembly line, but there was a necessary pace to keep the flow moving and to keep the assembly line supplied. Being an eager student, I wanted to prove I was capable of doing the job and put all my attention on the job task. In one particular situation I replaced the regular operator on the job, and I understood the pace was important. I worked conscientiously (as most new hires attempt to do) and thought I was doing well because my trainer was encouraging me. After what seemed like an hour or two (but actually had only been 20 minutes or so), my trainer tapped me on the shoulder and motioned me to step aside from the job. I was confused until he pointed to a large quantity of parts that had been accumulating because I had been too slow! I thought I had been working very hard and had been doing a great job, when in actuality I had gradually been falling behind. I also discovered (much to my dismay) that the regular operator had been double-checking all of my work to ensure I had not produced any defective products (and I later understood how important this checking was). The regular operator stepped back into the job and within a short time had the pile cleaned up and the line condition back to normal. This example taught me that even the best-intentioned trainee with good skills is not likely to maintain the pace initially and must be supported. I also learned that the trainer must ultimately be in control of the entire situation and is responsible for the final outcome.

session. One common mistake is to try to teach everything that is needed to do the job, in one session. This generally results in a dazed and confused look on the student's face because he or she has been overloaded with information. When teaching long or complex jobs, the trainer must first break the job down into manageable pieces and present the pieces gradually over time. This is similar to the challenge of teaching at line speed. A long or complex job requires the presentation of small amounts of material over a longer period of time.

Generally speaking, the average person can handle a training session of approximately 30 minutes in length, which includes the presentation of the job and the practice of the job by the student. The rough breakdown is about 15 minutes of teaching followed by 15 minutes of practice by the student. During the training the student is concentrating on listening, watching what is being done, and then focusing on doing what was seen and heard. Most people will have trouble recalling what they saw and heard more than about 15 minutes ago, and they will begin to worry they are forgetting, which makes the situation worse.

To put this into some perspective, a job with a cycle time of approximately 15 seconds or less can normally be taught in a single training session. This depends on the complexity and number of steps, but it is a general guideline. A job with a duration of approximately one minute may be taught in three or four training sessions. These sessions may be part of a large training block, but each segment should follow the pattern of presenting a section and allowing the student to practice what was learned while developing some level of mastery prior to moving to the next segment.

As we have mentioned previously, there are few hard and fast rules, and the trainer must always observe the result and adjust the training method accordingly. For some people you may not give enough at one time, and they will become impatient and want to move faster. A smaller portion may be too much for others. It is necessary to "read" the situation and make modifications during the training presentation.

It may be advisable to teach longer and more complex jobs in small segments in a sequence that is different from the actual work sequence. For example, let's say a job has four segments to teach. It may be better to teach segment number 3 prior to teaching segments 1 and 2. Perhaps segment 3 is easier to learn or requires the least amount of work. If the trainer only has a short time available for training, it may be beneficial to train this shorter segment out of the regular work sequence.

For our discussion when we indicate "training," we mean steps 1, 2, and 3 of the four-step method. We are referring to the portion of the training activity in which the knowledge of the work is transferred. Much more time is needed to actually develop full skill on the job *after* the knowledge and information are transferred to the student (step 4 of the four-step method). Skill development may take days, weeks, or even months during which the trainer must continue to provide support as needed.

Training When Time Is Limited

One thing is for sure—there will never be enough time available to do training the way you want. There are some special circumstances every trainer will face. These techniques are best reserved for times of some desperation—times when there is a shortage of skilled workers and you need critical to do whatever is necessary in the most important short-term to get through. It is critical for the trainer to focus on the most important content of the task with the time available.

The worst-case scenario is when there are several people absent at the same time and there are not enough trained people to meet the immediate requirement. One way to be effective with a limited amount of time is to identify in advance, simple, entry-level work that can be learned quickly. Toyota calls these "freshmen jobs," and they are the first jobs given to new hires and temporary workers used to supplement the full-time labor force. The skilled workers can be shifted to the more complex tasks, while the easy task is taught to a new hire or temporary person (who is often a full-time employee borrowed from another work group).

It is especially important when time is limited to distill the job down to the most important points. If you are in a bind, it is possible to quickly convey the crucial points of the job. Students will not become completely proficient with the work, but they will be able to fill the immediate need. You will discover that in training sometimes less is more—give the student less information overall, but make it the most critical information.

In this situation it is necessary to "do what you have to do," but the burden of responsibility is never shifted. If a team member is given limited training and left prematurely to do the work, the trainer assumes full responsibility for the outcome. If there is a quality problem, the trainer must take responsibility because it is the trainer who made the decision to put the team member on the job without complete training (even though the trainer may have had "no choice"). We certainly don't recommend this practice, but it is often a reality, and with careful consideration any negative impact can be minimized.

Trainers may be able to position themselves on the line in the following operation (nearby) so they can keep a close watch and provide some support to the trainee. Skilled trainers are always seeking ways to do the best they can with the reality they face in the moment. Be careful though, that your "reality" is not just a lightly veiled excuse for poor performance. Reality will always force you to make decisions. Make sure your decisions are the best ones possible and they produce the best possible outcome.

Jobs That Require Special Skills and Techniques

The Training Within Industry material originally referred to special skills and techniques as "knacks" or "tricks of the trade." In addition to knacks, there are specialized movements that are difficult to learn. One example is spray painting. Spray painting (especially of a high-quality finish) requires expert skill. The painter must control the speed of movement, the distance from the surface, and the angle of the spray gun as well as the triggering and release of the spray gun at the correct time. If the movement is too slow, runs and sags may develop. Too fast, and the resulting coating may be too thin. If the distance from the surface is too great, the surface finish may not be smooth and glossy. Holding the spray gun too close may result in runs and sags, and also the number of spray passes is increased because the spray area is reduced (this would add time and cost).

The traditional learning method would involve the trainee watching someone and listening to the explanations of the key points. Then the student would try the job while the instructor provides feedback. In this method the student would need to practice until he achieved the right "feel" and would then lock the memory of that feel in the brain and body. This can be time-consuming as the information is first perceived visually, transmitted to the brain where it is processed, and the signal for action is sent back out to the hand. This back-and-forth feedback loop between the brain and hand will continue until the correct result is achieved.

One effective method for shortening the practice time is for the trainer to guide the student's hand through the motions. The trainer stands beside the student and holds his hand as the motion is completed (always ask the student before taking his hand). With this method the student can see the correct action with the eyes and sense it with the body, and the signals are sent back to their brain. With a few repetitions the correct motion and feel are stored in the brain and body thereby reducing the try—see—adjust—try again—see—adjust—do, pattern to, try—feel and see—adjust—do. This is not a perfect method because the trainer is slightly out of position for his or her own muscle memory orientation. It may be necessary to guide the student's hand for only the most difficult tasks and not the entire job.

In addition to the guided-hand technique, the trainer may place greater emphasis on the specific key points by accentuating the motions or dramatizing them, pausing for effect at a certain point so correct positioning can be seen, or increasing the number of repetitions. The trainer may perform the motion more slowly and even stop mid-motion so the student can see the entire body posture. The trainer may indicate the positioning of the feet, the bend of the legs, the angle of the wrist and arm, and so on. Special techniques are virtually impossible to define in words. They must be seen and tried before they can be learned. The trainer must take extra care to fully understand the details when breaking down the job.

These special techniques are part of what we refer to as the "know how" of the job. They apply not only to manual manufacturing work but other types of work as well. For example, a Japanese vice president of engineering who was sent to set up the European technical center for Toyota said his most intense learning experience was when he was at the drawing table for six months side by side with an experienced interior trim designer. They both took portions of the same automotive dashboard, and the senior designer guided him through the design process. Much of what he was learning day in and day out were the special techniques of drawing as well as special techniques related to interior trim. The challenge of the vice president was to replicate that learning process for the new hires in Europe. One approach was to send them on "internships" to Japan for up to one or two years to learn from these master engineers.

Training When Oral Communication Is Limited

Today's work environment provides many barriers to oral communication as the primary means of transferring job knowledge. Many workforces are multicultural, and a common language is not spoken (this was a challenge in learning jobs from the Japanese at Toyota), and some work areas require that protective gear be worn (respirators or full body suits) that limits oral communication, while other work areas have very high noise levels. In these situations the trainer must learn to communicate the critical information without talking.

The communication of the work steps is fairly easy. The student will be able to see what is being done and can mimic that activity. The key points may be communicated with techniques such as pointing and pausing, or exaggerated motions, and even the reasons may be demonstrated without speaking using pantomime or demonstrating the outcome of key points that are performed correctly and incorrectly. Again we stress the need for trainers to be adaptable to the specific environment and to develop effective methods for the situation at hand, which is likely to vary from person to person and job to job.

In this situation let's assume there is a communication barrier such as the requirement that a respirator be worn, but there is no language barrier. It is possible for the trainer to orally communicate with the student—just not in the actual work area while the work is performed.[1] The trainer may use a videotaped recording of the job and explain the steps, key points, and reasons as the tape is played. This method is not recommended for general training because the videotape is limited in its viewing range, and it is difficult to see the details. The student is not able to move closer for a better look and may not see the detail necessary. This technique is good for explaining the high-level aspects of the work, but the details will need to be learned at the workplace.

There are some techniques that should be utilized during any training but which can be applied with greater emphasis, or as the primary communication mode, in these situations. One approach often used by Toyota trainers is the "pause-and-point" method to emphasize a key point. The pause is for effect—to indicate a specific thing or event. The pointing indicates what is being emphasized. An example is the placement of parts in a machine. The key points are related to the correct placement of the parts. A finger is pointed to indicate the correct orientation, or if the part is located on a pin, the finger is pointed to show placement on the pin.

There are several variations on this theme including holding up fingers to indicate the step number (hold up two fingers to indicate step 2) and using the fingers to trace a motion or pattern. Exaggerating critical motions or movements, dramatizing and gesturing, pointing, and other "sign language" may be used. In addition some techniques that have been discussed previously may be used as well, including breaking the job into smaller training pieces, increasing the number of repetitions, and guiding the student's hand as the task is performed.

Teaching Visual Tasks

Inspection tasks are unique in that they are largely visual—the eyes rather than the hands are making the movements. This is a challenge for the trainer because she will need to show the students where their eyes should

---

[1] There are communication devices for this situation that may be helpful, such as the headsets worn by motorcyclists. In an explosive environment, such as a painting booth, any electronic devices must be approved as safe for the environment.

be focusing, and also when the student performs the task, the trainer must confirm that the student's eyes are following the correct path.

We have observed numerous trainers teaching an inspection task. While telling the student to, "inspect the part," the trainer might hold the part, turn it this way and that, hold it up to view at an angle, and so forth, but will never provide the actual path for the eyes to follow. In the case of inspecting larger parts, we see trainers bending down to view at the correct angle, sweeping their hands across the surface, even stopping now and then to review a potential defect. This should not be done when trying to teach the inspection pattern because it is an interruption and a distraction from the training. For inspection tasks it is important to separate the inspection task, "how to look" from, "what to look for." Upon tryout of the job, the student will try to emulate the trainer, also moving the part this way and that, or bending down to try to copy the trainer's posture.

The first step for the trainer, then, is to identify the correct path for the eyes to follow. This is dependent on whether the inspection is a "spot" type or an overall surface inspection. Spot inspections are intended to identify specific areas where problems are likely to occur. These problems are location-specific—they will always occur in the same place. A problem with a missing screw, for example, can occur only where the screw is to be inserted. Other defects such as cracks or damage may happen in specific locations as well. For these situations the point-and-pause method mentioned previously can be used. The trainer points to the specific location when explaining the job, and the student will also point while performing the job. In fact, the act of pointing is part of the job and should be done as a regular part of the task. For spot inspections Toyota often uses a "yoshi," a Japanese word that translates roughly as "check." This is similar to airplane pilots conducting a preflight inspection. The pilot calls out an item, the copilot verifies, points, and calls out "check."

The act of pointing while looking requires a different connection in the brain and will aid in the prevention of "blind inspection," a condition that allows a person to look directly at something but not to see it. We have all experienced the situation in which a defect is passed to the customer is so obvious we all wonder how it could get past the opertor. This is why it happens. This effect is similar to muscle memory because the eyes are looking and the brain is "seeing" based on memory, but is actually not processing the current situation. It is a state of hypnosis and is a common occurrence in repetitious work. Pointing with the finger breaks the pattern in the brain and requires attention to the matter at hand. (It also provides a visual indicator to leaders that the task is being performed because the pointing is visible, while the eye movement is not.) For especially critical tasks at Toyota the operator may use a "grease pencil" to mark a location indicating that the task had been performed (of course this was done only on nonvisible surfaces such as tie-rod nuts).

There are two categories of inspection tasks. In-process inspection—an inspection step as part of another task—and inspection as the entire task. The in-process inspection may be specified as one major step of the task. For example the major step may be, "Inspect the air bag cover." If the entire task were an inspection (usually a more thorough inspection by an "inspector"), the task would be broken down into multiple major steps. The inspector would be responsible for a more complete inspection possibly including dimensional checks, color checks, surface finish, and so forth. For this discussion we are focusing on the visual portion of the in-process inspection, but the same concepts can be applied to inspection jobs.

Visual surface inspection requires the movement of the eyes over a specific pattern. The pattern must be defined based on the following criteria:

1. The pattern should include any spot locations where specific defects will occur.
2. The pattern is based on the focal width of vision (how much area can be seen at one time).

Figure 14–2 depicts an inspection pattern that includes both spot locations as well as an entire surface inspection. The visual path followed by the eyes is determined based on the location of spot checks and the focal width of vision.

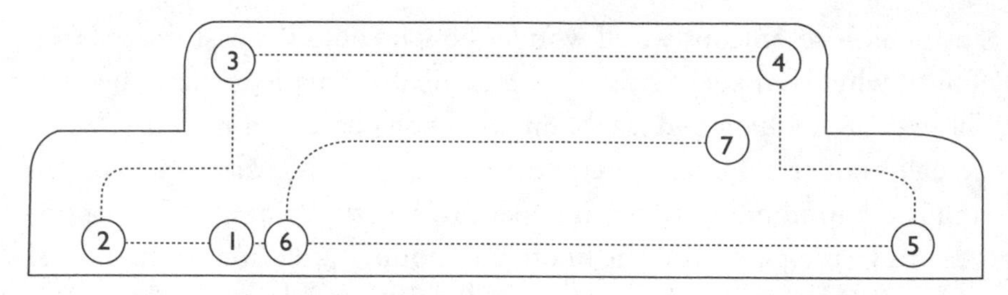

Figure 14–2. Visual inspection path with spot inspection locations

One of the challenges of visual inspection tasks is the relatively narrow focal range of human eyes. If we look straight ahead, we are able to detect motion at a relatively wide angle, colors at a narrower angle, and detail in a very small area. This is because the area in the center of the retina (called the *fovea*) responsible for detailed focus is very small. We can see things on the periphery, but not clearly. We believe we can "see" well at the periphery because our eyes are constantly in motion moving from side to side as needed. Look closely at this sentence, and do not shift your eyes. Notice how far above and below this line you are able to see *clearly*. Notice how far to the left and to the right of a single focal point you can clearly see without moving your eyes. Did you notice your eyes tended to automatically shift in the direction you were trying to see? Chances are if you stare at a letter in the center of this sentence, you can still "see" the letters at either end of the sentence. You should notice the letters at the far ends are not really distinguishable. You can see something there, but it is impossible to actually read any letters. The key is to determine the area of vision in which defects are distinguishable. We call this the *visible distinction range.*

Luckily, in most visual inspection tasks, it is only necessary to detect some surface variation while visually sweeping over an inspection path. If an anomaly is detected, it can be more closely examined. If, however, the inspection path is wider than the visible distinction range or the eyes drift from the inspection path, any defects outside the visible distinction range are likely to pass undetected.

Our peripheral vision range of distinction is greater from left-to-right than it is from top-to-bottom when following a vertical

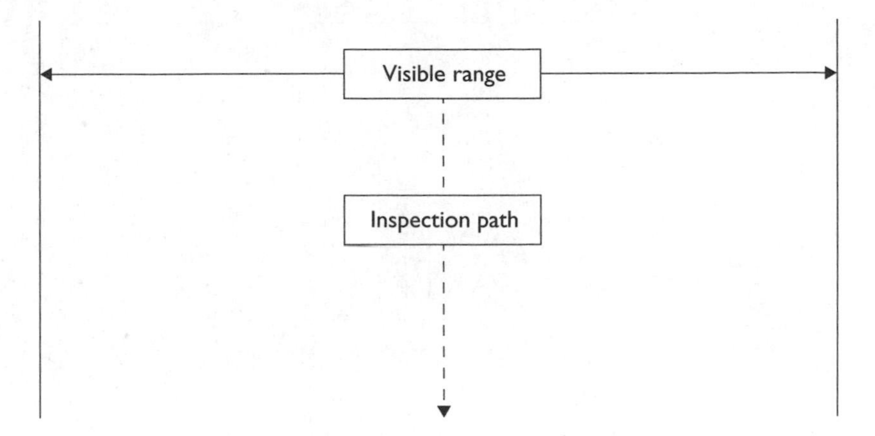

Figure 14–3. Visible distinction range with vertical inspection path

inspection path because of the side-by-side placement of our eyes. The average range of visible distinction is approximately four to six inches from the left side to the right side (see Figure 14–3).

When the inspection path is horizontal, the visible distinction range from top-to-bottom is reduced to approximately three to four inches (Figure 14–4). These variations must be considered when determining the inspection path. Some overlap should occur with each inspection path to avoid inadvertently missing any spots.

The trainer can demonstrate the correct path and visible range with her fingers. For a side-to-side path (Figure 14–4), the trainer can use the index finger and thumb to form an L shape with the tip of the thumb and index finger indicating the boundary of the visible range. For a top-to-bottom path (Figure 14–3), the trainer can use the index finger and pinky finger to form a U shape that will be approximately four to six inches wide. Of course, everyone's hands are different sizes, so for smaller hands a different combination of fingers may be necessary to indicate the visible range and path.

The major steps and key points for an in-process inspection of the part in Figure 14–2 appear below. (Tip: Using a sample part with the inspection points and paths indicated with magic-marker to show the correct path and step numbers is a good training aid.)

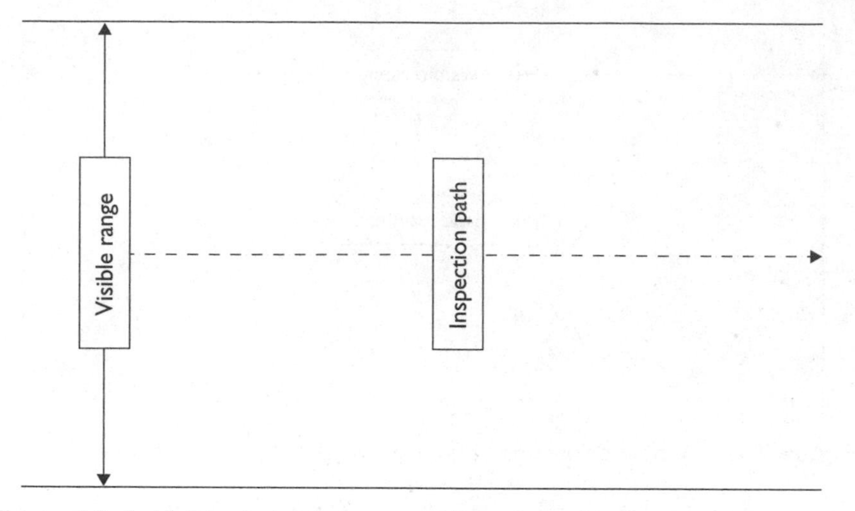

Figure 14–4. Visible distinction range with horizontal inspection path

Major step: Inspect the air bag cover.

Key points: (1) Follow the inspection path with fingers so it is possible to see if the correct path is being followed. (Reason—to make sure no area is missed and the most efficient path is used.) (2) Spot inspection of four locations. (Reason—these four locations are prone to repetitive defects.)

When demonstrating the major steps and key points, the trainer would begin at location 1 and, using the fingers to show the correct path, move them across the part to location 2. At this location the trainer would pause, point, and call "check," before moving on to location 3 with the fingers in a U shape. At location 3 the trainer again pauses, points, and calls "check," before proceeding along the inspection path with the fingers. The pause-and-point actions demonstrate the location of specific checkpoints.

This task could be broken down in different ways as well. The movement from location to location could be given as individual key points. We chose not to present the task in this way because seven key points would be quite a bit to remember and would make the training cumbersome. This is an individual decision that must be made by the trainer. If the trainer demonstrates the path and stops to point at each spot location, it is likely the student will easily learn to repeat the motion portion of the task—the "how to inspect" portion. The next phase of inspection training pertains to "what to look for," and "what to do if a problem is discovered." The next section explains how to develop on-the-job knowledge and judgment ability.

How to Develop Judgment Ability and On-the-Job Knowledge

Virtually every job workers must do in modern times will require the development of judgment ability and accumulated know-how that is learned on the job over time. Trainers often make the mistake of attempting to teach judgment ability while teaching the work task. This assuredly causes the training process to get off track and the student to become confused. For example; almost all jobs require some sort of in-process inspection, and an inspection task is made up of three parts—how to look (the task), what to look for (knowledge of defects), and the judgment regarding acceptability of defects found. The inspection task must be separated into its three components for training. The task portion is covered first (as described in the previous section), and the knowledge and judgment are developed afterwards—separate from the task training. So the student is taught *how* to inspect, but not what to look for or what to do if he finds anything abnormal. This is, at first, strange to students because they expect to learn what they are looking for.

Let's look at a typical training example to better understand where the problem is. The following dialogue is typical when the trainer attempts to mix the three elements of a training task into one training session.

The trainer begins the presentation of the major steps.

Trainer: There are 5 major steps for this job. The first major step is to inspect the air bag cover. When you are inspecting the air bag cover you need to look for any excess sealant, missing parts, and rivets that are not properly seated (pointing randomly at the air bag cover). Make sure you look at each rivet and make sure no sealant is on the air bag (rotating the part and glancing at it).

This example includes several common mistakes. First of all, the presentation mixes major steps, key points, and reasons into a continuous string. For our point here though we are concerned with the blending of tasks—the what to look for and the how to look for it. The "how" portion is very loosely described using terms like "you need to look" and "make sure you look." This is like telling someone to "have a nice day." What *exactly* does it mean? Another problem when teaching inspection tasks is the product being inspected may not have any defects (hopefully). How do you explain what the student should look for if it is not present?

The problem is the focus of the training is on the knowledge and judgment rather than the task—the actual inspection. It is our experience that if you do not learn an effective method of inspection, it does not matter whether you can classify the defects because you are not likely to see them. On the other hand, if you have a good method of inspection, the operator is likely to be able to find and recognize an abnormal condition—he or she just won't know what to do about it.

Let's review another dialogue that corrects the problems with this presentation. This time we will back up to the preparation of the student to explain how an inspection task is taught. Also this training session will concentrate on the inspection portion of the job only.

Trainer: Today I will be teaching you how to inspect an air bag cover. There are actually three parts to this job, and today I will only teach you one of them. I want to teach you how to do the actual inspection now, and later I will teach you what types of defects you will be looking for and how to determine whether they are acceptable or not.

There are two major steps for this part of the job. The first major step is to inspect around the cover plate. (Using his fingers, the trainer will trace a path around the perimeter of the cover plate where he is inspecting for excess sealant.)

The second major step is to inspect the rivets. (The trainer will point and pause at each rivet in a specific pattern.)

Now I'd like to show you the job again, and this time I will explain the key points. The first major step is to inspect around the cover plate. There are two key points for this step. The first key point is to follow a path from the bottom and move around the cover plate (demonstrating the path with his fingers). The second key point is to use your fingers to follow the path (demonstrating the technique).

The second major step is to inspect the rivets. There are two key points for this step as well. The first key point is to check the four rivets (pointing and pausing at each in order). The second key point is to point at each rivet with your index finger.

The training would continue in this manner until complete. The trainer would then have the student perform the job and would have the student begin the inspection operation. The trainer would remain with the student and ask the student to inspect each air bag cover and then to pass it to him. The trainer would also inspect the part, and if he finds any defects, he would stop and review the defect with the student. It is likely that the student will notice abnormalities on his own, but he will have no understanding of whether the condition is acceptable or not.

During this checking process, the trainer is building the student's accumulated know-how and judgment ability. When the trainer is certain the student is performing the inspection task correctly and no defects are passed on, he may ask the student to place any abnormal air bag covers into a defective parts box. The trainer and student can evaluate these at a later time.

When the trainer evaluates items discovered by the student that were set aside, he can take time to explain to the student what was found (name and cause of the defect), as well as to begin to develop in the student an understanding of levels of acceptability (good or no good). At Toyota samples of common defects are often stored in the work area for training purposes, and in some cases "boundary samples" (samples show the limits of acceptability for cosmetic imperfections) are maintained to aid in the development of judgment ability.

The development of knowledge and judgment ability may extend for several months. It is not necessary for the trainer to stay with the student at all times during this extended period. If the student is able to call for help (using the andon) or set the part aside until an evaluation can be made, he may work largely unassisted.

How to Teach Tasks Performed Infrequently

Repetitive jobs offer many opportunities to practice and develop skills and require top capability because of their frequency. There are other activities that occur very infrequently or are not intended to be a regular part of the job. For example when an automatic system fails, it is necessary to perform the operation manually. Manual operation of the system is not really supposed to be part of the overall task and therefore not something that is done regularly. Many activities may occur only monthly, semiannually, or less often.

How is training handled for these kinds of infrequent activities? Since the task is very infrequent, it is not necessary to have several people who know how to do the task, and the training need would be minimal. If the Job Instruction (JI) method were used in its entirety, it would require seven repetitions of the task for complete training (a minimum if all steps of the JI method are followed). When the task is done one time, it will not need to be repeated again for quite some time. Does the trainer wait until the next time the task is needed and then pick up on the training to repeat the next step? Would the trainer just repeat the process even though it is not necessary to do it again? No. This situation requires a slight modification of the Job Instruction method.

For these infrequent tasks Toyota leaders and engineers would prepare an operation instruction sheet (also called a work instruction sheet). The operation instruction sheet is very similar to a job break down sheet, but it does not have the reasons for the key points listed and instead has a section for diagrams, sketches, or photos that will clarify the operation. This document is used more as a reference for how to do the task than as a training aid. When it is necessary to perform the task, it is possible to review the instruction sheet and follow the directions enough to perform the task. The operation instruction is similar to a recipe for cooking. Someone with limited skill can follow along well enough to successfully complete the task.

Note that in an earlier chapter, when we discussed the difference between the standard worksheet and the job breakdown sheet, we said the standard worksheet is for waste elimination and the job breakdown sheet is for job instruction. We said the worker should not be referencing either sheet to do the job because they should have learned the job well enough to do it repeatedly within takt time. In the case of infrequent tasks, the operation instruction sheet is a tool for training but also a reference for the worker to do the job. Since they do the job so infrequently, they cannot be expected to remember everything in the long time between performances of the job.

Because of the infrequent nature of these tasks, they are generally completed by either the team leader or group leader, or another "off-line" resource. It is not necessary to teach multiple people to perform the task because it not a routine part of the job, and it is possible to complete the task by following the operation instruction sheet when necessary. When a task is completed infrequently, it is difficult for anyone to remember all the details. If the details are written down, it is easy to follow them. We should note that in some jobs there are fewer repeated tasks and a larger portion of infrequently performed tasks. In this case, there will be more use of Job Instruction (JI) sheets that are referenced to do the job.

Using Training Aids

Training aids can be used to help clarify the task or speed the learning process. For example, when teaching an inspection task, the inspection path and spot inspection locations are marked on a sample part to show the correct inspection path. Developing judgment is simplified if actual examples of defective parts can be shown to the student during the discussion. In Chapter 2 we discuss several ideas used at Toyota's Global Production Centers and in the work area. These training aids shorten the learning time and allow practice without the worry of creating defects.

Training aids may be "cheat sheets" or other visual items that assist with understanding. One example we saw during a Job Instruction class was a color-coded sheet to help identify key information. If the task being taught is completing a data collection sheet, a sample sheet with numbers written on it and indicating the steps helps the student remember the sequence and location of information. Always look for ways to convey information quickly, easily, and effectively. This becomes particularly important for infrequently performed tasks.

There Are Many Challenging Situations

The Job Instruction method is deliberate, organized, and detailed, and it will help you to produce excellent results. Yet, there will be no shortage of challenges. These challenges are what make the training effort so exciting. Trainers must constantly think about what they are doing and experiment with new techniques to improve their effectiveness.

Much of the book has used repetitive, routine jobs as examples, and even in these cases we see there is a great deal to learn. We have intentionally focused on the most basic training situations to illustrate the core training philosophy and methodology. We have also given examples of job breakdowns and analyses of skill requirements for jobs that are less routine. Unfortunately, you will face many difficult situations not covered in this book. These will require you to apply your own learning and creativity to those challenges.

Less routine jobs are obviously more complex and take much longer to master. The Toyota Technical Center in the United States has been working for years to simplify the training process to more quickly bring on new engineers as the technical center grows, and it has been one challenge after another. But the basic thinking process on how to develop people is the same. One piece of advice we can give you is to keep on trying. Working to develop a systematic approach to training is better than leaving training to chance. In the final section of this book we discuss how to verify that the training process is producing the desired result.

Part Four

Verify Learning and Success

We learn wisdom from failure much more than from success. We often discover what will do, by finding out what will not do; and probably he who never made a mistake never made a discovery.

Samuel Smiles

Chapter 15

Follow Up to Verify Learning and Ensure Success

Moving the Student Toward Self-Reliance

Now you are ready for the student to do the job on his or her own and move into the final step of the four-step method—follow-up. This step should be made as a gradual transition. The student should never be tossed directly into the fire. It is not necessary for the student to be 100 percent capable of performing the work before doing the job independently. In fact, their capability is more likely to be less than 100 percent because there are still additional items to learn (e.g., how to start up or program the equipment and full knowledge of quality expectations). In any case, the trainer must check the student's progress frequently at first and gradually reduce the follow-up as confidence in the student's capability is developed.

In the case of Toyota engineering, there is always a team leader whose job is to continue to monitor and train each engineer in the group. Leaders and engineers work together regularly, so it is easy to mentor on the job. Senior engineers are not monitoring junior engineers minute by minute as they may be at first in a repetitive manufacturing job, but they are generally with new engineers daily and seated in the same open office area. Toyota's philosophy is every team leader and manager is a teacher first.

The Trainer Is Always Responsible

The Job Instruction motto states, "If the student hasn't learned, the instructor hasn't taught." This simply means the teacher must continue to teach until the student is fully capable of performing the job. Once the student begins to work on his or her own, the trainer will either reap the reward of his or her training efforts or will suffer the consequence of a poor effort. This is the trainer's motivation to reflect and learn from each training experience and to improve. There is no doubt that a well-trained workforce has fewer problems than one that is not well trained.

Trainers may not relinquish responsibility for the student. Even if they ask someone to keep an eye on the student, they are still responsible. To ensure success, the trainer must keep a watchful eye on the student and monitor progress. Some trainers mistakenly believe this watchful attention is "looking over the shoulder" of the student, and that it will be perceived negatively. The trainer must bear in mind this is an act of caring, not an act of spying or trying to catch the student doing something wrong. The trainer desires a win-win situation. The student wins when he or she performs well, and the trainer wins when the student wins (and has fewer problems to deal with).

Always Support the Student

The Training Within Industry (TWI) material states, "Put him (the student) on his own." This should not be interpreted as, "*Leave* him on his own." Above all, the student must feel secure and cared for, and the trainer must feel certain of the student's capability. Unfortunately we often see inexperienced workers obviously struggling alone. We have changed this terminology to state, "Assign the worker a task," because it more clearly states what you will be doing. The trainer is obligated to set a clear and specific expectation: Tell the students what they need to do.

We pick up on our training dialogue where we left off in Chapter 13:

Trainer: Bob, I think you're doing well, and it's time for you to do the job.

Student: Oh, okay. What should I do?

Trainer: I'd like you to do the steps of the job we've gone over. I want you to maintain a steady pace just as you've been doing. I am going to stay here to help if needed and make sure your quality is acceptable and just in case you have any problems, but you will do the complete job.

Student: Okay, I'll give it a try.

Explain Who to Call for Help

It is not always possible for the trainer to stay with the student on the job. When this happens, the trainer should make arrangements with someone in the work area who can provide assistance to the student if needed. This person should be instructed to keep an eye on the trainee, and to verify the quality of her work, and to ensure her safety. The trainee, should be introduced to the support person and instructed to call on him or her if necessary. The trainer should specify to the student when they will be leaving the work area and approximately when they will return. An experienced worker on the job next to the student can handle this role effectively.

The training dialogue continues:

Trainer: Bob, I think you're doing a great job. I need to go to a meeting now. It should take about an hour. While I'm gone, Janet will be able to help you if there are any problems. I've asked her to keep an eye on you. I'll check with you when I get back to see how you're doing.

Student: Sounds good. Can I push the call button to get Janet?

Trainer: Yes, just press the call button if you have any problems at all.

Check Progress Frequently

At Toyota it is unlikely that team members would be put on a job to work by themselves if they weren't ready to do the job. Success on the job is too crucial to the overall operation for a trainer to take the risk of putting an incapable person on the line, particularly in the tightly timed environment of Toyota. We would estimate that in most other companies the majority of trainees are released to work alone prematurely. In the beginning it is important to check progress very frequently. Team leaders and group leaders are continually roaming the line at Toyota, and it is natural for them to check all operations on a frequent basis.

This is really an issue of risk minimization and support. The smart trainer knows that if follow-up is infrequent, the risk for problems increases. If the trainer checks the student every 30 minutes, the potential for defects is reduced to a 30-minute window. If the trainer checks every hour, the potential number of defects is doubled. The frequency of follow-up is best determined based on the confidence level of the trainer. If the student has demonstrated very consistent performance, the trainer will have a higher confidence level and the follow-up interval can be lengthened.

The trainer does not necessarily need to explain the follow-up to the student, but doing so provides the student with some reassurance he or she is being supported.

Our training dialogue continues:

Trainer: Bob, I think you're ready to work on your own for a while. I'll check back in half an hour or so. In the meantime, if you have any problems, remember to push the call button.

Student: All right. I'll do my best.

Trainer: (Later when checking back, the trainer verifies quality and whether the student is following standardized work properly.) Hi Bob. It looks like you're doing great! Is there anything you need?

Student: Thanks. Can you look at the sealant on these parts to make sure it's okay?

Trainer: Sure (confirming the quality). They look good. You could reduce the sealant just a little, but these are fine.

Student: Okay, thanks.

Encourage Questions

New hires are often shy about asking questions. They don't want to appear as if they don't know what to do. If the trainer asks, "Do you have any questions?" the student might reply with a quick "no." The trainer must invite questions and create an atmosphere where the achievement of understanding is desired. This is best done with a statement such as, "Bob, if you have any questions now or later, please feel free to ask. I want to make sure all your questions get answered." The trainer then may have to follow up with some specific probing questions related to key points, such as, "Can you look at the sealant and tell by looking whether it has been applied properly?"

Gradually Reduce the Coaching and Follow-Up

By now the team member is able to do the work with minimal support, but the trainer must continue to monitor progress until she is certain the student is fully capable. We have found from experience that bad habits or incorrect work methods can begin to creep in over time. Changes to the work method often occur without conscious thought by the trainee. For whatever reason, students make a change to a method, and very quickly the new method becomes a habit. It is important for trainers and leaders to continuously monitor work methods, but the frequency can be reduced as skill levels increase.

World-class athletes who achieve top ranking in their sports have coaches and continually work to perfect their performance. Coaches help to develop overall strategies for an athlete's style and also work on the detailed mechanics of the body movements. Tiger Woods is well known for changing his entire golf swing—twice! He is still performing the same task of hitting a golf ball, but he is making adjustments to the multitude of finesse elements within the swing.

The same concept applies to work. The trainer should continually coach the student to help him or her develop the smoothest, consistent work method with minimal effort and waste. It is the refinement of the method that makes a difference in the performance levels. It is not realistic for the trainer to teach and develop a deep level of skill during the initial training session. The initial session is for developing the fundamentals. Once the fundamentals are embedded in muscle memory, it is possible to work on finessing the technique. And in an environment of kaizen, you expect the job will be improved, and those working on the job must learn the updated methods, so learning never stops.

It is important to keep an eye on the overall performance measures as an indicator of changes in the work method. If quality, safety, or productivity indicators begin to decline, the leader must first verify that the correct work method is being followed. As noted, it is common for small and almost imperceptible changes in the work method to occur and begin to affect performance. The trainer and leader must have a keen eye and deep knowledge of the method to detect these changes. Toyota expects team leaders and group leaders to regularly audit the standard work by going through job by job and comparing what the person is actually doing with the standard work. In fact a standardized process is in place to audit the standard work job by job over a specific period of time. The group leader is typically expected to formally audit one job a week or even more frequently. This is intentionally designed as an opportunity for coaching and fine-tuning the performance of each team associate. If there is no formal system in place for coaching it is apt to stop as people feel they already know it all.

Use the Cascade Audit Method to Ensure Success of the Process

In every robust system there is a set of checks and balances to ensure that critical parts of the system are not compromised. The development of team member talent is a critical part of the system and thus should have some checks and balances. Ultimately the leader is responsible for the results of training whether she or he is personally doing the actual training or not. The leader is responsible for the development of the trainer and certainly has a vested interest in the outcome. Given this vested interest, it is alarming to find many leaders who want to pass responsibility for such a critical activity to others and then act as if they are absolved of the outcome.

It is important for everyone in the organization to use the "cascade method" for evaluating the effectiveness of the process.[1] Toyota uses the cascade audit method for the structure of leadership and the flow of information within the organization. The cascade audit method is based on the analogy of flowing water and fish migrating upstream. Information and capability is meant to flow like water downstream, and every leader must ensure that the flow is smooth and free of any turbulence or obstructions. Also it is important that any fish (ideas or problems) that need to swim upstream can do so and reach the level necessary to get implemented or corrected. When necessary, the water can rise above each level and can accelerate the spread of information. Issues or problems should also be elevated level-by-level, becoming more clear and urgent at each level.

The desired process allows information to flow freely to all members and any problems or ideas to surface and be addressed. Unfortunately in any system there are breakdowns. The flow is blocked in one direction or the other. It is crucial to find the obstructions and to remove them so the smooth flow is resumed. The challenge for most human beings is their unwillingness to admit weakness. Many of us choose to ignore weaknesses or pretend they don't exist. The Toyota Production System is supposed to be a "no fault" system. The objective is not to identify *whom* to blame for a problem, it is to find out where the *system* failed. Even so, people still have a tendency to hide problems because they feel a need to protect themselves. They are driven by fear and ego. They are afraid of the consequence of failure, and their ego prevents them from admitting there is a need to improve. This is one of the greatest challenges of any organization.

What we often view as "failure" is acceptable and even desirable within Toyota—if reflection and learning are part of the process. When people pursue perfection as a goal, they will always fall short. If people pursue continuous improvement as a goal, they will

[1] This idea is from Tim Szymcek, a former quality engineering and supplier development leader in Toyota's North American Manufacturing Operations and the owner of Predictable Quality Solutions, a quality consulting and product sorting company (www.predictable-quality.com).

quickly realize that learning from mistakes and growing in capability is a part of the process and is not something to be ashamed of or to be feared.

All leaders should work hard to foster an environment of mutual trust and support. A leader who finds a weakness in any subordinate must also assume responsibility for developing the subordinate and correcting the weakness. It does no good to find weakness, point it out, and then use retribution as a threat or expect it to be resolved on its own. The leader wants to find any weakness and correct it so the total system becomes stronger.

All leaders or managers should verify the success of each of their subordinates by verifying the ability of their subordinates. The evaluation is cascaded one level down as shown in Figure 15–1. To audit and verify the effectiveness of the certified Job Instruction (JI) trainer, we would evaluate the effectiveness of the workplace trainers. It would be necessary to observe the workplace trainers during a training session and also to evaluate their ability to break down jobs and to make and execute an effective development plan for all employees in their area. If the workplace trainers have good capability, it is assumed the certified Job Instruction trainer has effectively flowed the learning down to them and has helped them to correct any weakness. If the audit reveals any weakness in the workplace trainers, the next step is to confirm whether the certified Job Instruction trainer weakness had already been identified, and if there is a corrective action in progress.

If the certified Job Instruction trainer is unable to identify weakness in the workplace trainers, the responsibility for correcting this inability is with the Master trainer. Note in the figure that the department managers are not necessarily part of the training process, but they have responsibility for the results and a vested interest in the success of the process. Department managers should be auditing the effectiveness of the certified Job Instruction trainers and the workplace trainers and should be requesting support from the Master trainer to help resolve any weakness. In Chapter 16 we provide some evaluation forms that can also be used to audit the capability of certified Job Instruction and workplace trainers.

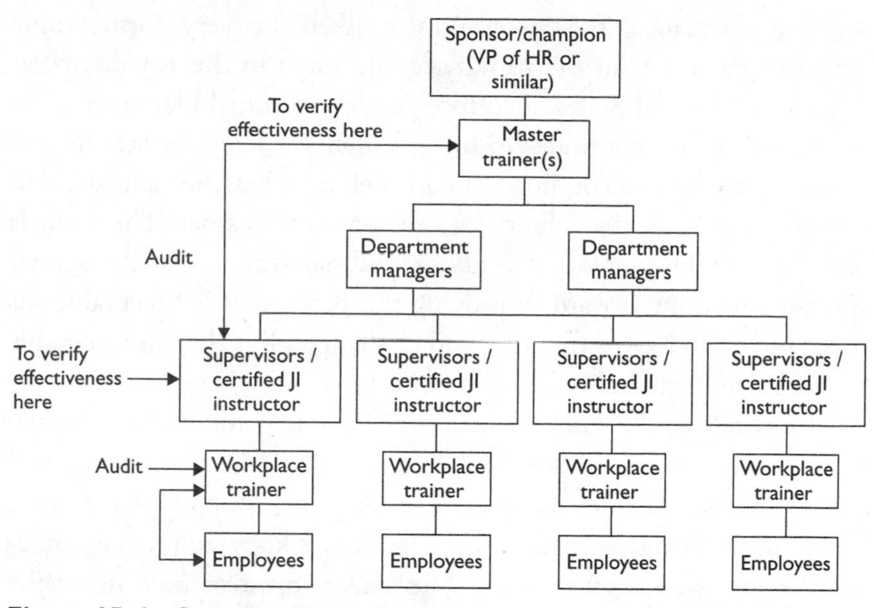

Figure 15–1. Cascade audit method

In the cascade audit method, the best way to find out about the actual performance in the workplace is to evaluate the situation one level below a specific leader. A manager does not go directly to the leaders who are responsible for the workplace to find out if they are doing a good job. They would make an evaluation of the people who report to the leader to determine the effectiveness of that leader. For example, the managers would not ask the certified Job Instruction trainers directly how they are doing until after they verify the status in the workplace for themselves. If the managers were to ask the subordinates directly, "How is your development process going?" they would likely get the response, "It is going great!" It is difficult for subordinates to report their own poor performance to the boss, and the manager should never accept the subordinate's assessment without verification.

To understand the real situation, the managers must first go to see for themselves, and then they can confirm what was observed with the subordinates. This may appear to be "checking up on" the subordinate and indicate a lack of trust. In Toyota the expectation is that everyone is surfacing problems, and if a subordinate is questioned about performance, they would most likely be very forthcoming regarding the issues in the workplace (although in the Toyota operations in the United States, a culture where individual blame seems to be the norm, this continues to be a challenge). The manager then is simply verifying the condition for himself and has the obligation to provide support to the subordinate to correct the issues. The audit is not about finding blame. It is about finding weakness in the system and then working toward improving the process. It is acceptable for subordinates to have difficulties and challenges, but they must be able to recognize them and to develop plans to correct them.

To conduct the audit, the leaders would carefully review the performance metrics of the work area to see if there are any broad issues that are affecting the overall results. For example, if the work area is not meeting the quality goal, the leaders know to focus on quality key points during the audit. The leaders must go to observe the employees in the workplace to evaluate their ability and knowledge. They should bring the job breakdown describing the key points and observe enough work cycles to feel confident they have a good representation of how the associates do the job. An audit card or form should be used to record any deviations from the standard methods, and then it is used to record countermeasures and when they are implemented. This evaluation method has two benefits:

1. The upper-level manager must actually go to the source to confirm the results *(genchi gembutsu)*.
2. In order to confirm the capability of the team member, the manager must be knowledgeable about the work.

This is a fundamental element of Toyota's success. Managers who are two levels above where the work is performed are intimately familiar with the work that is conducted at least two levels below their own position. In many cases because of documentation and standardization, it is possible for a manager more than two levels above to have a deep understanding of the work. For example, in a Toyota plant each team leader is expected to audit the standard work of at least one employee daily, and the group leader will select and confirm at least one job weekly. The assistant manager (who is one step above the group leader) is also expected to roam the floor and randomly audit one operation per group each week, and the manager would audit one job per month.

Having this knowledge of the work allows managers to follow up and to identify weakness in the capabilities of leaders and trainers. Ultimately the manager must assume responsibility for the overall outcome, and it is best not to leave such crucial evaluations to the opinions of those responsible for delivering the results.

So, if supervisors want to evaluate the effectiveness of a workplace trainer, they should visit the team members and verify their job performance. If a hospital administrator wants to verify the effectiveness of a head nurse, the administrator should go see firsthand the performance of the nursing staff. These evaluations include the preparation of all documents—a training plan, standardized work or standard methods, and job breakdown sheets among others.

One problem with the cascade audit method is sometimes subordinates do not want to get their boss in trouble. If your questioning leads to answers that would compromise their trainer or boss, you may get the standard answer. For example, if you ask closed-ended questions such as, "Was your training complete?" and "Did the trainer do a good job?" you are likely to get a response of "Oh yes. It was very good."

This audit method is not for determining blame, but for finding areas that need improvement. More focused questions to test for knowledge, such as, "Can you explain to me what the key points for this part of the job are?" or "Can you tell me what is critical for quality in this step of the job?" will yield much more valuable insights. It is important for leaders to be able to find any weakness in the process. Is the weakness in the breakdown of the job and identification of critical information? Was the important information available but not transferred effectively? Was the team member left on her own prematurely before she had sufficient skills? Finding the answers to these questions will allow you to identify areas that need to be improved.

Learning Systems Are Not Self-Sustaining

A term we hear frequently by companies introducing lean programs is *sustainability*. We are often asked, "How will you ensure sustainability of the learning that takes place from your training?" We are also frequently asked for an "exit strategy" and a guarantee that the process will be self-sustaining when we are "finished." Regardless of whether or not the consultant should exit at some point or another, we do know that learning systems are not self-sustaining. Sorry, but we have to confess the truth. Managers who expect good processes to be self-sustaining are viewing the processes as purely technical and do not understand the nature of human systems.

Let's take a simple example from your home. You teach your kids to brush and floss their teeth every morning before they leave home. You teach them a prescribed method for both in great detail. They do it while you are there and clearly understand what to do. You implement a system in which a check sheet is posted on the wall, and your kids are asked to check off each time they brush and floss. You then don't check up on them for one year. At the end of the year, do you think they will be brushing and flossing every morning? Do you think the check sheet will be diligently used? If the answer is yes, we want your kids. If you do not follow up, if you do not have a refresher, if you do not regularly verify the correct method, our prediction is that the behavior will not be self-sustaining.

This does not mean you want to be looking over your children's shoulder every time they clean their teeth. As Henry Ford said, "Quality means doing it right when no one is looking." You want people to do the job right when they are not being observed. But to maintain that quality level requires audits at regular intervals along with coaching.

Unfortunately humans are not like machines. They cannot be programmed to do the same repetitive task over and over with a minimum of preventive maintenance. They take a lot of maintenance. Follow-up is a critical part of the process. In this chapter, we considered follow-up of each individual trained. In the final chapter, we move to a higher level of follow-up for the overall training program and for the entire organization.

Chapter 16

Organizational Follow-Up

Now Please Try, and—Do Your Best

If reading all the details of breaking down work into tiny bits, and identifying key points for all those bits, and training and confirming, and training and confirming has you exhausted and overwhelmed, then you probably got something out of this book. Unfortunately the task may feel overwhelming. If it does not, then you are most likely underestimating the task. Fortunately there is a way forward. And it involves the basic Toyota principle of "learning by doing." Now it is time to move beyond thinking about it and on to doing something.

At Toyota all employees are asked to "please try," always with the expectation that they will "do their best." Talent development is a never-ending process. There is no upper limit on how much people can learn or improve. Other objectives (such as defect reduction) have upper or lower limits, but the development of people is truly an opportunity for *continuous* improvement. Your best result will continually get better if you keep trying and learning. You must develop the ability to do *hansei* (reflection) to become an independent learner. An external Master trainer can help you in the beginning, but at some point you must learn to learn on your own, to take your accumulated know-how and reapply it into building additional know-how. Master teachers have the ability to expand their own capability by self-reflection and learning.

Developing Resources by Going Deep and Then Wide

Now that we have been through the entire process, let's discuss how to actually go about developing the resources you need to pull this off. It is our opinion that it is very difficult to learn the people-development process from a book. There are hundreds of subtleties that are impossible to capture in a book. It is analogous to learning golf from a book. You may be able to intellectually understand the basics, but it is likely that when you actually step on the golf course it will be very different. Some poor swing habits will develop, and your game will not develop beyond a mediocre level without help from a skilled professional.

The professional will teach fundamentals and provide practice drills in a "classroom" setting (the driving range) until the basics are mastered. Then you will go out to the golf course (the real world) and learn the subtleties of the game. Which club should you use for a particular shot? When do you use a draw or fade shot? How do you change your approach based on the layout of the green and placement of the flag (which changes daily)? How do the stroke, body posture, and hand grip change when the ball is sitting downhill or uphill from your feet? What about the wind? How do you know where your putt will go? Reading the green is similar to developing judgment and accumulated know-how for job skills. And between lessons you will practice, practice, practice! Golf-great Arnold Palmer said, "It's a funny thing, the more I practice, the luckier I get."

So you can perform drills on the fundamentals of golf, but actual play involves learning to adjust to many unusual conditions. The same is true for training. Each student has a different learning capability and style. Each job will present special challenges. Even with great skill and a perfect plan, things are apt to change (like the wind). The trainer must make minor changes to his or her method as the training unfolds. But the more you practice the fundamentals, "the luckier you will get" in being successful when the inevitable special challenges occur.

To push the golf analogy a bit further, even the master pro like Tiger Woods has a golf instructor. Tiger knows he has blind spots and needs someone to observe his swing and to help him improve. And the same is true of trainers—you need someone to observe you and to help you continue to improve. We believe it is best to have someone who has a high degree of mastery of training and who has experience with many different training situations and with a demonstrated capability of teaching others. We recommend the use of an external "Master trainer" to support you through the initial steps of the process. The primary focus of the external Master trainer should be to help you develop internal resources and make you capable of taking responsibility for training others and helping them to improve.

Earlier in the book, we touched on the idea of developing depth of capability in a process and then spreading the process across the organization. We refer to this as "going deep and then going wide." It is necessary to develop depth of capability prior to attempting to spread the process across the organization. If you attempt to go wide across the organization before developing necessary strength, the outcome will likely be "watered down." Each successive generation of trainees is likely to have less capability because the teacher does not have the skill to teach the subtleties and the weaknesses are handed down. In *The Toyota Way Fieldbook* we speak of "microwaved" trainees who have been provided with little instruction and then are expected to teach others. You would not want to take golf lessons from a beginner, would you? Make sure your bench strength is deep before tackling the entire organization.

In step 1 of the following process, it is necessary to select an initial development focus area. This will be your driving range—a "classroom" to practice fundamentals and learn more about the subtleties of the game. We suggest you select an area that has some easier job tasks (you wouldn't play your first round of golf on the most difficult course) and that has strong leaders and potential apprentice trainers. There may not be a perfect choice for the initial development area. Choose the best one.

Be careful not to select the area with the greatest need (most problems) as your initial implementation area. It is likely that this area has weak leadership and does not have strong internal candidates with the capability to become effective trainers without a great deal of effort. More difficult areas should be tackled after you have mastered the fundamental skills and are capable of handling the more challenging situations.

Select potential candidates who will become Master trainers and Journeymen trainers (as we outline in Chapter 4). These people should have the desire and basic capability to deliver classroom type training. They will do some of the workplace job training, but they will primarily be mentors and coaches for the apprentice trainers who will be doing the actual employee training. The Master trainer will have responsibilities for coordinating the process, conducting the Job Instruction (JI) classes, mentoring trainers, and evaluating the results. Candidates for Master trainer should have good planning and execution abilities.

It is a general philosophy within Toyota that it is necessary to have two people who are fully capable and ready to step into any leadership position at any time. If you will have one Master trainer, it is necessary to develop three people who are capable of handling this role. Select no less than three people who have the basic raw materials for the job and have them participate in the initial development process. At the end of the process choose the best one to actually assume the responsibility of Master trainer. The two additional candidates can be great resources as you spread the process, and they would be able to advance to Master trainer level if the need arises. Identify the key people who will become certified Job Instruction trainers. They will have the responsibility for developing workplace trainers.

For the first round of development it is best to have at least four potential candidates for Job Instruction trainers in the class. Depending on the size of your organization, that number of trainers may be sufficient to meet your entire need. If you have a very large organization (like Toyota), you will need to develop additional JI instructors in subsequent development sessions. Having four in the first session provides a safety margin in case some of them decide not to continue, or if it turns out they are not capable. Always work to develop extra people (this is one case where overproduction is acceptable!).

In Chapter 6 we describe the multiyear process by which Toyota develops product engineers. Toyota recognizes that it is a craft, and the subtleties cannot be taught in the classroom. So Toyota creates structured experiences with mentors to teach the new hire to become an engineer over four to five years. We suggest that your trainers are also in nonroutine jobs, and developing an effective training program requires a long-term process of learning by doing under the guidance of a mentor.

Structure for Implementation

Any structure we suggest for developing an overall training program will fit some organizations better than others. There is no one-size-fits-all approach. But it is worth describing one well-designed approach as an example. At the least it will illustrate the thought process we would expect you to go through when developing your own training program. Building on the theme of going deep first, learning from this, and then spreading the learning wide, we are going to start with an initial area to begin developing internal training talent.

Step 1: Initial Development Focus Area

You need to start to develop your training resources by focusing training in one area of the plant. Select an initial development focus area (step 1 completed with support from outside Master trainer):

- Conduct a basic Job Instruction training class for potential certified JI instructors, Master trainers, workplace leaders, and workplace trainers of the initial work area.
- Everyone mentioned above must complete the basic Job Instruction training course and become certified as workplace trainers (potential Master trainers and certified JI instructors must then have additional training to teach the Job Instruction class).
- Practice application in the work area to deepen skills:
    - Job breakdowns
    - Training plans
    - Actual training sessions
- External Master trainer provides coaching and mentoring during training events (using Job Instruction training evaluation guide shown in Figure 16–1).[1]

[1] All forms are available for download at www.thetoyotaway.org.

- External Master trainer provides an evaluation of the capability for each trainer:
    - Evaluates capability by using cascade method (confirming capability of student).
    - Each Certified trainer must successfully complete the core requirements (Figure 16–2).
- Potential Master trainer(s) are responsible for supporting and continuing evaluation of this work area (supported by continued mentoring and follow-up by external Master trainer).

Step 2: Second Wave of Development

Now you will have a chance to improve on what you did in the first area as well as train your second group of JI instructors. Select an additional work area and repeat the process (step 2 is completed with support from external Master trainer):

- Conduct basic Job Instruction training class for workplace leaders and workplace trainers of second work area.
- Second group of potential certified JI instructors are selected and attend training by external Master trainer.
- Potential Master trainers and certified JI instructors from step 1 should attend the training again as observers.
- Practice application in the work area to deepen skills:
    - Job breakdowns
    - Training plans
    - Actual training sessions
- External Master trainer provides coaching and mentoring during training events (using Job Instruction training evaluation guide shown in Figure 16–1).
- External Master trainer provides an evaluation of capability for each trainer:
    - Evaluates capability by using cascade method (confirm capability of student).
    - Each trainer must successfully complete the core requirements (Figure 16–2).

- Potential Master trainer(s) are responsible for supporting and continuing evaluation of this work area (supported by continued mentoring and follow-up by external Master trainer).
- All qualifying certified JI instructors and Master trainers receive certification of capability by the Master trainer and move to next level (become certified to teach the Job Instruction class).

Step 3: Develop Internal JI Instructors and Master Trainers

Teach certified JI instructors and Master trainer candidates to deliver the Job Instruction training course (step 3 completed with support from outside Master trainer):

- Present extended train-the-trainer class with potential Master trainers and certified JI instructor candidates as students to learn delivery of Job Instruction class. (40 hours).
- Practice presentation of Job Instruction training class in the next work area selected for training (each certified JI instructor and Master trainer will conduct a portion of class):
  - Workplace trainers and leaders from the selected work area are the students.
- Certified JI instructors and Master trainers are each assigned to mentor a workplace trainer or leader:
  - Observe Master trainers and certified JI instructors during training and provide feedback using training evaluation guide (Figure 16–3).
- Certified JI instructors and Master trainers are each assigned to evaluate an apprentice trainer or leader:
  - Evaluate the capability of each student using the trainer evaluation guide (Figure 16–1).
  - Trainers receive certification when the requirements are successfully met.
- Potential Master trainer(s) are responsible for supporting and continuing evaluation of this work area (supported by continued mentoring and follow-up by external Master trainer).

Step 4: Further Develop Internal Trainer Resources in Parallel Deployment Areas

Expand application to two additional work areas:

- Certified JI instructors and Master trainers deliver Job Instruction training class to leaders and workplace trainers of subsequent work areas (step 4 completed with support from internal Master trainer and evaluation from outside Master trainer).
- Practice presentation of Job Instruction training class with next work areas (each certified JI instructor and Master trainer will conduct a portion of the class).
- Workplace trainers and leaders from the selected work area are the students.
- Each certified JI instructor is assigned to mentor a workplace trainer or leader:
  - Observe workplace trainer or leader when training team members and provide feedback using training evaluation guide (Figure 16–1).
- Each certified JI instructor and Master trainer will evaluate a workplace trainer or leader:
  - Trainers receive certification when the requirements are successfully met.

Step 5: Continue to Develop Workplace Trainers and Leaders

Repeat the process until all workplace trainers and leaders have been trained in the Job Instruction method:

- Ensure that the process does not become diluted as it is passed down.
- Each trainer must prove proficiency before receiving certification. Use workplace trainer certification guide (Figure 16–2).

Implementation Milestones

It is difficult to say exactly how long it will take to completely establish the process in your organization. It depends on how large your organization is, how many individual jobs there are, and how many leaders

Job Instruction Training Evaluation Guide

Trainer:	Job:	Date:

Preparation for training:

Yes/No		Comments:
	Job breakdown sheet complete?	
	Work area was set up for training?	
	Neat and orderly?	
	Tools and equipment ready?	
	Safety?	

Step 1: Prepare the student

	Put the student at ease?	
	Told them the job name?	
	Found out what they already know?	
	Got the student interested in learning the Job?	
	Placed the student in the correct position to learn?	

Step 2 : Present the operation

	Demonstrated the job one major step at a time?	
	Repeated the operation stressing the key points?	
	Repeated the key points explaining the reasons?	
	Instructed clearly, completely, and patiently?	
	Did not give more than student could master at one time?	

Step 3 : Try out performance

	Had the student do the job while correcting errors?	
	Had the student explain the major steps?	
	Did the job again while explaining the key points?	
	Had the student explain the reasons?	
	Continued until the student understood the job?	

Step 4 : Follow-up

	Assigned the person a specific task?	
	Identified who to see for help?	
	Indicated when they would check back?	
	Encouraged questions?	

Process check:

Did the student adequately learn the task?

Was there any confusion?

Did the student struggle with any part of the task?

Ask the trainer what they would do to improve the training.

How will they incorporate these corrections into the follow-up?

Figure 16–1. Job Instruction training evaluation guide for workplace training

Workplace Trainer Certification Evalution Guide						
	Evaluation of activities					
Fundamental skills	1	2	3	4	5	Complete Y/N
Develop training plan						
Job breakdown						
Training events						
Successful follow-up						
Completion of fundamental skills requires a minimum of three acceptable examples of each skill						
	Evaluation of activities					
Special training skills	1	2	3	4	5	Complete Y/N
Long or complex jobs						
Limited verbal communication						
Teaching at line speed						
Teaching special skill or technique						
Visual tasks (inspection)						
Developing judgment ability						
Use of training aids						
Completion of special training skills requires a minimum of three acceptable examples of each if applicable						

Figure 16–2. Workplace trainer certification guide example

Master Trainer and Certified JI Instructor Class Delivery Evaluation					
	Day 1	Day 2	Day 3	Day 4	Day 5
Practiced each day segment					
Followed the course outline					
Maintained time schedule					
Effective coaching					
Job breakdown					
Training plan					
Mentoring ability					
In classroom					
In workplace					
Complete ability to deliver Job Instruction training?					

Figure 16–3. Evaluation sheet for Master and Certified trainers

and trainers need to be trained. And the process is implemented while people do their regular jobs in addition to the new responsibilities for talent development. The internal resources in your company will not be able to dedicate all of their time to this process, and you will most likely be using the same resources for other activities such as lean implementation. The speed at which you spread the process across the organization is not as important as the resulting depth of capability of the people. Development takes time. In fact, it goes on forever. It is important, however, to have the foundation in place and to have trainers developed. Figure 16–4 shows a possible timeline for implementing the process outlined in the previous section. This should give you a general idea of the timing for your process. If your resources are relatively limited, perhaps your timeline will be extended. It is more important to establish appropriate depth of capability before spreading the training across the organization, but you must continue to work toward an organization-wide process.

Proposed First-Year Talent Development Implementation Schedule	Month 1	Month 2-4	Month 4-6	Month 6-7	Month 7-9	1 Year
Step 1: Initial Development Focus Area						
Select potential Master trainers (including backups)	○					
Select potential Journeymen trainers (partial)	○					
Select initial development focus area	○					
Select apprentice trainers from development area	○					
Conduct Job Instruction class (external trainer)	○					
Develop training plans for development area		○				
Break down the jobs for the development area		○				
Practice training for trainer skill development		○				
Evaluate effectiveness of results			○			
Step 2: Second Wave of Development						
Select potential remaining Journeymen trainers		○				
Select second development focus area		○				
Select apprentice trainers from second development area		○				
Conduct Job Instruction class (external trainer)			○			
Develop training plans for second development area			○			
Break down the jobs for the second development area			○			
Practice training for trainer skill development			○			
Evaluate effectiveness of results				○		
Step 3: Certifying internal JI instructors						
Conduct Job Instruction train-the-trainer class (external trainer)				○		
Include all qualified potential Master trainers and Journeymen				○		
Step 4: Further Develop Internal Trainer Resources in Parallel Deployment areas						
(Two additional work areas simultaneously)				○		
Select additional development focus area				○		
Select apprentice trainers from additional development area					○	
Conduct Job Instruction class (internal trainer)					○	
Develop training plans for additional development area					○	
Break down the jobs for the additional development area					○	○
Practice training for trainer skill development						
Evaluate effectiveness of results						
Step 5: Continue to Develop Workplace Trainers and Leaders						
Annual process review						○→
Continue spreading to additional work areas						○→

Figure 16–4. Proposed first-year talent development implementation schedule

How to Approach Talent Development for Nonroutine Jobs: An Engineering Example

In this book we have been emphasizing the routine portions of nonroutine jobs and how you can break those down to teachable pieces. There is still a need to develop people to do the entire job, and for nonroutine jobs this requires a holistic look at the job and a great deal of OJT mentoring. Let's consider how Toyota does this in the case of developing engineers.

At Toyota a critical part of the value chain is engineering new vehicles. In the auto industry customers expect a regular offering of fresh new vehicles, and Toyota will typically completely redesign a model every five years. New vehicles may have a standard power train, but what the customer sees will be almost completely different. Two to three years into the vehicle life cycle there is a major "freshening." On the one hand there is a regular cadence to product development, and that has provided an opportunity to standardize much of the development process. But with so many models, product development engineers are constantly juggling several major projects at one time.

The design task is not just to engineer one prescribed part like a bumper, but to integrate the particular part with all the surrounding parts—integrate with manufacturing, integrate with suppliers, integrate with stylists, make sure it is safe for the driver, and make sure it meets targets on cost and quality—all within a very tightly prescribed schedule. Toyota has an intensive process of value engineering to reduce cost that often requires integrating separate parts into one so the engineer must understand all of the related parts. If you were to take the design of bumpers alone and break it down to the smallest detail, there would be thousands of things to consider over the multiyear development program. We have seen in Chapter 10 that a good deal of these tasks have been documented in a know-how database.

Obviously we do not want to do job breakdowns for thousands of tasks. So we need a more thoughtful approach with a clearer picture of what the engineer needs in terms of knowledge and skills and how to best provide those to the engineer.

	Elementary level (<1 year)	Intermediate expert (2–9 years)	Expert (>10 years)	General manager level
Fundamental skills	CATIA, PROE, CAE intro Visualization sketching Planning design Beginner SQC	1-year intensive CATIA or PROE Advanced sketching (geometric) Intermediate SQC	Team leader training Special elite training Advanced quality training	Professional study class New GM training New head of office training Manager level SQC
Core job-specific knowledge	Design for cost (by division) Division intro education Specific specialty training*	Special expert training (OJT with mentor) Specific specialty training (classroom)†	OJT in specialty (general manager/ senior engineer at location) Specific specialty training (classroom)†	Practical business management education (lectures, e-learning) OJT support (GM/senior on location)
Ancillary task knowledge	Planning basics (yrs 1–2) Report writing (yrs 1–2) Understand design support systems (e.g., prototyping)	Other field's techniques Cost planning (second year)	Understanding business costs/general management training (required for new team leader and new general manager	Management budget
Policies and judgment	New member company introduction Data security (e-mail) Beginner intellectual property	Labor and legal issues (yrs 2 and 6) Getting patents Dealing with other companies' patents	Labor and legal issues (yr 10) Consider developing third-party business system	Management observing laws
Accumulated know-how	Factory experience Practical human labor experience (work in factory) Work in sales dealership	Freshman project (year 2) Know-how database OJT with mentor	Continued-OJT with higher-level mentors	Continued-OJT with higher-level mentors

* Specialties include engine, body engineering, controls engineering, materials engineering, electrical engineering, and so on.

† For example, for controls, includes basic development, testing, C-programming, construction planning, documentation, rechecking and debugging, managing software projects (this training goes from year 2 throughout the career).

Figure 16–5. Example topics from Toyota training plan for product development engineers (subset of full curriculum)

Toyota has a great starting point on this using a training curriculum that has evolved over decades. It is summarized in Figure 16–5. Actually this is a simplified version of a large matrix that is on four pieces of 11- by 17-inch paper. The simplified version we present here is not complete, but we are using it to give examples of the different types of knowledge and skills engineers at Toyota need to have. In essence this provides the high-level skills and knowledge breakdown required by Toyota engineers.

We have broken this down into our five categories: fundamental skills, core job-specific knowledge, ancillary task knowledge, policies and judgment, and accumulated know-how. Toyota does not use this terminology internally, but there is a very good mapping of Toyota's own categories to the framework we have used in this book. For example, what we refer to as core job-specific knowledge was found in Toyota's matrix under "technical division" classes. The engineer is assigned to a technical division that is the "functional specialty" of the engineer (e.g., body exterior, body interiors, chassis, engine, materials, controls engineering, electrical engineering, etc.). Most of what we refer to as ancillary skills are described as "business techniques" and "intellectual property" in Toyota's matrix. Following is a discussion of the Toyota training and development program timeline.

Year 1: General Knowledge about the Company and an Appreciation of Key Customers of Engineering

In Japan "freshmen engineers" are all hired at the same time, right out of a top university. Hundreds of engineers start on the same day and meet in a big auditorium. At this point the engineers have not been assigned to a division, so it is not certain in what precise specialty field they will be working. The first year of general training includes three to four months of working on the shop floor building cars as a freshman team associate. The engineers are taught jobs using the JI methodology. They do not necessarily work in the same area in which they will later specialize. The point is to get a general understanding of the Toyota Production System, the demands of a routine manual job, and an appreciation for one of the key customers of the product development engineer—the shop floor worker who will be building what the engineer designs. When it comes to design for assembly and manufacturability, the engineer will have a very different perspective after this experience.

The engineers also spend several months in sales working at a dealership and selling cars. Part of this time is spent in door-to-door sales in Japan. New engineers get an appreciation for what customers look for in a car as well as the challenge of making a sale. When they finally do engineering, they always will have a vivid picture of trying to sell Toyota vehicles (usually without a lot of success in that early period).

One of the fundamental skills of all engineers at Toyota is sketching, by hand, not with a computer. It is said in Toyota that an engineer who cannot manually sketch cannot engineer a vehicle. Even in today's computer age, it is thought at Toyota that if you cannot sketch by hand, you cannot make a drawing with a computer system. In Ann Arbor, Michigan, where Toyota develops American product engineers, there is a weekly sketching class for 30 minutes led by an experienced engineer. Students are given something to sketch, and the teacher then critiques the sketches and grades them. The students must continue to go to this class every week until their level of sketching is acceptable. Some of the fundamental skills of sketching could be taught using the JI method. Ed Mantey, vice president of engineering at the Toyota Technical Center, explained, "Sometimes I look over the young engineers' shoulders at their computer-aided design (CAD) screen, and I know the design will not work. I ask, 'Did you sketch this out? Did you manually draw the relationship to other parts?' Of course the answer is no." There is some native ability in sketching, and in the selection process the recruit is asked to sketch something as part of the new hire evaluation process. Note that even after the first year in Japan there is an advanced set of classes that focuses on geometric sketches.

The "ancillary tasks" learned in the first year include planning basics and report writing. Toyota uses a unique form of report writing called A3 reports, which are described in *The Toyota Way Fieldbook*.[2] Engineers

[2] Jeffrey Liker and David Meier will be working on an additional book on problem solving that will provide greater detail on the use of A3s.

also have to understand the various design support systems like prototyping. The new engineers learn about basic personnel policies of the company. Also, data security and intellectual property are key policy domains for engineers.

In the first year engineers are beginning to learn critical know-how that they will build upon over their careers. Mostly the know-how is gained from experiential learning like working in the factory and at the dealership. Ask Toyota engineers who have worked for 20 years at Toyota, and they can vividly recount experiences they had during their early experience in the factory, and in struggling to sell cars.

Years 2–9: Becoming a Real Engineer

Toyota does not view a university graduate as an engineer. The company knows that top universities in Japan select the best students from high school, and it also knows that engineering students get a broad background of basic education from reading and writing and math to fundamental engineering sciences like thermodynamics and structural mechanics. And of course, engineering graduates have some degree of computer literacy. So they have some fundamental skill training that will accelerate their learning process at Toyota, but they do not know how to be an engineer and certainly not a Toyota engineer.

Toyota believes every engineer should be able to draw on the computer in addition to the manual sketching. The company does not believe in the model in which engineers lead only technical projects and leave the actual drawing to CAD specialists, though it does have CAD specialists acting as technicians. In Japan, engineers spend their second year assigned to a drawing department and using CAD. They learn from CAD specialists. This is a fundamental skill for a Toyota engineer. Notice through experiences in the factory and sales and the design room they are also learning to respect the people who do the more routine work of the organization. During that period the other workers teach the engineers, and this experience helps them to appreciate the challenges of their jobs.

Engineers are assigned to their technical division by year 2, and the CAD work will be included in their engineering specialty. They also get assigned a "freshman project" within that specialty, which is a real and challenging engineering task done under the supervision of a mentor. For many it is the first time they have actually engineered something real. The freshman project is another one of those lifelong memories.

After the second year the young engineers are working full time within their specialty. They are part of a work team led by a team leader. The work team is just one of a number of work groups to which the engineers belong. Some are cross-functional module development teams that are doing simultaneous engineering (between styling, other engineering specialties, and manufacturing, for example). But this team is within a function, and the team leader's job is to teach the young engineers how to be a Toyota engineer for that specialty. Team leaders know that one of their primary jobs is to be a teacher, and their performance appraisal will consider how well the students are performing.

There are many classes engineers attend, often two-hour classes, which are frequently taught by senior engineers. The classes are focused on specific technical topics within a specialty (e.g., injection molding and polymer characteristics). A lot of the job-specific knowledge is from OJT under the team leader. Toyota's policy is that it takes two vehicle program cycles for someone to be considered a "full engineer." Ed Mantey explained, "It takes an engineer a four- to five-year time frame to go through two programs and be equal as a full engineer wherever you are in the world—to design a part, negotiate with suppliers, negotiate with styling, work with purchasing—an engineer who can do all those things including [designing] functionality of the part." Ed Mantey is responsible for body and electrical engineering, and in his area alone there are about 60 classes engineers must take.

Beyond 10 Years: Learning to Be an Expert and Maybe a General Manager

Beyond 10 years it is expected that engineers have developed deep technical knowledge in their specialty and usually at some point are assigned a second related specialty. Beyond 10 years, the engineers need to continue to hone their knowledge and skills and become real experts. A key part of becoming a real expert is teaching others—developing future generations of experts. Expert engineers learn how to be team leaders and how to develop younger engineers. Some expert engineers will develop patents and can get funding to spin off a subsidiary to act as a third-party business. There are a variety of opportunities for engineers to stay on a "technical track" becoming "senior engineer" and to focus on the craft of engineering—getting better and better and teaching others—without taking on a lot of administrative responsibilities.

Some engineers will shift to an administrative track and become assistant general managers of a department and perhaps a general manager. They attend professional study classes that are taught by general managers and senior executives. Again we see the strong value Toyota places on learning on the job with experienced mentors guiding the way. It is important to note that at Toyota the most important job of any manager is to teach. It has been drilled into Ed Mantey's head that "the biggest success of any manager is the success of the people they have taught." And Ed Mantey requires all of his general managers to teach formal classes to more junior engineers in addition to their day-to-day mentoring responsibility.

Over time as Toyota has been globalizing and developing engineering centers for other regions, like the Toyota Technical Center in Ann Arbor, Michigan, and a similar center in Brussels, there is a greater need to formalize the training process. In Michigan we are seeing a more focused effort to isolate fundamental skills, develop standardized training methods, and expand the know-how database. It is still a work in process. The watchword at Toyota is always kaizen.

Can JI Training Be Successful in a Nonlean Organization?

We know of a number of companies who became serious about JI training before undertaking a serious transformation to lean methods. There is a cart before the horse problem here. Can you be lean without highly skilled people, and can highly skilled people function effectively in a non-lean environment? We think the answer is no to both parts of the question. So how do we get out of this conundrum?

First let's understand the problem. Remember that thing called the Toyota Production System? Toyota was not kidding when it said it was a *system.* A system means that the parts are interdependent. Figure 16–6 illustrates some of the interdependencies. We have argued that JI training is a necessary ingredient to developing exceptional people. And we also have explained how JI training builds on standardized work. If there is no standardized work, then you have no way of knowing what to train people to do.

Standardized work depends on defined standards and on a degree of stability in the workplace. For example, one of the problems we have seen in manufacturing when JI is attempted without a stable workplace is that the standard work suggests that the person reach to get a part from a container on a certain place on the rack. But, since the plant is using push scheduling, the standard location on the rack is already filled with overflow of another part, and the part the worker needs is somewhere in a stack of containers piled up on the floor. There was nothing in the standard work or the way the workers were trained that said, "Search for the container holding the part." This case illustrates how a stable workplace depends on having a system set up to support flow and pull. A push scheduling system will lead to instability in quantities and locations of materials and variation in workload, and any defined standards will become meaningless. Flow and pull depend on *heijunka*—leveling. It is not a coincidence that the foundation of the Toyota Production System is leveling.

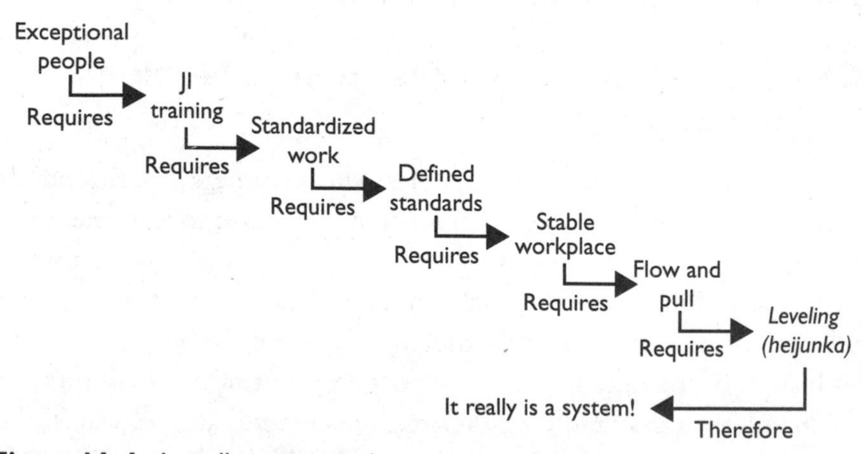

Figure 16–6. It really is a system!

So how do we approach JI if we do not have lean systems? The answer goes back to the notion of going deep and then wide. We would always suggest you start with the basics of the lean system before developing an elaborate system of training. We suggest you pick an area, which becomes your model for standardized work, flow, pull, and leveling and then start to spread the process more broadly. The model area can then be the learning laboratory to begin JI training. This has the dual advantage in that the Master JI trainer you develop can first begin by learning the Toyota Production System (TPS). Understanding TPS in our experience is a prerequisite to being a skilled JI trainer—at least at the senior level. It is possible to have team leaders who can do JI training of individual jobs with a more limited understanding of TPS.

And how do you get started and develop your first TPS expert? The answer is to turn to the basic principles of Job Instruction training. You need a similar method: a skilled trainer of TPS with a clear understanding of fundamental skills, an opportunity for them to learn by doing, first learning the pieces under supervision, then putting together the pieces into a whole system. At this point, the new trainer can start to work independently. All this needs to be supervised and supported by someone who has been there. As in JI for manual jobs, the new trainer should not be left on their own but should be supported and taught new skills.

All Leaders Have Responsibility for Developing Others

At Toyota one of the primary responsibilities of all leaders is that of developing subordinates. Leaders have a vested interest in the development of their people. If their subordinates have a low capability, it will affect the leader. All leaders must be trained in the Job Instruction method so they are able to effectively mentor trainers and team members. If a trainer has a weakness, the leader must help to develop the trainer. If the trainer is weak, the team members will be weak and the performance results will be poor.

We describe the role of the team leader in the engineering example in Chapter 6. Toyota has a matrix organization in product development.

It has a key role called the chief engineer who is responsible for the vehicle. For example, Toyota will say, "It is the chief engineer's car." The chief engineer is responsible for the Camry program, for example, from concept to production. The chief engineer has a small staff of assistants (three to five people), but all the other hundreds of engineers working on the program report up a functional hierarchy (interior trim, body sheet metal, chassis, electronics, etc.) to a general manager of the function. The body interiors' engineer reports up the body interiors management hierarchy. The team leader is part of that functional hierarchy. The primary purpose of the functional hierarchy is to ensure "towering technical competence" among the engineering specialists.[3] This means the main objective of the functional management hierarchy is to develop deep expertise in the engineers. And the team leader on the front line is there to develop the junior engineers.

This might suggest that the chief engineer is freed up from this responsibility. After all, the chief engineer is responsible for an entire vehicle program and does not need to worry about developing engineers when there is an entire functional hierarchy doing it. But that is not the Toyota Way of thinking. The chief engineer has the opportunity to develop engineers working on the vehicle development program itself. As an example, Akio Nishimura was the chief engineer for the 2006 FJ Cruiser program. He explained the way he uses a relatively new innovation in product development called the *obeya* (big room). The *obeya* was developed as part of the Prius hybrid development project, and only senior engineering leaders met in this room to manage the program.[4] Nishimura explained how he uses a larger *obeya* to house the 70 or so working level engineers doing the detailed engineering. He said that while originally the *obeya* was for senior decision makers, he uses it for developing engineers. It is an open-office arrangement, and his desk is there along with those of the working-level engineers. He says that he is there most of the time when

---

[3] James M. Morgan and Jeffrey K. Liker, *The Toyota Product Development System: Integrating People, Process, and Technology* (New York: Productivity Press, 2006).

[4] Described by Morgan and Liker as well as in *The Toyota Way,* (New York: McGraw-Hill, 2004).

he is in Japan. It gives him an opportunity to follow the work of the younger engineers and coach and teach them in real time. What better opportunity to learn engineering than on an actual vehicle program with a super engineer who has risen to the rank of chief engineer as your coach and teacher?

Using Layered Audits to Confirm Effectiveness

There is a saying in Toyota that, "No problem is a problem." This means that no process can be perfect. There are always opportunities to improve, and if you look at the process and see only perfection, you will not improve. In this section we describe a method for verifying the effectiveness of the talent development process.

In general we are not audit enthusiasts—at least not for the sake of just checking a box and indicating that the audit is complete as we see so often. Audits are waste. They do not add value to the product or service. When assigned an audit process, people often lose sight of the purpose and see it as just another job to perform. Or they see it as a way to get people to do something they do not want to do. But when properly used as an improvement tool, audits can play an important role. The purpose of audits is to identify potential problems and to take appropriate actions to correct them. If an audit is used to identify problems and corrective action is taken, there is some value to the process, but audits should not be used as the primary indicator of the success of your talent development process.

We have said on numerous occasions in this book that the performance measures in any work area will provide an indication of the training effectiveness. Audits should not be the primary tool used to detect problems. An audit should provide a more precise and detailed understanding of the specific issues after the broader indicators raise concern. Audits can help to pinpoint an individual with a performance issue or a trainer who is missing key points when breaking down the job.

The idea of layered audits is to have each layer in the organization verifying the effectiveness of the next level below. Since the bulk of employees in any organization are on the front line, most of the responsibility for auditing is at the first level (the team leader position at Toyota). Of course the team leader is often the workplace trainer (who may be inclined to cover any deficiencies), so it is also necessary to conduct an audit from a higher level from time to time. The supervisor (group leader) is responsible for auditing one job in each team every week (selecting a different job every week). The audit process is basically the same as the one used by the team leader. Using the job breakdown as a guide, the team leader or supervisor will observe the work to see if it is being done correctly. Then he or she will ask specific questions regarding the key points of the job. Open-ended questions such as, "Can you tell me the quality key point for that step?" and "Can you tell me why that is important?" will confirm that the information and ability has flowed down to the team member.

Spreading the Process

In this book we have made a point of the value of being able to determine the importance of some work elements in relation to others and to focus efforts on the most critical things. This applies to determining the initial area to begin the process, determining the most important aspects of the work content, determining which portions of the job should be taught first, and to determining how to spread the process across the organization effectively. We have discussed the need to develop depth of capability before attempting to widely spread the process.

How will you know when it is time to spread the process? You mustn't wait until perfection is attained in one area before moving into other areas. But when has enough capability been achieved in one area to then move into others? You must determine what is critical and what must be mastered before spreading into other areas. This is similar to determining when a trainee is ready to work independently with support and follow-up. We would love to be able to provide you with a checklist and tell you, "When people can do this, they are ready to move on," but the fact is that learning to make these decisions is part of your development process. You must be able to assess readiness. You must be able to determine how much support and follow-up will be necessary. You must set your own expectations for achievement. If we set an expectation for you, it is likely you will strive to reach that level and no better.

The objective must be more than to just get to the goal line—to "get it done." The goal must be to repeatedly improve the results and to strengthen the organization by continuously working to develop the full capability of every member. You must set your own expectations for the process, and when you reach that level, you will recognize there is another level. There is no limit to the capability people can reach in this process. Any limit is only a self-imposed limit for that moment.

The critical key to success is to follow the pattern of learning a new process, making an effort to try out the new skill, and then reflecting on the result and learning from your experience. If something did not work out the way you anticipated, try another approach. With time and experience you should develop a wealth of accumulated know-how that will provide you with numerous alternative approaches when you are faced with challenges.

Every great teacher knows it is necessary to first be a great student in order to become a great teacher. Being a teacher will require even more learning. All leaders must strive to teach all they know, and since they will constantly be learning, they will also constantly be teaching. From this never-ending cycle everyone is continuously growing in capability and understanding.

This cycle of continuous learning and teaching will provide the prosperity mentioned in the Chinese proverb at the beginning of this book. Investing in people and developing talent in everyone will break the cycle of struggle and defeat and replace it with a cycle of success and growth. It has been said that, "Nothing comes without a price," and we believe this is true. We believe the investment in the development of your human capital will return a yield that is far greater than the cost of the investment. You must decide for yourself whether it is worth it to work hard preparing the soil, planting the seeds, tending the plants, and protecting the crop so that a good harvest is possible. There are no guarantees, and there will be many challenges, but in the end it will provide years of prosperity.

Please try, and do your best!

Index

Page numbers in **bold** indicate full page figures or tables.